Copyright and e-learning

a guide for practitioners

Second edition

Every purchase of a Facet book helps to fund CILIP's advocacy,
awareness and accreditation programmes for information professionals.

Copyright and e-learning

a guide for practitioners

Second edition

Jane Secker with Chris Morrison

facet
publishing

© Jane Secker 2010
© Jane Secker with Chris Morrison 2016

Published by Facet Publishing
7 Ridgmount Street, London WC1E 7AE
www.facetpublishing.co.uk

Facet Publishing is wholly owned by CILIP: the Chartered Institute
of Library and Information Professionals.

Jane Secker and Chris Morrison have asserted their right under the
Copyright, Designs and Patents Act 1988 to be identified as authors
of this work.

British Library Cataloguing in Publication Data
A catalogue record for this book is available from the British Library.

ISBN 978-1-78330-060-0 (paperback)
ISBN 978-1-78330-113-3 (hardback)
ISBN 978-1-78330-149-2 (e-book)

First published 2010
This second edition 2016

Text printed on FSC accredited material.

MIX
Paper from
responsible sources
FSC® C013604

Typeset from authors' files in 10/14 pt Linotype Palatino and Myriad
Pro by Flagholme Publishing Services.
Printed and made in Great Britain by CPI Group (UK) Ltd,
Croydon, CR0 4YY.

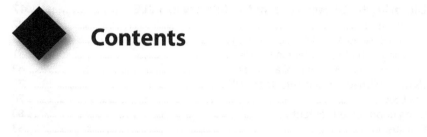

Contents

Figures, tables and case studies

Figures

Tables

Case studies

Preface to the second edition

In a recent conference workshop I asked staff working in higher education to choose from a list of adjectives that might describe copyright and new technologies such as social media, and to consider any words that might apply to both. The exercise revealed that a perception remains that many of those in education regard copyright laws as restrictive, slow to evolve and somewhat out of step with the digital age, while technology is seen as exciting, constantly evolving, and responsive to the user. This perception was one that I had been keen to counteract when first writing this book in 2009. However, the exercise also highlighted that the intersection between copyright laws and new technologies remains an area of considerable interest, but one of much concern to people. During the workshop the group discussed how the two concepts had more in common than it might appear, yet the grey areas, the areas particularly where the law is open to interpretation, worry people. What emerged from the workshop for me was the need to challenge the notion that technology and copyright exist outside the control of society. We need to remind educators that copyright laws and new technologies are intended to serve society, not just to provide financial rewards to the creative industries but also to allow new research and education to flourish. We also need to be mindful that technology is not neutral but a construct of the society we live in and shaped by all sorts of factors, including commercial interests. The quote (often incorrectly attributed to the Canadian philosopher of communication theory, Marshall McLuhan)[1] that 'we shape our tools and then they shape us' illustrates how both technologies and copyright laws are determined by societal norms. Therefore, if there is a belief amongst educators that either of these are working against society and hindering the free flow of information in the education system, then this needs to be addressed. There are already far too many misunderstandings about copyright, and while it is overly simplistic to view it as a simple set of rules, this book attempts to distil good practice based on practical experiences and equip practitioners with a framework to tackle queries that arise in their day to day work.

The book explores a subject that has fascinated me for over a decade: the overlap between copyright laws, education and new technologies. It has been substantially updated since the first edition, which was written in 2009. This new edition benefits from my collaboration with Chris Morrison, who is currently Copyright Licensing and Compliance Officer at the University of Kent. Chris and I serve on several external committees together and have a shared interest in copyright, digital literacies and new technologies. Therefore the second edition of this book benefits not only from a second writer, but is also a result of our conversations about the role of copyright in the digital age. We both recognize the need to balance the rights and rewards of authors and creators with copyright exceptions so that new ideas, creativity and education can flourish.

This edition includes substantial updates to several of the chapters, in light of changes to copyright law. For example, in the UK, several new exceptions to copyright were introduced in 2014 following the Hargreaves review of intellectual property three years earlier. Copyright issues have also arguably been brought more sharply into focus in the intervening period, in light of attempts in the USA particularly to crack down on internet piracy and hacking. The death of the high profile internet rights campaigner Aaron Swartz, who was potentially facing 35 years in prison for downloading large extracts of the JSTOR database, has highlighted the tension between academic publishers with paywalls and copyright restrictions and the open access movement. Unsurprisingly, the pace of technological change has necessitated updates to several chapters, as new services have been launched.

We noticed that the terminology used to describe the subject matter of the book had changed in the intervening years and so we have updated the book to try to reflect the new language that is used, particularly to describe internet technologies. Chris and I had lengthy discussions over whether the use of the term 'e-learning' was still relevant, given that much learning now involves some form of technology. However, in the end we decided to retain the title of the book, but throughout the book the wording has been updated to reflect the pervasive nature of technology in education. E-learning is far less of a distinct concept in 2015 and terms such as 'technology-enhanced learning', 'online learning' or simply 'learning' are used interchangeably in this edition. Another significant change to terminology appears in Chapter 5, which now considers copyright in the connected digital environment. It uses the term 'social media' in place of 'Web 2.0', which was commonly used in 2009, but has become synonymous with the web today. Finally we are delighted to include several new and updated case studies in this edition to the book, which have been written by some of the same authors and some new authors. The case studies provide a valuable addition to the book, illustrating copyright and e-learning in practice from a range of different institutions and countries.

Jane Secker

Note

1   The quote is likely to be from Father John Culkin SJ a Professor of Communication at Fordham University in New York and friend of McLuhan. However, many people think McLuhan said if not this, then something very similar.

Acknowledgements

Many thanks to all the people who helped me with this book, including Helen Carley and Damian Mitchell at Facet Publishing for encouraging and supporting me to write a second edition, and Chris for agreeing to co-author it. Thank you also to our copy editor for Facet, Lin Franklin. The second edition of this book felt at times like climbing a mountain, where the summit was always seemingly just out of reach. Eventually, through hard work and a lot of discussion, tea and chocolate, we have produced something of which we are truly proud, and which is far more substantial than the updates to the first edition that we originally envisaged.

We would particularly like to acknowledge the authors of the case studies, which are real-life examples and add valuable illustration of the topics covered by the chapters. The authors include: Monique Ritchie

(Brunel University, UK), Kate Vasili (Middlesex University, UK), Trevor Dawes (Washington University in St. Louis, USA), June Hedges (University College London, UK), Melanie Johnson (University of Auckland, New Zealand) and Mark Dilworth (Zurich International School, Switzerland).

Many other individuals supplied valuable advice and information for this book including: Lizzie Gadd (Loughborough University), Ralph Weedon (University of Strathclyde), Lisa Bungeroth (Universities UK), Claire Kidwell (Trinity Laban Conservatoire of Music and Dance), Alex Kohn (McGill University, Canada) and Dominic Young (The Copyright Hub).

We are grateful to the many individuals who completed the higher education scanning survey presented in Chapter 2, and thanks are also due to Laurent Liote from LSE for his help in creating the survey. Thanks also go to Jo DeVito and David Duffield from the Copyright Licensing Agency (CLA) for supplying additional data for this chapter.

We would also like to thank our employers, the London School of Economics and Political Science (LSE) and the University of Kent, and also our colleagues, who have always provided valuable advice and assistance.

Finally a big thank you to Tim, Lorna and Sam for their patience and support while we were writing this book and for the endless cups of tea!

Jane Secker and Chris Morrison

Introduction

Material on the subjects of copyright and e-learning is essential reading for those working in education today. Whether you are a staff development officer, a teacher or an administrator, digital technology and the internet will have impacted on the way in which you work. This impact has been felt in both formal and informal learning in school classrooms and staff development units, in almost all educational establishments in the last 15 years. Information and communication technologies (ICTs) have offered teachers new ways of finding, creating and distributing content to learners, extending the physical classroom to include some form of digital space in which teachers can place resources. Educational technologies provide students with new ways of completing assignments, new types of assignments and new ways of interacting with their teachers and peers; learners who study at a distance from their institution can discuss ideas using online forums or can work together on projects using a collaborative writing tool such as a wiki. The development of ICTs has provided students with access to learning and resources at a time and place convenient to them. Those working in student and staff support, in libraries, IT, training and educational development have perhaps seen the greatest changes, with the creation of new roles and responsibilities specializing in educational technologies. Increasingly both learners and teachers are working in what is described as a new learning environment, a description that makes reference to the digital or virtual space.

The classroom of the 21st century often has integrated technology such as smartboards, wireless networks, recording and lecture capture tools. Our learners increasingly use technology in the classroom, bringing with them laptops, smartphones and tablets with in-built cameras and recording devices, leading them to have different expectations, skills and experience from students of the past. Thus, as the teaching and learning environment changes, so too does the way we teach. However, in this new and exhilarating world of online teaching and learning, copyright is often an issue that is overlooked, or perhaps considered as an afterthought. Whereas online learning is seen as fun and exciting, copyright is perceived as being boring and restrictive; it can be perceived as a barrier that stops teachers putting into practice their teaching innovations. For those charged with offering copyright advice, it can sometimes seem as though they are the person inhibiting exciting new developments. It is also fair to say that if teachers do consider copyright issues, it is usually late in the day, meaning that any problems that occur can be more difficult to resolve. Yet, with some foresight and understanding of the legislative framework in which education operates, copyright need not be a barrier to using new technologies. If online courses are designed with copyright issues in mind at the outset, using principles of 'open practice'[1] then it should not prevent teachers from providing students with the information that they need in a timely and appropriate manner.

This book aims to provide practical advice about a variety of copyright issues for those working in the broad field of online learning. It seeks to challenge the notion that copyright is always an obstacle to teaching with digital technology, or that copyright laws are out of step with the ways in which modern teachers and students wish to work. Ten years ago in the UK, educational organizations such as HEFCE (Higher Education Funding Council for England) and Jisc published guides on copyright and e-learning but aside from this book, there have been few subsequent publications. This contrasts with the growth in publication of copyright guides written to support librarians and archivists, including recent editions from three UK authors Cornish (2015), Pedley (2015) and Padfield (2015). This book aims to bridge this gap and provide an updated guide for practitioners working in the online learning field. It is based on best practice developed by leading institutions that are supporting students in a blended learning environment and includes seven case studies. As learning technologies have spread from higher education to schools, colleges and other learning organizations, a good understanding of copyright and other intellectual property right (IPR) issues remains essential across the sector. This book will help staff to be more confident that they are using technologies in a way that respects copyright laws and that they are not exposing their institution to the risk of legal challenges from publishers and other rights holders. We also hope that it helps staff to understand how copyright exceptions and licences can help to provide access to resources for their students. It also attempts to provide a framework for dealing with copyright queries and for offering training and support in your own institution. Finally it provides a wealth of further reading and resources. However the book does not replace the legal advice that institutions are advised to seek if they are in any doubt over copyright issues.

Who should read this book?

The intended audience for this book is anyone working in education who uses some form of digital learning technology to support students. This includes both teachers and educational support staff such as learning technologists, librarians, educational developers, instructional designers and IT staff. It is aimed at the entire education sector from primary and secondary schools (known as K-12 in some countries) to higher education, although many examples come from the higher education sector where copyright education and support is usually better resourced. The book may also be relevant to those developing learning resources in the commercial sector, where online learning is increasingly used for staff development. In the public sector, libraries, museums and archives and government departments are also developing and using online learning and so they too should find this book of interest. The book may also be helpful to those working in related areas, such as the health service, who are developing e-learning materials.

It is anticipated that the main audience for this book will be people living in the UK, although where possible an international perspective is included. Technology has broken down many physical barriers to allow access to learning worldwide, so teachers and learners might be geographically separate. Meanwhile, copyright laws are concerned about where an educational establishment is based. Therefore, those providing e-learning support to international students need to consider carefully the copyright laws of their own country. If materials are made available by a UK institution copyright infringement would usually be pursued through courts in the UK. However, if material is being hosted outside the UK an awareness of the laws of other countries is required. Furthermore, if a teacher moves from one country to another, for example from the USA to the UK, they are well advised to familiarize themselves with the law in the new country. The authors work in the UK and therefore the guidance provided is based on the laws of the UK. In recognition of differing copyright legislation around the world, international examples have been included where relevant. These examples come predominantly from the English-speaking world including the USA, Canada, New Zealand and Australia. The book recognizes that UK copyright law has to comply with European directives and will be impacted by further work to reform and harmonize copyright legislation across the European Union (EU). However, with the exception of Ireland, other European countries are not considered in any detail.

Finally, this book is intended as a best practice guide, and no part of it should be considered to constitute legal advice. The authors are not lawyers and have deliberately written this book as a guide for practitioners, rather than for lawyers or copyright experts. There are some references to legislation and case law, but other books cover these topics in far greater detail. In addition, educational establishments are advised to seek legal advice on problematic copyright issues, particularly those that are likely to lead, or have led to, litigation. It is also advisable to develop clear internal IPR policies in line with the institution's appetite for risk and approach to open practice. Your institutional legal team or legal advisers can help to devise policies such as terms of use and a 'notice and takedown policy' that apply to the virtual learning environment (VLE). More information including example policies are provided in the section 'Further resources' of the book.

Definitions

Before proceeding any further it would be helpful to define some of the terms that are used throughout this book, in order to provide context and avoid potential confusion. The authors both work at UK universities and therefore use terminology commonly used in the UK higher education sector. If you are new to any of the acronyms it is suggested that you refer to the Glossary. The authors are aware that terminology can be problematic as it is often country specific and in the field of technology it is constantly evolving.

E-learning, online learning, learning or educational technologies

E-learning – 'electronic learning' or 'online learning' at its broadest level – is defined as the use of computer technology to support teaching and learning. However, this definition suggests that simply using a computer in any part of learning, for example in order to word-process an essay, might be e-learning, and this is not the case. A more accurate definition of e-learning is that it is the use of computer technology as an integral part of the learning, teaching or assessment process. These technologies are often called 'learning technologies' or 'educational technologies' and the staff that support them might be called learning technologists or educational technologists. In this book the terms e-learning and online learning are used interchangeably to reflect how terminology has evolved in the last six years since the first edition of this book was published.

The most common type of learning technology is some form of e-learning system or platform. In the UK these are called VLEs; elsewhere in the world people use the terms 'course management systems' or 'learning management systems'. VLE is used throughout this book to refer to these systems. The VLE provides a secure online space where resources, learning activities and assessments are made available to students, often for specific courses or modules. Password protection is almost always in place, so that placing material on a VLE ensures that it is restricted to students and staff in the institution. In some instances technology may be replacing some of the face-to-face or classroom-based activities, such as a lecture or a seminar. However, in many instances the online resources and activities complement face-to-face teaching. There are increasing numbers of institutions, particularly in higher education or providing continuing professional development (CPD), which now offer courses delivered almost entirely online. This allows students to carry out their learning at a time and place of their choice rather than attend the institution in person. It should be recognized that the terms 'e-learning' and 'online learning' include a broad spectrum of models of education.

E-learning platforms

E-learning platforms, or VLEs, are used by the majority of higher and further educational institutions in the UK today. In the schools sector VLEs are becoming increasingly common and are often implemented and supported by local education authorities.

Proprietary commercial systems and free, open-source solutions are used in equal numbers in higher, further and school level education. In the commercial and health sectors e-learning can be supported by a dedicated platform or through using an intranet. E-learning is used for formal education, informal learning and for CPD and staff development activities. In many cases, some form of face-to-face training complements the online support. In general e-learning platforms are password protected so although material is placed on a network, it is not made available on the internet to a wider audience.

Blended learning

Blended learning is a term related to e-learning, used to describe a blend of face-to-face and online learning. True e-learning is in fact fairly rare, and many institutions provide online support to complement their face-to-face teaching. Where 'blended learning' occurs students usually attend traditional lectures or seminars but have access to a variety of online resources. They may undertake online assessments and use discussion forums, but they are not distance learning students. This mode of education is highly flexible, allowing students to catch up if they miss classes. Blended learning is now the default model in higher education in the UK. Access to online resources via the VLE helps students who work and study part-time, students who live some distance from the university campus and students with disabilities who may not be able to access the campus or traditional resources.

Copyright and intellectual property rights

Copyright is one of a number of legal rights known collectively as intellectual property rights (IPRs), which give exclusive rights to the creators and owners of ideas, information and creative works. Related IPRs include patents, trade marks, design rights and database rights. These are not discussed in any detail in this book, which concentrates on copyright. Copyright covers written materials (known as literary works), artistic, dramatic and musical works, works of architecture, sound recordings, film and video, photographs and websites. This list is not exhaustive and the full list of copyright works as defined in UK law are set out in the Copyright, Designs and Patents Act 1988 (CDPA). Copyright laws exist throughout the world and international copyright agreements such as the Berne Convention (first signed in 1886) ensure there is automatic protection against the copying and selling of works beyond their country of origin. The laws often date back to the early days of publishing, yet in most countries the law has tried to reflect the emergence of new technologies. Copyright laws do not cover ideas in themselves and to qualify for copyright protection the expression of ideas needs to be 'fixed' in some way, for example in written or recorded format.

Throughout this book we also use the term UK copyright law, which is in fact a misnomer, as the UK has three legal systems: English law, which applies in England and Wales; Northern Ireland law; and Scots law, which applies in Scotland. However the relevant copyright legislation is the Copyright, Designs and Patents Act 1988 (as amended) known as the CDPA, which applies across the UK. Substantial changes were made to this act in 2014 and the section 'Further resources' includes a link to the act, where the amendments can be seen. Copyright infringement cases are usually resolved under civil rather than criminal law, so people are unlikely to be sent to jail for copyright infringement unless it is deliberate and commercial in nature.

Copyright officers

At several points in this book we use the term 'copyright officer'. In the UK, there is no requirement for an educational establishment to have a copyright officer and similarly there is no formal definition or qualification for copyright officers. A recent survey found that in the library and cultural heritage sector in the UK, 64% of institutions had a person with specific responsibility for copyright matters (Morrison and Secker, 2015). The job descriptions of such people vary considerably, as does their background. Many copyright officers in UK higher education establishments sit within the library or information services division. However, there is considerable variation in the expertise of these people, the type of queries they are asked to deal with, and the ultimate responsibility and strategic influence that they have within their organization (see Chapter 6).

Born digital content and digitization

Another important concept central to this book is that of 'born digital' content, a notion which separates content created in digital format from that which is digitized from a print or analogue source. Born digital content is discussed in greater detail in Chapter 4.

Overview of the content

Chapter 1 provides an overview of copyright and other IPRs as they relate to e-learning in several English-speaking countries. It has been substantially updated to cover recent changes to copyright legislation in the UK and elsewhere in the world. It also provides background information about the development of online learning, and its relationship to face-to-face teaching and distance education. This chapter explores how the digital environment differs from the classroom and considers issues such as copying for educational purposes and what the law permits. Finally it provides details about new developments in copyright such as the open access and Creative Commons movements. The case study comes from Brunel University, which appointed a copyright officer to tackle these and other issues in 2004.

Chapter 2 considers how to re-use text-based content in e-learning. It examines the situation in the UK where the Copyright Licensing Agency (CLA) licences permit published materials to be digitized for education. Results from a survey conducted in 2009 and repeated in 2015 into scanning activity in higher education are presented. These demonstrate the significant growth in scanning of published works in the intervening period and the challenges encountered by higher education librarians to deliver copyright compliant content to teaching staff. The chapter also briefly considers the situation in other countries, specifically the USA, and the digitization of archival or other unpublished works and the copyright issues associated with orphan works. Two case studies are included in this chapter, one from Middlesex University examining scanning and copyright services provided by their library, and one examining electronic reserves in the USA.

Chapter 3 looks at digital media: video, images and sound, and how these types of resources might be used in e-learning; it considers, for example, the digitization of off-air recordings under the Educational Recording Agency (ERA) licence and the use of on-demand TV services. It also explores the use of lecture capture and the copyright and IPR matters raised by this technology. It considers the creation of digital media in-house and provides a useful list of digital media resources available to the education community. The case study is from University College London (UCL) with a discussion of some of the complexities of negotiating rights to deliver content worldwide using open licences.

Chapter 4 looks at 'born digital' resources and outlines the copyright issues concerned with this type of content. Increasingly, born digital content is embedded with a variety of digital rights management technologies designed to limit the ways in which that content can be re-used. This chapter covers specific concerns that need to be addressed when using different types of digital resources, including external websites, licences for electronic resources and lecturers' own content. It includes a case study from the copyright officer at the University of Auckland in New Zealand who describes the operation of the library's course reading list service.

The digital environment is changing rapidly and Chapter 5 examines copyright in the connected environment, specifically focusing on social media and emerging trends such as massive open online course (MOOCs). The chapter provides an overview of these technologies and the changing digital environment. It then considers questions such as whether to rely on third-party-hosted services, where the copyright lies in works with multiple creators, and the copyright implications if individuals contribute content to social media services. The chapter provides examples of how several social media services handle copyright in order to protect their own rights and how they handle others uploading content to their services. Examples from some of the most popular sites such as Flickr, Facebook and Wikipedia are included. The chapter includes a case study from Zurich International School examining how students are encouraged to use emerging technologies in a responsible way that respects copyright law.

Finally Chapter 6 discusses copyright education and training for staff and students in educational establishments, referred to as 'copyright literacy'. Arguably the key to developing effective, high quality online learning relies on embedding an understanding of copyright and intellectual property laws into the institution's culture through staff development. However, students also need a greater understanding of copyright issues as they use technologies in their studies and go out into the workplace. The chapter considers who should deliver copyright education, the support that they require, the intended audience and ways of providing it – for example, the different approaches to copyright education needed by teaching staff in comparison with administrative staff or PhD students. Methods of delivery are considered, including face-to-face workshops, online learning, and the role of printed guides and leaflets. Finally this chapter considers how to deal with copyright queries and provides sources of further advice and support. It includes a case study from the authors, who have developed an interactive games-based approach to copyright education, which has proved highly effective as a way of engaging learners.

One of the strengths of this book is that it includes case studies from several high profile UK universities, and from educational establishments in the USA, New Zealand and Europe. The case studies explore issues raised in each chapter in more detail and provide specific examples of best practice. They are:

◆ Case Study 1 The copyright officer at Brunel University London
◆ Case Study 2 Digitizing course readings at Middlesex University
◆ Case Study 3 Electronic reserves and copyright in a US university
◆ Case Study 4 Open course creation at UCL
◆ Case Study 5 The Course Reading List Service of the University of Auckland, New Zealand
◆ Case Study 6 Zurich International School, Switzerland – e-learning and copyright
◆ Case Study 7 Copyright the card game: a games-based approach to copyright education.

Throughout this book the authors assume that readers have no previous knowledge of UK copyright law or the questions relating to copyright and e-learning. References are included at the end of each chapter and suggested further resources are included at the end of the book. A glossary is provided, which explains technical terms and acronyms (although these are spelt out in the main text on the first occasion of their use). Wherever possible the authors have tried to avoid legal jargon and offer pragmatic advice based on good practice in the sector and their collective experience.

Note

1   Open practice or practices are defined in the Glossary and discussed in detail in the book (see Chapter 1, page 41).

References

Cornish, G. P. (2015) *Copyright: interpreting the law for libraries, archives and information services*, 6th edn, Facet Publishing.

Morrison, C. and Secker, J. (2015) Copyright Literacy in the UK: a survey of librarians and other cultural heritage sector professionals, *Library and Information Research*, **39** (121), 75–97.

Padfield, T. (2015) *Copyright for Archivists and Records Managers*, 5th edn, Facet Publishing.

Pedley, P. (2015) *Practical Copyright for Library and Information Professionals*, Facet Publishing.

Abbreviations and acronyms

ALA	American Library Association
AUCC	Association of Universities and Colleges of Canada now known as Universities Canada
BIS	Department for Business, Innovation & Skills (UK Government department)
BUFVC	British Universities Film & Video Council
CAL	Copyright Agency Limited (Australian reprographic rights organization)
CCC	Copyright Clearance Center (US reprographic rights organization)
CDPA	The Copyright, Designs and Patents Act 1988 – the copyright legislation in force in the UK
CILIP	Chartered Institute of Library and Information Professionals
CLA	Copyright Licensing Agency (UK reprographic rights organization)
CLARCS	Copyright Licensing Agency Rapid Clearance Service
CLNZ	Copyright Licensing New Zealand
CONFU	Conference on Fair Use
CPD	continuing professional development
DACS	Design and Artists Copyright Society
DCLG	Department of Communities and Local Government
DCS	Digital Content Store; pilot service for universities in the UK from CLA, to be a central store of digital readings
DOI	digital object identifier
DRM	digital rights management

ERA   Educational Recording Agency
EU   European Union
HEI   higher education institution
HESA   Higher Education Statistics Agency
ICLA   Irish Copyright Licensing Agency
ICT   information and communication technology
IPO   Intellectual Property Office (UK Government department)
IPR   intellectual property rights
Jisc   Joint Information Systems Committee
LSE   London School of Economics
MOOC   massive open online course
NLA   Newspaper Licensing Agency
PPL   Phonographic Performance Limited
SCONUL   Society of College, National and University Libraries
SEPS   Second Extract Permissions Service
TADC   Talis Aspire Digitised Content
UCISA   Universities and Colleges Information Systems Association
UNESCO   United Nations Educational, Scientific and Cultural
            Organization
URL   uniform resource locator
VLE   virtual learning environment
WIPO   World Intellectual Property Organization

Glossary

Copyright Hub A non-profit organization launched following the Hargreaves review of intellectual property in the UK. The Copyright Hub is building technology to link copyright works, owners and users digitally, with the intention of making the process of getting and giving permission quicker and easier for everyone.

Copyright officer Many organizations in the cultural heritage sector employ a named individual who takes responsibility for copyright issues including training, advice, policy development and compliance checks. In the UK there is a range of professionals who take on this role, and a number of job titles. Quite a high percentage of them are library and information professionals. There is no recognized qualification for this role.

Dark web World wide web content that exists on dark nets, that hide the IP addresses of the servers that run them. Thus they can be visited by any web user, but it is very difficult to work out who is behind the sites. You cannot find these sites using search engines such as Google or Bing.

Deep linking The process of linking to a page within a large website, bypassing the home page of the site. Deep links are often more likely to change, for example when a website is reorganized, and some organizations expressly prohibit deep linking in their website terms and conditions.

Digital literacies Jisc defines digital literacies as the capabilities that fit someone for living, learning and working in a digital society. They overlap with other learning literacies such as information literacy and media literacy and are underpinned by functional ICT proficiency. The capabilities include the appropriate use of technology for communication, collaboration, learning and scholarship, knowledge creation and an awareness of your digital identity and wellbeing.

E-reserves A US term for making available extracts from library materials in electronic format for students on specific courses. 'Reserves' is the US term for a short loan collection and hence 'electronic reserves' are electronic short loans.

Fair dealing A concept enshrined in UK law that relates to how a fair and honest minded person might treat a work and whether that treatment would have a negative impact on the owner of the work. Many of the exceptions to copyright in the UK are subject to fair dealing, which involves making a judgement for each individual case.

Fair use US term, often confused with fair dealing, which allows for exceptions to copyright law for societally beneficial purposes including education. Unlike fair dealing it involves the application of a broad fairness test, rather than stipulating a finite list of possible uses such as quotation or criticism and review.

Moral rights The right to be identified as the author of a work (the right of paternity), the right to object to derogatory treatment of a work (the right of integrity), the right not to be identified as the author of someone else's work (false attribution), and the right to privacy of certain photographs or films. In the UK, under the CDPA, moral rights need to be 'asserted' in a formal written statement otherwise they do not apply. They are intended to protect an author's creative identity and in some countries last beyond the duration of copyright, so ensure that a work cannot be falsely attributed even for older, public domain works.

Notice and takedown policy Institutions that make content available on the internet often use these policies to mitigate against claims of copyright infringement. This is a process that allows rights holders to inform the website owner of a possible copyright infringement, and states that the website owner will remove the content while an investigation takes place. Sample policies from several organizations are included in the section 'Further resources'.

Non-commercial usage Often difficult to define in practice but is described by Creative Commons as activity that is 'not primarily intended for or directed towards commercial advantage or monetary compensation'. Many copyright exceptions around the world specify that usage should be non-commercial and this test relates to specific activities rather than the broad goals of individuals or organizations. Generally, educational activities are considered non-commercial as the primary aim is not to make a profit.

Open educational resources Open educational resources are usually digitized materials offered freely and openly for educators, students and self-learners to use and re-use for teaching, learning and research.

Open practice(s) A range of open educational activities, such as developing and using open educational resources, developing open courses such as MOOCs, practising open scholarship through sharing research openly (open access) and using open-source technologies.

Public domain Material where the copyright has expired is considered to be in the public domain. For example, in the UK a published literary work is said to be in the public domain when the author has been deceased for more than 70 years.

Risk management Approach used by organizations to deal with potential issues involving risk, based on an assessment of the likelihood they will occur and the impact of the consequences. With regards to copyright matters it involves considering a range of factors, including the type of work being used, its economic value, the likelihood of a rights holder finding out about an infringement, the type of remuneration they might expect, and the likelihood of a court action being taken. Risk is about more than just economic damage and involves consideration of the potential damage to an organization's reputation.

Risk-based approach Making decisions based on consideration of a range of factors as described above. It involves tolerating that some infringement may happen and that there are appropriate measures in place to mitigate the consequences.

Third-party rights or material Content that is owned by someone other than the person copying, communicating or receiving it. For example, a lecturer prepares a PowerPoint presentation and includes several images she has taken from the internet which belong to another organization. In this case the third party is neither the lecturer nor the student receiving the PowerPoint, but the organization that owns the image sourced from the internet.

1 E-learning and copyright: background

Introduction

This chapter considers copyright in the digital environment, and its relationship to recent developments in education. It provides an overview of the major differences between copyright laws in several English-speaking countries in the world and how they apply to online learning. The focus of this book is on the UK, but it briefly discusses copyright laws in the USA, Australia, Canada and New Zealand. While the book does not replace any legal advice that those developing online learning might need to obtain, it considers how copying can be undertaken for educational purposes. This chapter focuses on various exceptions to copyright law (activities such as copying that can be done without the rights holder's permission) and the impact of copyright issues on face-to-face teaching. The chapter also defines e-learning (or online learning) for the purposes of this book. This definition includes the use of the internet, intranets and secure computer networks such as VLEs, course management systems and other online learning environments. This chapter considers the different effects copyright law has on teaching in the digital environment when compared with the classroom. It also explores new developments in scholarly publishing, including the open access movement and open-source software, along with the development of open licensing schemes such as Creative Commons. This chapter includes the first case study in the book, from Brunel University, where the institution appointed a copyright officer in response to the copyright challenges they were facing.

Recognizing the copyright dilemma

Much of what teachers wish to do in an online learning environment is similar to what they have traditionally done in the classroom. They give students learning activities such as reading, critiquing a work of art or consulting a manuscript source. Students may work individually or in groups. However, online technologies provide huge opportunities to broaden the reach of education by allowing students to participate in learning regardless of their geographic location. Digital technology also allows students to work together asynchronously at a time and place convenient to each learner. Used effectively, e-learning is far more than simply the use of an online document repository, it can be an engaging, online, interactive learning environment. Many of the copyright challenges to e-learning relate to the creation of an online library of resources. Digital technology offers the teacher the opportunity to provide students with perfect copies of copyright works such as digitized books, music files or a piece of digital video. Early digital library research projects, such as those funded by Jisc (the Joint Information Systems Committee) in the 1990s as part of the Electronic Libraries (e-Lib) programme, recognized the complex copyright issues that the digitization process could cause.[1] Many early digitization projects in libraries throughout the world deliberately concentrated on using material that was out of copyright, thus avoiding the need to seek copyright permissions. Seeking such permission is time consuming and potentially problematic if the owner of a work cannot be traced. However, in the UK, Jisc launched several projects as part of e-Lib to tackle this issue head on, looking at what at the time was called 'on-demand publishing' and 'electronic short loan'. These various projects ultimately led to the establishment of a service called Heron (which stood for Higher Education Resources On-demand) funded initially by Jisc. In 2002 Heron became a commercial service providing digitization and copyright services to higher education primarily in the UK until 2015. The services have subsequently been acquired by the Copyright Licensing Agency (CLA) and Heron will be wound up in 2016 and incorporated into new services offered by CLA. These developments are discussed in greater detail in Chapter 2. Needless to say the reason that Heron was developed in the first place was as a response to the growing demand to provide students with digitized access to copyright content.

Through early projects in e-learning and digital libraries, Jisc became increasingly aware of the legal ramifications of working in a digital environment. Consequently it launched Jisc Legal in 2000 to provide advice and support on a wide range of legal concerns for the further and higher education community. Until the end of 2014 the Jisc Legal website (www.jisclegal.ac.uk) provided a wealth of legal advice and guidance over the use of technology in education, including copyright issues. In January 2015 the service was reduced following funding cuts and replaced by the Jisc Customer Services Division, which has seven geographically based teams around the UK. The team employs a subject specialist focusing on technology and the law, although since late 2014 the helpdesk support for copyright and IPR queries has been more limited. However, Jisc still provides written guidance on legal issues, and *A Quick Guide to Intellectual Property Rights in the Digital World* is one of the resources produced by this team in 2015 (Jisc, 2015). Other suggested resources for keeping up to date in this field are listed in the section 'Further resources'.

The development of e-learning in the UK

Before considering copyright issues any further, this next section will briefly provide an overview of developments in the field of online learning. A list of general readings on this topic is provided in the section 'Further resources'. Technology has become increasingly important in education and training, with the proliferation of digital tools to support administration and online learning, and the widespread availability of high-speed broadband in many places around the world. Technologies to enhance and support teaching and learning have had the greatest impact in the higher education sector, with significant investment from funding bodies such as Jisc, which has provided the infrastructure through the Janet network and research and development funding for projects and initiatives. The Janet network is dedicated to the needs of education and research in the UK; it connects the UK's education and research organizations to each other and the rest of the world through links to the global internet. Thus every higher education institution (HEI) in the UK has invested significantly in digital technologies to support teaching and learning. Students' face-to-face learning is primarily supported through the use of online learning platforms (known as VLEs in the UK and learning or course management systems elsewhere in the world). The 2014 survey on technology-enhanced learning in higher education in the UK by the Universities and Colleges Information Systems Association (UCISA, 2014) showed that Blackboard Learn is the most widely used commercial institutional VLE in the UK (used by 49% of responding HEIs), however 62% of institutions use the open-source system Moodle. In the past five years there has also been a growth in the number of online courses offered to students who may rarely or never attend a UK HEI, or who may be taught at an overseas campus. VLEs are the main teaching platform used to support the increasing globalization of the UK higher education sector. The number of massive open online courses (MOOCs) offered in the higher education sector has grown in recent years; these are free online courses offered by traditional universities, but open to students from around the world. MOOCs present specific copyright challenges. They are considered in the case study in Chapter 3 and discussed in more detail in Chapter 5.

In reality, entirely online learning, as defined in the Introduction, is rare, but most educational establishments have recognized that providing online support for learners and face-to-face teaching offers many rewards for teachers and learners. The use of technology is largely linked to the need to provide students in higher and further education with greater flexibility as to where and when they can access learning. As a result of the funding cuts and introduction of fees in the higher education sector there are now far higher numbers of students who work while studying, so students increasingly need to take advantage of convenient, electronic access to course content. Meanwhile, academic institutions can reduce their administrative burdens by distributing content online rather than in paper format.

In the further education sector most colleges also have VLEs, the most common platform being the open-source system Moodle. Essentially what these systems provide is a relatively easy-to-use platform to distribute content to learners, with built-in educational tools or activities to engage them and facilitate learning. These include discussion tools, assessment tools, file uploads and collaborative workspaces. There has been a significant decline in public funding in the further education sector in the past five years. However the Further Education Learning Technology Action Group recommended in June 2014 that a minimum of 10% of all publicly funded programmes should be delivered online by 2015–16, demonstrating that there has been a significant investment in online learning in this sector. Jisc are currently working on a programme to implement this recommendation in the FE sector (Jisc, 2016).

In the school sector the use of learning technologies has been slower to develop. There was some progress from 2006 to 2010 following investment from central government through Becta, but funding cuts following the general election in 2010 led to the closure of this agency. Becta's role was to ensure that technology was used effectively in the British education system and it ran events and produced numerous resources to help encourage the use of e-learning. Developments in the school sector in this period were driven by the UK Government's e-strategy *Harnessing Technology* (DfES, 2005), which was launched in 2005 and sought to provide a 'cradle to grave' approach to using technology in learning. The e-strategy also set the expectations that:

◆ by spring 2008 every pupil should have access to a personalized online learning space with the potential to support an e-portfolio (provided by their local authority)
◆ by 2010 every school should have integrated learning and management systems (a comprehensive suite of learning platform technologies).

Following the election in 2010, the Department for Education's approach to technology-enhanced learning has been largely silent. Nevertheless, as a result of earlier investment 'learning platforms' or VLEs are increasingly common in UK schools along with the use of other classroom technologies such as interactive whiteboards. However, the current government policy has focused on enhancing the computing curriculum and developing the capacity of teachers to support 'digital literacies' (see the Glossary for more details) rather than on using online learning.

Online vs. 'blended' learning

Many HEIs were drawn into investment in online learning technology by the potential of supporting students at a distance, which until there were developments in technology had remained the preserve of specialist institutions such as the Open University. The potential of entirely online learning has become a reality in the last five years, and can be seen as a way of expanding student numbers without the need for additional teaching space. It also meets the growing demand for education throughout the world, but the financial investment associated with fully online distance education is significant. In 2005 the UK 'e-university' collapsed at a reported cost of over £500 million. This led some institutions to reconsider how they might use technology and focus on what is often called 'blended learning'. This is defined in the Introduction as the support of on-campus face-to-face students with an e-learning platform that enables them to access lecture materials, resources and readings and communicate with their peers and tutors outside the classroom. This model has become increasingly common as higher education has expanded and the way students manage their studies has changed. Since 1992, there has been significant expansion in higher education in the UK and many other English-speaking countries, and participation levels in higher education in the UK are now approximately 50%. With increasingly large class sizes and more students studying while working part (or even full) time, online and blended learning open up higher education and provide students with flexibility to learn at a time and place convenient to them. Thus, technology has been linked to the widening participation agenda in the UK, in which students from non-traditional backgrounds enter universities. Student retention can be a key issue and many e-learning systems include administrative functions that allow student participation to be tracked to alert tutors to potential problems with student engagement early on.

In 2012–13 the higher education landscape changed again in the UK following the introduction of full fees for undergraduate students, whereby most students pay up to £9000 per year for their tuition. A report by Universities UK noted a 6.3% decline in student numbers (Universities UK, 2014) although it recognized a growth in the UK's international higher education market share. In the last five years there has been a growing globalization of the UK higher education market with some institutions developing entirely online courses for students based overseas, and others expanding internationally by setting up overseas campuses, or working in partnership with other universities around the world. In 2013–14 Universities UK reported that there were 638,850 students studying for UK qualifications, but based outside the UK – the highest number of students was based in Malaysia. This figure has grown by 65% since 2008 and while more than half are registered with an overseas partner institution, almost

120,000 are studying by distance, flexible or blended learning (Universities UK, 2015). Research was also commissioned by the UK Government's Department for Business, Innovation & Skills (BIS) in 2014 to explore the value of transnational education to the UK economy. This study found 63 HEIs (of around 150 universities in total) reporting that they run active transnational education programmes, which bring in revenue of almost £500 million (BIS, 2014). Since 2010 there has also been a growth in the number of private for-profit higher education providers. This creates specific copyright challenges, blurring the line between not-for-profit education and commercial activities.

E-learning and digital resources

Learning technologists have long advocated that VLEs should be interactive environments to enhance learning, where students complete activities and assessments rather than simply access content. However many teachers still use a VLE simply as a digital document repository. Materials such as PowerPoint slides, lecture notes and essential readings are often uploaded onto the learning platform and these have replaced hard copy handouts in most institutions. A typical HEI digital course site therefore acts as an electronic file store for materials which were previously included in course handbooks or given out in the classroom. In recent years institutions have invested in lecture capture systems, so not only can students access slides from a presentation, but a recording of the lecture will also be made available to them. In 2012 51% of HEIs reported having institutionally supported lecture capture tools; by 2014 this figure had risen to 63% (UCISA, 2014, 28). Expectations about the quality of video and audio production have increased in line with the sophistication and accessibility of recording and content delivery technologies. Therefore many learning technology teams now work alongside more traditional audiovisual technicians to provide quality services in this area as the technology improves and the costs are reduced. Media streaming services are now available in 65% of all HEIs (UCISA, 2014) allowing video and audio to be delivered over university networks.

The wide availability of digital resources, be they useful web-based resources, e-journals or e-books, leads many teachers to try to include as many different types of learning resources as are appropriate within the

VLE for the convenience of their students. Librarians are aware that students and academic staff visit the library building less frequently than in the past to access resources, as many prefer the convenience of access from their own devices at their chosen location as allowed by institutional authentication systems. It is therefore no surprise that teachers who use the VLE want to include direct links to access full-text materials, for example from the course reading list. Reading list management systems were used by 55% of HEIs in 2014 (UCISA, 2014), which makes it relatively easy to add links to online resources, through integration with library systems. However, many teachers remain unaware of the complex licensing arrangements negotiated by libraries that allow them to access resources such as e-journals and e-books. In fact with more sophisticated authentication procedures and federated search tools, many teachers are not aware when they are using subscription resources rather than content freely available on the internet. The desire to provide students with as many resources as possible to help their learning can inevitably lead to copyright issues. Teachers will argue that they are simply trying to help students get access to material, but the ease with which content can be downloaded from the internet or a library subscription resource, or even scanned from hard copy, makes it all too easy to break licence agreement terms and conditions or infringe another's copyright. The general perception that there is an overarching exception for educational or not-for-profit use prevails in education, particularly outside higher education.[2] Additionally many teachers incorrectly believe that because they are distributing content to students via a secure network this provides them with greater legal protection than making material available on the open internet.

Our learners: 'the Google Generation'?

Before turning to copyright laws, it is also worth briefly mentioning the ongoing research that has looked at the characteristics of students today. Several studies (Prensky, 2001; Research Information Network, 2007; Rowlands et al., 2008) suggested that young people have a greater level of comfort around using technology than earlier generations leading to the coining of the term 'digital natives' (among others[3]), though some researchers have disputed the concept of digital natives finding it too simplistic (Jones et al., 2010). White and Le Cornu (2011) proposed the idea of a continuum to describe how people interact with the web as one of 'visitors and residents', which is neither age nor background specific, but dependent on people's motivation and context. While it is true to say that in much of the developed world many young people have greater access to technology, perhaps more worryingly, there is also some evidence to suggest that young people have a different (or lack of) understanding of copyright law than those from previous generations. Rowlands et al. (2008, 301) qualified findings from earlier research which suggested that young people did not respect intellectual property, saying they found this to be only partly true. However, they noted: 'Young people feel that copyright regimes are unfair and unjust and a big age gap is opening up. The implications for libraries and for the information industry of a collapse of respect for copyright are potentially very serious.' Meanwhile in 2013 the Intellectual Property Office (IPO) in conjunction with the National Union of Students (NUS) conducted a survey of over 2000 students in the UK into their attitudes towards and knowledge of IPR, including copyright (NUS, 2013). The findings suggested that most students did not feel they knew enough about IPR for their future careers and that IPR education is generally not embedded in their course in most institutions. Students believed IPR education focused almost entirely on plagiarism issues and only in law departments is copyright covered in any detail. These findings suggested that students recognized the value of learning about IPR, particularly with the increasing focus on innovation and entrepreneurship where students want to understand how to protect their own ideas.

Clearly students expect their learning resources to be freely available to them, either on the internet or in their online learning environment. The payment of fees has brought this more sharply into focus. However, many students have a limited understanding of why copyright might present those delivering or supporting their teaching with challenges. In the future we may start to see this change with an increased focus on entrepreneurship and innovation, and as students become more interested in how to protect their own ideas. Chapter 6 will discuss copyright education and suggest ways it can be delivered for different audiences, including students.

Copyright and educational copying

This section introduces the legal frameworks in which educational practitioners operate. It will compare how copying for online learning can be undertaken within the law in the UK, and then contrast this with the law in Ireland, the USA, Australia, Canada and New Zealand. For practical reasons this book cannot provide a comprehensive overview of the legal position across the world. Therefore, the focus is deliberately on the major English-speaking jurisdictions in the world to provide advice for e-learning practitioners in those countries. Other books that provide detailed copyright advice for specific countries are listed in the section 'Further resources'. Copyright legislation in the former Commonwealth countries (including Canada, Australia and New Zealand) is based on UK law and so is broadly similar. The key differences in the laws are discussed later in the chapter. In the USA, the law differs significantly because the 1976 Copyright Act includes the concept of 'fair use' to cover legal uses of copyright content without the rights holder's permission, whereas in the UK the tradition of 'fair dealing' is used (see 'fair dealing' section on pages 18–19). Fair use is generally seen as a more permissive approach to copyright for it allows copyright material to be copied for any educational use as long as a set of 'fair' criteria apply. Fair dealing, on the other hand, also requires application of a test of fairness, but only applies to a finite list of activities as defined in the legislation (such as criticism and review, or illustration for instruction). There has been some discussion in Europe about introducing the concept of fair use, but to date it seems unlikely to be adopted following significant push back from rights holders. Its introduction in the UK was also explicitly rejected in the Hargreaves Review (2011). Significantly, in the UK and many other countries, much educational or classroom copying still requires institutions to take out a licence from the respective reprographic rights body, as UK law does not include the 'fair use' concept.

An important query often raised by teachers who are developing content they want to deliver throughout the world concerns the jurisdiction that applies when they are copying material. Does the law of the country in which they work take precedence over the law of the country where the content is accessed by the end user? The most pragmatic way to approach this is that if you are developing an online course at a UK institution the laws of the UK apply (or if you are developing a course in a US educational institution US law applies). This is the approach that many institutions take when considering whether exceptions apply even if students might be accessing this material from a different country. This is primarily a risk-based position prompted by the un-harmonized nature of global copyright laws; the nature of this disjointed system is presented in great detail by Kenneth Crews in his World Intellectual Property Organization (WIPO) report on the impact of limitations and exceptions on libraries and archives (Crews, 2015). While further in-depth examination of the fragmented nature of cross-border access to copyright content is outside the scope of this book, it is worth noting that many licences have territorial restrictions in them and this is currently the focus of European policy debate over the creation of a European Digital Single Market (European Commission, 2016). These restrictions in particular apply to licences and services offered by commercial organizations, such as broadcasters and audiovisual production companies, whose business models rely on providing content at different times, different costs and in different formats from country to country. An example of how this has affected education is the ERA licence in the UK, which provides access to free-to-air broadcast material, but only for students geographically located within the UK. E-resource licences (see Chapter 4) increasingly provide access to authorized users based in a range of countries but this has proved a challenging task for collective management organizations like the ERA attempting to negotiate cross-border licences for entire classes of creative work. In the UK the CLA has sought to address this issue through a trial extension to its higher education licence that covers students based at overseas campuses. The pilot is still ongoing; one of the requirements is that students need to be registered at the UK institution to be covered by this licence. Further details about educational licences in the UK are discussed later in this chapter as well as in context throughout the book.

Distance learning has always required a specific focus on copyright issues, and units or institutions dedicated to distance education (like the Open University) have rights and permissions departments to clear content for use, and considering application of exceptions. However, as we have seen earlier, many HEIs have ventured into the realm of online education to improve the effectiveness of their teaching and capitalize on the international market for UK education. As a result the model for traditional educational establishments has changed from one where learning materials were either made available at a physical location (a library) for on-campus students, or were deliberately compiled for off-campus students in conjunction with distance learning teams who were adequately resourced to consider copyright issues. This responsibility now often falls on the shoulders of teaching staff who want to provide compelling teaching content in digital format, but find it difficult to respond appropriately to the many legal questions (including about copyright) that arise. However, the potential for digital technology to empower both teachers and students in this new context is significant, and with the appropriate training and support (see Chapter 6), copyright need not be a barrier to creative teaching.

In general there are a number of ways that copying works can be undertaken without infringing copyright laws. These include copying:

◆ very small amounts of a work (copyright protects a substantial part of a work although no definition of what 'substantial' might be is provided in UK law and it does not relate simply to quantity)

◆ where copyright has expired; copyright protection is limited by duration to a set number of years (a summary of durations as they apply to different kinds of works is listed in Table 1.1), thus copying of a work which is out of copyright and in the 'public domain' is permitted

◆ under a statutory exception; for instance, copying in accordance with 'fair dealing' in the UK for the purposes of quotation, criticism and review

◆ under a collective licence, which gives permission from a broad range of copyright holders to carry out activities restricted by default under law – for example the CLA offer licences for the education sector to permit multiple copying of published works within limits

◆ under some other form of licence issued by the rights holder, such as a licence agreement for an electronic resource or direct permission obtained for use of a specific piece of content

◆ an 'orphan work' using the UK's Orphan Work Licensing Scheme or the EU Directive on orphan works (see above and Chapter 2).

It is interesting to trace how different countries have dealt with educational copying since the advent of the internet, and particularly how they allow teachers and educational establishments to make material available via an online learning platform. While not attempting to be comprehensive, the later part of this chapter includes details from a selection of English-speaking countries. It aims to highlight how technology is causing governments around the world to reconsider their copyright laws and try to bring them up to date. Yet, despite the need for changes to accommodate and support teaching practices, the pressure to amend the law often seems to be coming from well resourced, commercial lobbyists. In particular the media industries such as global publishing, music and film companies that flourished in the 20th century are attempting to combat internet piracy and illegal file sharing by persuading policy makers to strengthen copyright law. In trying to clamp down on this type of copying, legislators could well be causing further problems for educators who simply want to allow students and researchers to be able to access information in the most convenient format. As educational content is increasingly provided in digital format, the copyright and licensing regime in countries throughout the world has proved burdensome for administrators and librarians. However there are signs that a more progressive copyright regime might be evolving as demonstrated in the changes in the UK following the Hargreaves Review. Hopefully future debate will reveal a route to a fairer balance between the needs of education and the need for copyright owners to receive just rewards for their endeavours, and that this will be recognized by governments around the world as they undertake copyright reforms. Nonetheless, those in education need to be mindful that there is a powerful lobby from commercial publishers and the movie and music industry that continues to push back against copyright exceptions. An important aspect of copyright education is to instill ethical use of copyright material in educational institutions in order to challenge the view that exceptions undermine the creative industries' ability to exploit copyright works.

A brief introduction to UK copyright law

These next sections will explore copyright in greater detail, looking at why the laws exist, what types of works are protected, and for how long and what activities are permitted for educational purposes in the UK. This part of the book has been updated following amendments in the UK to the Copyright, Designs and Patents Act 1988 (CDPA) in June and October 2014, which provided several new education-related copyright exceptions and amendments to a number of existing exceptions. These changes[4] followed an independent review of intellectual property law launched by the Prime Minister in November 2010 and conducted by Professor Ian Hargreaves of Cardiff University (Hargreaves, 2011).

This book focuses on copyright and e-learning and is therefore not intended as a comprehensive guide for librarians to copying under the law. See the section 'Further resources' at the end of the book, but notable authors who have produced invaluable guides for UK librarians or archivists include Padfield (2015), Pedley (2015) and Cornish (2015). The works of Padfield and Cornish are useful supplements to this book as they include questions and answers to common copyright dilemmas that those dealing with copyright queries are frequently asked about. Meanwhile Pedley's *The E-Copyright Handbook* (2012) is particularly useful for those interested in relevant case law on digital copyright. This book seeks neither to replace nor replicate these existing publications, but rather to provide a focus on how copyright issues impact specifically on online learning.

The first ever copyright law was implemented in Great Britain at the start of the 18th century. This was intended to provide intellectual and financial incentives for the production of cultural works by providing limited protections to those who create, and invest in the creation of them. The legislation – called the Statute of Anne – was introduced into British law in 1709 and its creation was prompted by the invention of the printing press and the need to regulate copying of literary works. The first words of the statute said that it was 'an act for the encouragement of learning' and even though copyright law has changed a great deal since then it still has a major impact on those working and studying in educational establishments. Since 1709 policy makers around the world have tried to strike the balance between adequate copyright protection against theft and piracy, versus sufficiently generous educational and societally beneficial provisions that foster the free flow of ideas. The need for balance was the main focus on the Hargreaves Review (2011), which sought to modernize UK copyright laws in the digital age. In the UK, copyright does not require a registration process and provided that works meet certain criteria, they then qualify for automatic copyright protection on their creation. These criteria state that the work must be:

◆ original
◆ fixed or recorded in some form

◆   created by a qualified national (effectively this means any person).

Copyright offers protection and certain exclusive rights to the owner or owners of the work. These exclusive rights are the right to:

◆   copy the work
◆   issue copies to the public (essentially to publish the work)
◆   rent or lend the work to the public
◆   perform, show or play the work in public
◆   communicate the work to the public (which means to put it on the internet or broadcast it)
◆   make an adaptation of the work or do any of the above in relation to an adaptation.

Usually the primary author (or authors) owns the copyright to a work, but this is dependent on the nature of the work (see Table 1.1). In the case of literary works such as books, it is often fairly clear who the author is. However, identifying the owner of copyright for works such as films and sound recordings can become more complex. For example in the case of a musical sound recording, the author of the work (the recording) is the producer, and the company that made the arrangements for the recording (e.g. paid for the studio) owns the copyright in it. The performances as captured on the sound recording give rise to an additional set of 'performance rights' for the featured artists. This is all in addition to the separate copyright protection afforded to the underlying musical work and

Table 1.1 *UK law on duration of copyright by type of material (CDPA 1988)*	
Type of material	**Duration of copyright**
Literary, artistic, dramatic and musical works	70 years from the death of the author, or 70 years from publication/performance if no named author
Sound recordings	70 years from the date of recording
Films	50 years following the last to die of: the principal director, producer, author of screenplay, composer of soundtrack
Broadcasts	50 years from the date of broadcast
Typographical layout	25 years from publication
Unpublished works	70 years from the death of the author or 31 December 2039 – whichever is longer

the lyrics (in the case of a song), the authors of which are often different people to the producer or the artists. In the case of films the producer and the principal director are the author of the work. Cornish (2015, 121–9) provides an excellent overview of the issues surrounding copyright ownership, many of which were complicated by the changes to UK copyright law throughout the 20th century. Anyone trying to identify the copyright holder in any given work should be aware that as a property right, copyright can also be transferred (sold) to someone other than the author. In many cases the copyright owner of a work can be identified from the copyright symbol placed somewhere prominently on the work (for example, © Jane Secker with Chris Morrison 2016), but its use is not a prerequisite for copyright protection in the UK or for much of the world.

Cornish (2015, 42–3) provides greater detail about the duration of copyright and should be consulted for specific queries such as protection for authors from outside the European Economic Area and protection for works with multiple authors. Even when copyright has expired, moral rights may remain. The moral rights are the right to be identified as the author of a work (paternity), the right to object to derogatory treatment of a work (integrity), the right not to be identified as the author of someone else's work (false attribution), and the right to privacy of certain photographs and films. See the Glossary for more details.

In addition to the protection that a copyright work receives in the country where it was first published, there are several international copyright agreements that provide protection for works internationally. For further details of these agreements such as the Berne Convention, the UK's IPO provides a useful overview (IPO, 2014).

Content produced by UK civil servants, ministers and government departments (including legislation and government reports) is known as Crown Copyright material. Most copying and publication of Crown Copyright material was previously allowed under a waiver, but is now explicitly permitted under the terms of the Open Government Licence (National Archives, 2015). This now permits unrestricted copying of the material following amendment of the Public Sector Information Directive in 2013. The Open Government Licence is discussed in Chapter 4 (pages 132–3); in essence, provided you acknowledge the source and do not reproduce government logos or insignias, you are free to copy, adapt and exploit UK government information.

The Hargreaves Review

Before we consider copyright exceptions and licences it is worth considering the recent changes to the law in the UK to provide some context. Although the UK Copyright Act has been modified many times since 1988, significant amendments relating to education were finally made to the CDPA in June and October 2014. This followed the review of intellectual property by Professor Ian Hargreaves, which came after several failed attempts in the preceding decades to redress the balance in the copyright regime and modernize it for the digital age (Hargreaves, 2011). For example, in December 2005 HM Treasury launched a widespread review of UK intellectual property laws, known as the Gowers Review. The recommendations made by the Gowers Report (HM Treasury, 2006) were widely criticized as not going far enough to recognize the pace of technological change and they were never implemented in UK law. Consequently in November 2010 the Prime Minister announced another review of intellectual property laws to make them fit for the digital age and to ensure they supported innovation in the interests of economic growth. This time the recommendations from the review led to amendments to the law following several rounds of consultations with stakeholders. This included the education community and representatives of rights holders and other commercial and non-commercial organizations.

Professor Hargreaves made ten recommendations and the government responded to the Hargreaves Review in August 2011. In 2013 the first changes were enacted via the Enterprise and Regulatory Reform Act, which made provision for the handling of orphan works – works where it is not possible to identify or contact the author. Meanwhile the Copyright Hub[5] was launched in July 2013 (see Chapter 5, page 203, for more details) and the new exceptions finally came into force on 1 October 2014.

The issue of 'orphan works' has caused many problems in education and cultural institutions. Orphan works consume a considerable amount of staff time in attempts to track down rights holders to obtain permission to copy the materials. On occasions where the rights cannot be traced, an institution needs to assess the risks involved in copying the material without permission for each individual case. Institutions also need to maintain records to demonstrate that all possible avenues were explored. The launch of the Orphan Works Licensing Scheme by the IPO in October 2014 gave institutions one route to using orphan works in a risk free way.

However, there is also now an orphan works exception following a European directive that allows use of certain orphan works by educational and cultural institutions. For more information see Chapter 2, pages 81–2.

One of the most significant aspects of the 2014 copyright reforms in the UK was the provision that certain exceptions could not be undermined by the terms of a contract between rights holder and end user. This was particularly important to the education sector in relation to the licensing of electronic resources, where the terms of a licence are often more restrictive than the provisions of the law. For example, the law allows people to make a single copy of an article for their own non-commercial research or private study but an electronic resource licence may prohibit this. The effect of the changes to the law in October 2014 was that any term of a contract or licence that attempted to undermine an exception provided for by law in the UK could be ignored. However it is still early days to ascertain what this actually means in practice. For many academic librarians working under the provisions of a range of licence agreements there is a level of anxiety about whether they can ignore a legal contract they or their employers have agreed to. The issue has also been further complicated where commercial publishers use some form of digital rights management (DRM) technology to prevent copying or exploitation of the work under an exception (see Chapter 4, pages 125–7, for more information). In early 2016 these matters were subject to ongoing discussions between the IPO and the Libraries and Archives Copyright Alliance (LACA).

'Fair dealing'

If you wish to use a copyright work for educational purposes in the UK you could do this under a direct licence, where permission is obtained directly from the rights holder, or a collective licence from a reprographic rights organization such as the CLA. Alternatively you could choose to rely on a copyright exception if licences are unavailable or inappropriate, although this will require consideration of the CDPA to ensure that the proposed activity is permitted by law. Licences are effectively a risk free approach to copying, because you have permission, meanwhile copyright exceptions rely on an element of judgement. UK law (like many other copyright laws throughout the world) has a provision known as 'fair dealing', and most educational copying done under an exception to copyright law is subject to this provision. It requires a judgement to be made over how a 'fair-minded and honest person would deal with the work' and case law is relevant here in determining what might be 'fair'. Fair dealing is in fact a defence that could be used in court rather than a right under law. This is particularly important because it puts the onus on the person using the defence to make sure it actually applies. Since 2014 fair dealing can be applied to all types of copyright works (including films, sound recordings or broadcasts) and permits the making of limited copies for the following specific purposes:

◆ non-commercial research and private study
◆ quotation, criticism and review
◆ the reporting of news
◆ government administration
◆ illustration for instruction
◆ caricature, parody, or pastiche.

In all cases, where feasible you must provide a sufficient acknow-ledgement. Much photocopying and scanning of published works undertaken in an educational context falls under the fair dealing provisions; for example, single copies made by teachers for their research or by students as part of their private study. However, distribution of copies via the VLE or similar network constitutes multiple copying and thus is unlikely to be considered as fair dealing. Having said that, fair dealing defences do cover some activities beyond single, personal copies as the next section on specific educational exceptions in the UK explains.

Educational copying and UK law

Anyone wanting to make copyright material legally available in educational establishments in the UK has to do so under either a licence or an exception to copyright. In order to stay within the law and make the best use of your resources you need to understand the relationship between the two.

Licences can be for specific works or collections of content, or they may be 'blanket' licences that cover whole classes of work (e.g. musical works or published editions). The most commonly encountered licensing bodies providing blanket permissions to UK educational establishments are summarized in Table 1.2.

Table 1.2 *Licensing bodies providing blanket permissions to UK educational establishments*

Licensing body	Class of work	What is allowed
The CLA (Copyright Licensing Agency; www.cla.co.uk/)	Books, magazines	Limited copying and use in a VLE such as Moodle
The ERA (Educational Recording Agency; www.era.org.uk/)	UK TV broadcasts	Recording and storage allows use of Box of Broadcasts (BoB) service http://bobnational.net/
NLA Media Access (Newspaper Licensing Agency; www.nlamediaaccess.com/)	Newspapers, magazines	Press clippings (including digital content)
The DACS (Design and Artists Copyright Society; www.dacs.org.uk/)	Artistic images (including photos)	Reproduction of artistic works
PRS for Music (www.prsformusic.com/), formerly two separate organizations: the Performing Right Society and the Mechanical Copyright Protection Society	Musical works and sound recordings	Public performance, audio products, online services; performance, communication and reproduction of musical works on behalf of songwriters and composers
PPL (Phonographic Performance Limited; www.ppluk.com/)	Musical sound recordings	Public performance of musical sound recordings on behalf of the copyright holders (record companies, producers and performers)
Filmbank (www.filmbank.co.uk/)	Feature films	Showing film and TV in non-educational context

In addition to dealing with the licensing bodies listed in Table 1.2, institutions can purchase licences for specific electronic library resources, teaching objects and software packages directly from suppliers or via aggregators like Jisc Collections and Eduserv (for more details on born digital resources see Chapter 4).

In the UK, Sections 29 to 36 of the CDPA include specific exceptions that relate to education where it is not possible or appropriate to get a licence.

Table 1.3 sets these out in more detail (although as this is a summary you should refer to the original wording of the legislation when assessing a copyright issue).

Table 1.3 *Exceptions in the CDPA relating to education*

Copyright exception	Brief description	Limitation and caveats
Section 29: Research and private study	Allows individuals to make single copies of limited extracts of copyright works for non-commercial research or private study. No contractual override.	Subject to fair dealing. Cannot be used for sharing material on a VLE. Individuals must make their own copies. Cannot be used to circulate copies to students.
Section 30: Quotation (criticism and review)	Allows 'fair dealing' usage of quotations for any purposes including 'criticism and review'. No contractual override.	Subject to fair dealing. Works must have been made publicly available (this does not cover unpublished material).
Section 31A & 31B: Accessible copies for disabled users	Allows copying to provide equal access to copyright works for users with any type of physical or mental disability, as individuals (s.31A) or institutions (s. 31B). No contractual override.	Covers all types of copyright work. No contractual override. Does not address use of DRM technologies or technical protection measures.
Section 32: Illustration for instruction	Allows limited, non-commercial 'fair dealing' use of copyright material for the purposes of teaching. No contractual override.	Subject to fair dealing. Covers all copyright works including sound recordings, films and broadcasts.
Section 34: Performing or playing a work for educational purposes	Performing, playing or showing work in course of activities of educational establishment.	Members of the public cannot be admitted. Does not permit copying of the work.
Section 35: Recording of broadcasts	Allows recording of free-to-air broadcasts by or on behalf of educational establishments for non-commercial purposes. Only applies where no licensing scheme (ERA) available.	ERA licensing scheme takes precedence. Non-commercial educational use. Allows off premises access only via secure electronic network.

Continued on next page

Table 1.3 *Continued*		
Copyright exception	**Brief description**	**Limitation and caveats**
Section 36: Educational copying of published works	Allows copying and use of multiple copies of extracts from published copyright works. Only applies where no licensing scheme (i.e. CLA) available.	Cannot exceed more than 5% of a work in a year per institution. CLA licensing scheme takes precedence if the work is in CLA's licensed repertoire. Includes incorporated works (e.g. illustrations).

Although the CDPA makes a provision for educational copying, relying on the exceptions to the law involves a degree of risk. The CDPA does not specify which technologies can be used to make copies, so digital copying is permitted. However, the distribution of copies of a work via a network was clarified to be an exclusive right of the right holders in 2003 when the UK law was amended by the Copyright and Related Rights Regulations (Statutory Instrument No. 2498). This amendment:

◆   redefined broadcasts to specifically exclude internet transmission (or podcasts)
◆   gave copyright holders the exclusive right to 'communicate a work to the public'
◆   defined this right as making the material available by 'electronic transmission' – via the internet and/or broadcasting the work.

Before this amendment it was technically illegal to view websites, as doing so created temporary copies on the viewer's computer, but the amendment stated that copyright is not infringed by:

the making of a temporary copy which is transient or incidental, which is an integral and essential part of a technological process and the sole purpose of which is to enable:

(a) a transmission of the work in a network between third parties by an intermediary; or
(b) a lawful use of the work.

Chapters 2–5 of this book consider in greater depth the ways in which licences and exceptions apply to certain types of content and context in the UK, although it is worth discussing the broader implications of the recently updated legislative environment. One of the objectives of the recent UK copyright reforms was to legitimize existing educational practice and provide the flexibility to avoid copyright being a barrier to the use of new tools and practices in learning and teaching. Section 32 of the CDPA – 'illustration for instruction' – is one of the most important additions to the law because until 2014 there was no provision for the reproduction of copyright material in teaching 'by means of a reprographic process'. This meant that using copyright content in PowerPoint slides and electronic whiteboards for teaching without permission was illegal and there was no provision for the copying of sound recordings or film. Effectively this left traditional 'chalk and talk' reproductions of existing works as the only practical, legal option, although it was widely recognized that use of technology to present copyright content to students in a classroom was widespread and caused little harm to copyright holders. This section of the CDPA also updated the provisions for use of copyright content for the purposes of answering or preparing an examination question – an exception that has also been widely used by those creating dissertations or theses. The amendment in 2014 actually narrowed the scope of this exception by removing the condition that 'anything done for the purposes of an examination' was permissible and instead applied a fair dealing test. However, it is likely that for the most part the activities undertaken under the previous, more wide-ranging exception are still valid under the newly worded legislation. As before, the exception only relates to the preparation or answering of the exam question, so subsequent use of the material such as posting a thesis containing third-party copyright material is not covered under this exception, although it may be under Section 30 – criticism and review, quotation and news reporting. See Chapter 4, pages 158–9, for more information on the online submission of theses.

The practice of quoting from other works is fundamental to the process of learning, but up until 2014 there was no exception that specifically mentioned the term 'quotation'. Instead Section 30 of the CDPA allowed limited portions of works to be reproduced for the purposes of criticism and review (and for news reporting), so the use of the work had to relate to a critical evaluation of the work or a related concept (such as the values and thoughts embodied in it). Following the Hargreaves Review, the law was amended to say that people could quote a reasonable proportion of a copyright work for any purpose as long as it had already been published and the use passed the fair dealing test (not any more than was needed, not affecting sales or exploitation and with attribution where practical). For the vast majority of students, quotations of short passages of text would already have been allowed under the standing concept of criticism and review. However, the exception now covers other potential uses in an e-learning environment, such as including material in exam tests, or teaching materials (although as mentioned earlier there is likely to be some overlap with Section 32, 'illustration for instruction', where both exceptions might apply). As the introduction of the concept of quotation is so new and there has been little UK case law, it is by no means clear what is and is not acceptable. Of particular relevance to those looking to make teaching materials available is whether an image (protected as an artistic work) could be said to be 'quoted' if it was reproduced in its entirety. EU case law suggests that in some cases reproduction of a photograph could be a quotation. This is discussed in more depth in Chapter 3, pages 91–2.

Section 34 allows copyright works such as films, TV programmes and music to be shown or performed in educational establishments as part of their educational activities. Therefore showing or performing a copyright work at an educational institution would not be covered by this exception unless it was done for the purposes of teaching or assessment.

Section 35 allows educational establishments to record broadcasts for the purposes of teaching and learning as long as there are no licences available for this activity. Although this exception can be used for subscription TV and radio, the recording of free-to-air broadcasts in the UK is licensed by the ERA. The ERA licences and the ways of getting access to broadcast content in education are mentioned in more detail in Chapter 3.

Section 36 allows educational establishments to make multiple copies of limited extracts from copyright works (with the exception of broadcasts or images that are not incorporated into other works) in order to support teaching. The limits before the 2014 copyright reforms were so low (1% of a work per quarter) that they were rarely, if ever, used. The updated limits now cover up to 5% of a work per institution per year, but as before do not apply if there are licences available to cover the copying. In the UK the CLA and Newspaper Licensing Agency (NLA) licences cover books, journals and newspapers, respectively, so the exception does not relate to anything within those organizations' repertoire where a licence is available. Educational institutions wanting to take advantage of Section 36 need to consider that although the percentage limit of an extract is similar to that of the CLA Licence, the conditions of the exception are different from the available licences. One major difference is that the 5% limit on a particular copyright work applies to the whole institution, so two or more teachers must not copy from the same work even if they are copying different extracts for different groups of students. In any event, it is important for institutions to incorporate an understanding of Section 36 alongside the application of the CLA Licence within their standard processes and procedures. The history and practical applications of the CLA Licence are discussed in more detail in Chapter 2.

Before 2014, copies for students with a visual impairment could be made under the Copyright (Visually Impaired Persons) Act 2002. This allowed single copies of copyright works (literary, dramatic, musical or artistic work or a published edition) to be made for visually impaired persons for accessibility purposes if they were not available commercially. The act has now been repealed following the Hargreaves recommendations that this should form a new exception and be extended to persons with all types of disabilities, not just visual. Section 31 of the CDPA now allows copying to provide equal access to copyright works for users with any type of physical or mental disability, either as individuals (s. 31A) or institutions (s. 31B). Copying for students with disabilities is also explicitly covered by the CLA Licence and the copying does not need to be reported, unlike other scanned items.

Case Study 1   The copyright officer at Brunel University London

Monique Ritchie

Introduction

In 2004–5, Brunel University Library created a new dedicated post to manage copyright in the academic environment, with a focus on digital copyright: the copyright and digital resources officer. Like most educational institutions, recent changes to copyright law and licensing schemes, and the increased use of e-learning environments and e-resources, threw copyright to the forefront of strategic planning. There was a strong recognition among library and senior university management that the digital age posed particular challenges at a time when the University's e-learning strategy was evolving rapidly. It became increasingly apparent that a university-wide copyright consultancy service was required to manage licence administration and copyright advice faced with an increasingly intricate licensing and legislative framework.

In 2012–13, the copyright officer assumed additional research support responsibilities in response to changes affecting academic research around open access and research data management and the post became a dual one: research librarian and copyright officer.

Remit, scope and position in the institution

The remit is broad, with the copyright officer responsible for providing support on copyright and IPR issues to all staff and students, academic and non-academic. However, the post sits within the library staff structure as, despite the close links with external departments and colleges and institutes, key stakeholders are primarily engaged in teaching, learning and research functions. The library naturally occupies a central position in relation to these, and is quite often the first port of call for questions – library or non-library related.

Initially, the Director of Library Services directly oversaw the direction and focus of the role as it had linkages with the University's strategic planning process. Once established, and following internal restructuring in 2008–9 to address changing university priorities, management devolved to the Academic Services team, working alongside subject liaison librarians and the institutional repository team. Further internal and institutional restructuring found copyright, digital readings and the institutional repository moving to Content Services, responsible for electronic resources, library systems and e-strategy in 2013–14, with the role based in a newly created Research Support Services sub-team. The copyright officer works closely with the Collection Services team responsible for interlibrary loans, reading list processing and acquisitions.

While copyright is no longer based in the same team as the subject liaison librarians who provide comprehensive support to the University's learning, teaching and research aims and objectives, the copyright officer continues to benefit from their close links with academic staff, and they also assume some copyright support responsibilities.

Within the institution, there are links with the Legal, Governance and Information Office, Computing and Media Services and the Learning Technology Team, and directly with academic staff within colleges and research institutes. The role therefore involves working with a wide variety of colleagues at many levels.

Role and responsibilities

The copyright officer deals primarily with the following areas:

◆ copyright licence administration
◆ creating and implementing copyright policy and procedures
◆ copyright compliance monitoring
◆ copyright clearance
◆ copyright consultancy (guidance on copyright and IPR issues, with a focus on digital copyright)
◆ designing and delivering staff development and user education on copyright and IPR in a teaching, learning and research environment.

The copyright officer is responsible for ensuring that the University meets the requirements of copyright law by administering licences and providing advice and training. The role directly supports the University's teaching and learning strategy, playing a significant role in making digital resources of all kinds available to staff and students, developing services and helping to ensure that initiatives in this area are seamlessly integrated from a user's perspective. The Digital Readings Service, which delivers digital readings licensed by CLA to the VLE, is one such initiative.

Core parts of the role of the copyright officer are ensuring that staff and students are aware of the terms of the licences, developing support materials and disseminating information in the form of web pages, staff development sessions, handbooks and newsletters. Copyright clearance is perhaps the smallest part of the role, possibly because Brunel encourages and provides support to staff to obtain their own, and before the post was created, many staff and departments were accustomed to doing this themselves. External liaison with similar post holders at other institutions is encouraged.

Although it may appear that the research and copyright elements of the Brunel role are unconnected, in fact they are symbiotically linked. First, there are significant copyright and intellectual property issues affecting all aspects of the research lifecycle, from conceptualization of a research project or idea to the publication and curation of research outputs and beyond. This dual role provides a unique opportunity to link support and target a community which is typically more difficult to target than the education community.

Second, the highly individualized and 'siloed' nature of research makes providing services and training to the research community challenging compared with the teaching or administrative communities, where centralized support is more embedded. Research support has proved to be a way in, as researchers seek advice on demand based on their individual schedules and needs, such as when applying for funding or publishing.

Problems, issues, challenges

The key areas of difficulty relate mainly to the CLA Licence and the legislative framework. Licensing terms and conditions are complex, requiring interpretation or condensing into manageable bite-sized formats for staff. Administratively, the CLA Licence requires separate processes from other content and its reporting and collection maintenance requirements are onerous, although there have been recent improvements and a commitment to working closely with the sector to improve licensing conditions.

Changes to copyright law in 2014 have further complicated copyright support, as some aspects of copyright practice and interpretation have now become less clear, particularly around fair dealing statutory exceptions for examinations and instruction. The use of certain content types, like images and broadcasts, is still fraught with difficulty. Some positive changes in the legislation, such as the exception allowing 5% of unlicensed works to be used for teaching in a 12-month period, are not being used because of the impracticability of managing processes institutionally and workload implications.

When the VLE was upgraded to a new version in 2007, which required training for most staff, 50 sessions were delivered to staff during that year. Sustaining a copyright training programme of this intensity is not feasible and so training is provided to e-learning support staff who cascade support to academics with back-up from the copyright officer. In 2015–16, centralized training is to be delivered through a central academic practice programme co-ordinated by the Brunel Educational Excellence Centre.

Brunel has found that academic staff, who are the primary users of the CLA Licence in their teaching, and to a lesser extent in their research, simply do not have the time to absorb the complexities of the licence and work out how to apply them to their needs or attend training sessions. Many staff are balancing heavy teaching, research and administrative workloads and the reality for most is that planning course content and relevant readings is often done under pressure. It is not uncommon for reading lists to be put together ad hoc, even a week before they are needed. In fact, from an academic's viewpoint, it is arguably the best method to guarantee the currency and relevance of readings, although from a library perspective this is the worst possible way, as the acquisitions process takes time, particularly when many lists come in at once.

Brunel tackles copyright compliance holistically, by focusing on embedding good practice into processes, rather than on the rules and regulations, and by simplifying administration for staff. A key example of this is the introduction of a simple requirement for staff to prepare and submit reading lists to the library for resourcing. Library staff then resource the content, consulting academics when there is a conflict or clearance is needed. Staff no longer need worry about what is legal, they can simply prepare lists based on the most appropriate content for their teaching needs and library staff advise accordingly. However, this approach is demanding and resource intensive for the library.

Technological advancements in teaching methods and evolving 'reading lists' that are less text based and feature multimedia and other content types (e.g. YouTube) more frequently increase demands on copyright support.

Conclusion

Compliance with multiple terms and conditions in complex licences is resource intensive and the workload it generates increases exponentially each year with increasing use of e-learning environments and other emerging technologies where the rules are different.

Overall, it is a very challenging task to ensure that the institution complies with copyright legislation and terms of blanket and contractual licensing. These licences are not yet flexible enough to allow academics to make use of the best resources available, without getting bogged down in working out what is legal or not. At Brunel the view is that copyright, even with recent changes to legislation in 2014, can at times hamper the ability to teach and conduct research effectively in the increasingly competitive international higher education environment, which has an impact on the creative output of students and researchers and ultimately on the economy.

Ireland

Irish copyright laws are broadly similar to those in the UK, although Ireland's Copyright and Related Rights Act dates from 2000 rather than 1988. As with the UK, Irish copyright laws have been amended in recent years following European directives. Educational institutions are required to take out a licence to cover multiple copying of copyright works from the Irish Copyright Licensing Agency (ICLA; www.icla.ie). Licences are available for schools and for HEIs. The licences cover photocopying, scanning and digital distribution of Irish works for secondary schools and HEIs. The ICLA also has reciprocal agreements in place for scanning of titles from the UK, Australia, Canada (including Quebec), New Zealand and South Africa. It has a list of participating US publishers and the licence also covers newspapers from Ireland and the UK. The licence specifies that institutions can make 'digital copies' (defined as scanning unaltered from the original) of copyright works that:

◆ are already owned by the institution
◆ do not exceed the limits of the paper licence (5% or chapter of a book, one article from a journal, a short story or poem not exceeding ten pages from an anthology)
◆ do not include printed music, newspapers, maps, charts, books of tables, artistic works (other than those essential to illustrate a text), in-house journals or 'privately prepared teaching materials'.

The licence also specifies that:

◆ no changing or editing of the material is permitted
◆ digital copies should not be posted on the web or sent by e-mail or linked to such that it can be accessed by unauthorized parties
◆ no copying to storage devices of the digital materials is permitted
◆ gathering of the copies is only permissible for back-up purposes and not for construction of a repository or database of resources.

Scanning under the licence causes some concerns in Irish institutions that are not able to restrict users from copying the files to a storage device – such as a USB stick or their own computer. Irish copyright laws were amended some time before those in the UK so that licences and contracts for digital publications (such as electronic journals or databases) cannot override the exceptions to copyright provided by statute. However, Kretschmer et al. (2010, 101) pointed out that no case law exists in Ireland and no empirical studies have been carried out to establish the impact this provision has on the Irish copyright industry.

Australia

In Australia the Copyright Act 1968 remains in force although significant changes were made to the law in 2000, which impacted on the copying that could be undertaken for educational purposes. Since the Copyright Amendment (Digital Agenda) Act 2000 came into force in 2001 it has been possible to scan copyright works for educational purposes under a licence from the reprographic rights organization, Copyright Agency Limited (CAL; www.copyright.com.au). The CAL website provides guidance for those in education and the education licences are blanket licences similar to those issued by the CLA in the UK since 2005. The licence covers photocopying, scanning and digital copying of text or images and allows any form of 'reproduction' or 'communication'. This includes adding to or changing the content, or presenting it in a different context. There are many similarities between the UK and Australian licences, which largely reflect the similarities of the legislative environment.

However, the CAL licences are more permissive than the CLA Licence in the UK, permitting 10% of a literary or musical work to be copied or one article from a journal issue. Artistic works can be copied in their entirety and copying from both published and unpublished works is permitted. Copies can only be distributed to registered students on a course and the material must also contain a copyright statement. Australian CAL licences also differ from the UK's CLA licences in the obligation to report data. Whereas UK universities have agreed to full data reporting on all items they scan under licence since 2005, data reporting is not a requirement of the Australian licence and compliance is monitored largely through periodic surveys. Further information and answers to frequently asked questions about the CAL licences are available from the agency's website (CAL, 2015).

Screenrights (www.screenrights.org) manages a licence that allows educational institutions to copy and share broadcast content, such as documentaries shown on television. There are also arrangements in place for music licensing of educational establishments.

New Zealand

Although the New Zealand Copyright Act 1994 allows schools, public tertiary (higher education) institutions and non-profit private training establishments to copy material from published works for educational purposes, the amounts permitted are limited. Therefore New Zealand has a similar licensing scheme to those in the UK and Australia. This permits copying beyond these limits and is issued by Copyright Licensing New Zealand (CLNZ; www.copyright.co.nz), which is the reprographic rights organization in New Zealand and offers licences for education and other sectors. Scanning under the CLNZ licence and copyright issues are discussed in Case Study 5 about the University of Auckland, presented in Chapter 4. The licence is similar to the Australian CAL licence in that the limits are 10% or one chapter of a work. However, the New Zealand CLNZ licence only covers copying from print originals. Pages copied from websites or electronic retrieval systems can be stored in the learning management system (VLE) under the Copyright Act 1994, providing certain conditions are met. Until recently each licensee provided sample data for all content copied under the licence during the period of one year, once in the five year term of the licence. New Zealand universities are currently piloting a different system, whereby each university has agreed to install e-reporting software that will automate the survey process and report more frequently with more accurate data. This will be reviewed at the end of 2016. In 2013 CLNZ referred a new licence and a significant increase in the licence fee for New Zealand universities to the New Zealand Copyright Tribunal. The reference followed a breakdown in negotiations after the universities refused to agree to the increased licence fee. The universities considered the proposed increase, from $6 to $20 per year per student, to be unreasonable given that journals and books were increasingly available in digital format. Further sources of advice about

New Zealand copyright law are included in the section 'Further resources'; the Copyright Council of New Zealand and the Library and Information Association of New Zealand Aotearoa provide useful information.

Canada

Canadian copyright laws are based on UK law, and therefore include common principles such as fair dealing and similar exceptions to copyright for educational purposes. Since 2007 the Canadian Government has been attempting to review its copyright laws, which has led to considerable public concern about copyright issues. Known as C-61 and C-32, the reforms have been criticized by many including Michael Geist, a University of Ottawa law professor, who led a movement that gained enormous popularity through a Facebook group. For example, amendments to Canadian law to outlaw the circumvention of digital rights management systems have been met with much opposition. Campaigners argue that circumvention for non-infringing purposes, such as fair dealing or uses permitted by educational and library exceptions in the Copyright Act, must be allowed.

In order to address these questions the Canadian Government convened the Gatineau Copyright Roundtable in July 2009. It was attended by copyright experts and representatives from bodies such as the Association of Universities and Colleges of Canada (AUCC) – now known as Universities Canada (www.univcan.ca/). In 2009 the AUCC recognized that copyright reforms were needed to support e-learning, and believed that educational uses of materials freely posted on the internet should be permitted. They therefore advocated that copyright laws should be amended to facilitate technology-enhanced learning and not to disadvantage online learners. In 2012, Bill C-11, otherwise known as the Copyright Modernization Act, was adopted, resulting in significant amendments to the Copyright Act. These included expanded exceptions for educational institutions and libraries, archives and museums, and reduced statutory damages for non-commercial infringement.

In 2012 Canadian universities had a similar dispute to that in New Zealand over copyright licensing with their reprographic rights organization, Access Copyright (which covers all of Canada, with the exception of Quebec), over the price of the annual licence. Access

Copyright had claimed that universities were unable to opt out of their licence, but a Supreme Court of Canada decision – in Alberta (Education) vs. Access Copyright – found that some copying for educational purposes did fall firmly under fair dealing. This decision, in combination with expansion to fair dealing in Bill C-11, led Canadian universities to question the value of the licence. Many Canadian universities have subsequently opted out of the licence, and rely on the fair dealing guidelines adopted by Universities Canada. These guidelines (Universities Canada, 2015) outline the amounts of copyright material that may be reproduced for educational purposes and under which circumstances, without payment of fees or obtaining permissions. However, some legal experts caution that the amounts referred to in the policy have no firm basis in law. Access Copyright is currently suing one Canadian university, while another university is embroiled in a lawsuit with the Quebec rights collective Copibec.

Access Copyright now offers a wide variety of licence options, to cover photocopies, e-mail attachments and the distribution of digital readings. There are several resources on Canadian copyright law listed in the section 'Further resources'. The Canadian Library Association maintains a Copyright Information Centre on its website and Michael Geist's blog (www.michaelgeist.ca) is another good source of up-to-date information.

The USA
Copyright legislation

In the USA the current legislation dates from 1974, but several other acts have been issued that those working in education need to be aware of. Copying for education under the Copyright Act 1974 is certainly less restrictive than in other countries in the world. The concept of 'fair use' is enshrined in the law, and differs substantially from the UK concept of 'fair dealing'. Specifically 'fair use' is a broad legal doctrine, which covers copying of copyright material for educational and other societally beneficial purposes. In the late 1990s many US librarians were involved in the Conference on Fair Use (CONFU) to set out guidelines of what could be copied under this provision. This coincided with many university libraries establishing electronic reserves services. Electronic reserves are either scanned or digital copies of copyright works made available to students via the library. The term 'reserves' is taken from the US word used commonly for short loan collections. Traditional paper 'reserves' were either books or copies of articles kept in the library for reference only access to allow large numbers of students to access them. Electronic reserves services were originally developed in parallel with online learning, and required students to access the material in the library via dedicated terminals. However, increasingly these services are now integrated so readings are delivered via the VLE. Some US universities rely on the fair use provision to deliver copyright material to students, and only seek copyright permission for material that is repeatedly used in a course of study. Others are more risk averse and routinely seek permission to digitize material for electronic reserves either directly with publishers or through the US reprographic rights organization, the Copyright Clearance Center (CCC). The CCC offers a blanket licence to institutions that wish to cover the copying they undertake. Unlike in the UK, most US government materials are not covered by copyright and unrestricted copying is permitted (see Chapter 1, page 16).

Other relevant US legislation

The Digital Millennium Copyright Act (DMCA) came into force in 1998 and specifically prohibits the circumvention of any 'technological protection measure' that a copyright owner might put in place, so the use of the digital material by students or teachers may be restricted if a publisher had used some form of digital rights management technology. The DCMA also added a provision known as 'safe harbor' which limits the legal liability of internet service providers from copyright infringements carried out by users of their service. This safe harbor provision has been instrumental in allowing the growth of internet services containing large volumes of third party copyright material. Meanwhile legislation dating from 2002 has also impacted on the delivery of copyright works in the USA, specifically with relation to distance learners. TEACHAct (covering technology, education and copyright harmonization) allows copyright works to be delivered to distance learners without permission from the rights holder and without the payment of fees. It covers the digitization of analogue works to produce digital materials if a digital version is not available for purchase.

Some of the specific requirements of this act are: only not-for-profit educational institutions are covered; the educational institution must have an institutional copyright policy; the educational institution must provide copyright information to faculty, other staff and students; the material must have a notice to inform students of the copyright policy; and the material can only be distributed to enrolled students.

The TEACHAct formalized what had been a grey area in US legislation. It allowed US institutions to make digital copies of published content available to students via a secure network (ALA, 2015). However, the act has not been without controversy and in 2008 several large publishing houses embarked on legal action against universities that they believed to be in breach of copyright. Both the University of California and Georgia State University have been pursued in court by publishers who believed their copyright had been infringed over the interpretation of fair use in regard to electronic copies for educational use. In the instance of Georgia State cases were first filed in 2008 and it was not until 2015 that the case was finally dropped. Case Study 3 in Chapter 2 examines the practice of one US university which takes a less risk-averse approach to copyright issues.

Copyright and scholarly communication

While technology moves at a fast pace and constantly offers teachers new ways of delivering different types of resources to students across a network, copyright law is often perceived as being slow to change and out of step with what is technically possible. Arguably copying material for educational purposes has also been an area of unspoken tension between publishers and academics. Many academic authors are themselves rights holders and as content creators they wish to see their work protected and derive a modest income from their publications. However, reproducing, copying, modifying and amending the work of others has always been a fundamental part of scholarship. Very little research is undertaken without building on the findings of previous studies and conventions such as quotation, citation and referencing were developed to recognize and acknowledge the works of others. So it is inevitable that teachers use others' ideas in the classroom, particularly in the arts, humanities and social sciences, where debate, opinion and argument are an essential part of the learning process. Yet technology has led many in the publishing, film and music industries to try to tighten copyright laws in conjunction with the application of technical protection measures (or digital locks).

This tension between the ease with which people can now share knowledge and creativity, and the concerns of those who have prospered under the more regulated and controlled information environment of the pre-internet age, has created an ideological battleground and copyright is at its heart. While rights holders talk of piracy and the risk this puts to jobs in the creative sector, advocates of the potential for humanity to share knowledge and creative outputs talk about freedom. The most famous and tragic example of these two viewpoints clashing involved the programmer and activist Aaron Swartz, who was a key figure in the creation of the Creative Commons licences (see below). He also helped to defeat the US Stop Online Piracy Act (SOPA) legislation in 2012, which was intended to control piracy on the internet. Swartz was caught systematically downloading JSTOR (see Chapter 4) articles on the campus of the Massachusetts Institute of Technology (MIT) in the USA in 2011. The subsequent prosecution through the US criminal justice system led Swartz to take his own life in 2013. Although this is an extreme example it demonstrates the level of investment that many people have in continuing this ideological battle. The rise of Sci-Hub, an illicit scholarly publishing file sharing service, is the latest incarnation of this battle in the education and research sector – see Chapter 5 for more detail. In the face of ever-tighter copyright restrictions some academics and IPR experts have launched initiatives to attempt to redress the imbalance that they believe now exists. A few of these initiatives are worthy of mention and discussed briefly next.

Creative Commons

The Creative Commons movement was founded in 2001 by Lawrence Lessig and a group of cyber law and IPR experts. Lessig is Professor of Law at Stanford Law School and founder of the school's Center for Internet and Society. The movement, sometimes called an alternative to copyright, is founded on the belief that modern copyright laws have become overly restrictive and are stifling creativity: 'A single goal unites Creative Commons' current and future projects: to build a layer of reasonable, flexible copyright in the face of increasingly restrictive default rules' (Creative Commons, 2009).

Creative Commons licences offer creators various choices, including to apply limited restrictions, an approach called 'some rights reserved'. This allows content creators to attach licences to their work to indicate that they are happy for it to be used in certain circumstances. Awareness of Creative Commons has grown considerably since the decision was taken to use these licences on Wikipedia in 2009. It is also now possible to search Google for content licensed under Creative Commons and the popular photo-sharing website Flickr uses Creative Commons licences as a key feature of its service. There are six types of Creative Commons licence, comprising four licence components: Attribution (BY), Non-Commercial (NC), No Derivatives (ND) and ShareAlike (SA). A summary of the six licences and their constituent components is given in Table 1.4.

As a content creator, a teacher can attach a Creative Commons licence to their work to indicate that they are happy to share it under certain

Table 1.4 *Creative Commons licences*

Licence type	Abbreviation	Description
Attribution	CC-BY	Lets others distribute, remix, tweak and build on creators' work, even commercially, as long as they credit them for the original creation. This is the most accommodating of licences offered. Recommended for maximum dissemination and use of licensed materials.
Attribution – ShareAlike	CC-BY-SA	Lets others remix, tweak and build on creators' work even for commercial purposes, as long as they credit them and license their new creations under the identical terms. This licence is aligned with the 'copyleft' free and open-source software licences, which ensure that derivative works can never be put under more restrictive licensing terms than the original. All new works based on the original work carry the same licence, so any derivatives will also allow commercial use. This is the licence used by Wikipedia, and is recommended for work that incorporates content from Wikipedia and similarly licensed projects.

Table 1.4 *Continued*

Licence type	Abbreviation	Description
Attribution – Non-Commercial	CC-BY-NC	Lets others remix, tweak and build on the creators' work for non-commercial purposes, and although new works must also acknowledge the creator and be non-commercial, creators do not have to license their derivative works on the same terms.
Attribution – No Derivatives	CC-BY-ND	Allows for redistribution, commercial and non-commercial, as long as it is passed along unchanged and in whole, with credit to the creator.
Attribution – Non-Commercial – ShareAlike	CC-BY-NC-SA	Lets others remix, tweak and build on the creators' work for non-commercial purposes, as long as they credit the creator and license their new creations under identical terms.
Attribution – Non-Commercial – NoDerivatives	CC-BY-NC-ND	The most restrictive of the six licences, only allowing others to download the creators' works and share them with others as long as they credit the creator, but they cannot change them in any way or use them commercially.

conditions. Teachers can also use the Creative Commons Search to identify material that they can use in their teaching. The most recent version of the licences, The Creative Commons 4.0 Licence, is an international licence designed to be used in any territory around the world. You can find out more about the licences from: http://creativecommons.org/.

The Open Movement

The open movement originated from the development of open-source software and this section discusses how this movement relates to technology and copyright issues. Open-source software as defined by the Open Source Initiative (2009) needs to meet ten criteria, including free distribution, providing access to the source code and having a free licence to distribute the software. It is an alternative to commercial, proprietary (controlled by a sole proprietor) software and was largely the inspiration for the Creative Commons licences and the open access movement. In the

UK in 2014 over 60% of institutions used open-source solutions for online learning and the open-source VLE Moodle is widely used in higher and further education. A growing number of other open-source learning tools are also available such as e-portfolio software, social networking tools such as wikis and blogging platforms, and content management systems. The use of open-source software gives institutions greater control over the software that they use and the licensing fees that they are charged, but this has to be weighed up against the costs of employing technical staff to set up and maintain the software.

While open-source software might have been seen by some as a niche area for the technically or legally minded, two subsequent open movements have done much to raise awareness about copyright issues in education: open access and the open educational resources movement. Peter Suber, one of the leading voices in the open access movement, provides a useful definition: 'Open access (OA) literature is digital, online, free of charge, and free of most copyright and licensing restrictions' (Suber, 2015). Suber provides a valuable overview of the open access movement, which is largely beyond the scope of this book. However, the establishment of open access repositories to capture the research output of universities has done much to highlight the importance of understanding copyright issues. Many higher education funding bodies around the world are now mandating authors to deposit publicly funded research outputs into an open access repository. Additionally, academics are starting to question whether they should assign copyright in their own publications to a commercial publisher. Arguably the biggest concern of the open access movement has been the restrictive licensing models of large publishers that effectively lock the general public out of accessing the outputs of publicly funded research. Many in the open access movement maintain it is not anti-copyright. In fact websites such as the SHERPA/RoMEO website (University of Nottingham, 2015), developed by Jisc and hosted by the University of Nottingham, have done much to raise awareness of publishers' copyright policies and help ensure that content deposited in open access repositories is there with permission from the publisher. A key advantage of open access publications for the e-learning community is that research output can be used (often by simply linking to it) without the need to pay additional permission fees to publishers.

Meanwhile the open educational resources movement has its origins in

2001 when MIT launched its OpenCourseWare Initiative (http://ocw.mit.edu/), which was a pledge to make all their teaching materials available online for free. The term open educational resources was first used by the United Nations Educational, Scientific and Cultural Organization (UNESCO) in 2002, which described open educational resources as:

> typically made freely available over the Web or the Internet. Their principal use is by teachers and educational institutions [to] support course development, but they can also be used directly by students. Open Educational Resources include learning objects such as lecture material, references and readings, simulations, experiments and demonstrations, as well as syllabi, curricula and teachers' guides.
>
> UNESCO, 2002

The Organisation for Economic Co-operation and Development (OECD) describes open educational resources as 'digitised materials offered freely and openly for educators, students and self-learners to use and reuse for teaching, learning and research' (OECD, 2007). It is important to be clear about the distinction between the terms 'free' and 'open' and how they are used together in this context. 'Free' materials may be offered for no cost but under strict copyright protection without permission to repurpose, adapt and re-use. 'Open' educational materials are deliberately licensed by the creator for re-use by others, sometimes without the need to reference the original author, and without restriction on how and in what context the materials can be used. However, free materials, even online, are not necessarily open.[6] The term 'open practice' (Beetham et al., 2012) is increasingly being used in higher education to describe a range of open educational activities, such as developing and using open educational resources, developing open courses such as MOOCs, practising open scholarship through sharing research openly and using open-source technologies. Open practices inevitably involve staff developing an understanding of copyright and licences and provide an opportunity to discuss the issues in this context. The copyright questions associated with delivering open education and open courses are explored in more detail in Case Study 4 about UCL (see pages 106–10) and in Chapter 5.

Conclusion

This chapter first explored what online learning is and how teachers might wish to use content in the digital environment. It also considered how e-learning differs from traditional face-to-face teaching and why when we put course materials online, copyright issues become more pertinent. It has examined how the UK and several other countries approach copyright law, the exceptions that exist and their impact on online education. The chapter has shown how developments in technology are driving reforms to the existing copyright regimes throughout the world. In many countries a satisfactory balance has yet to be achieved between protecting the economic wellbeing of rights holders, and the needs of educators to be able to share, copy and disseminate information freely. Recent copyright reform suggests that the needs of education can be balanced more fairly against the need for copyright owners to receive just rewards for their endeavours. However, educators need to be mindful that copyright exceptions may only go so far, and online learning can be seen by rights holders as both a potential new market, but also a threat to their ability to exploit copyright works.

Notes

1   The background to this programme is discussed in greater detail by other authors (Rusbridge, 1998; Secker, 2004), and is outside the scope of this book.
2   The higher education sector tends to be better resourced than other sectors and consequently more likely to employ copyright experts to advise staff and students.
3   These include 'the Net Generation', 'the Google Generation' and 'Generation Y'.
4   At the time of writing the legislation.gov.uk website had still not been updated to reflect these changes but links are provided to the Statutory Instruments and an unofficial consolidation of the Act in the reference section. Consolidated versions can also be found in legal databases such as LexisNexis and Westlaw.
5   copyrighthub.org – an industry funded initiative to streamline licensing of copyright works on the internet.
6   The difference between the two definitions of free is often expressed as 'free as in speech, or free as in beer'.

References

ALA (2015) *Distance Education and the TEACHAct*, American Library Association, www.ala.org/advocacy/copyright/teachact [accessed 6 April 2015].

Beetham, H., Falconer, I., McGill, L. and Littlejohn, A. (2012) *OpenPracticesBriefing*, briefing paper, Jisc, https://oersynth.pbworks.com/w/page/51668352/ OpenPracticesBriefing [accessed 6 April 2016].

BIS (2014) *The Value of Transnational Education to the UK*, BIS Research Paper 194, Department for Business, Innovation & Skills, https://www.gov.uk/government/uploads/system/uploads/ attachment_data/file/387910/bis-14-1202-the-value-of-transnational-education-to-the-uk.pdf [accessed 6 April 2016].

CAL (2015) FAQs, Copyright Agency Limited, http://copyright.com.au/faqs [accessed 6 April 2016].

Copyright, Designs and Patents Act (1988) (amendments from 2014 still pending at the time of writing), www.legislation.gov.uk/ukpga/1988/48/contents [accessed 6 April 2016].

Copyright, Designs and Patents Act (1988) (unofficial consolidated version as amended in October 2014), www.gov.uk/government/uploads/system/uploads/attachment_ data/file/308729/cdpa1988-unofficial.pdf [accessed 6 April 2016].

Cornish, G. (2015) *Copyright: interpreting the law for libraries, archives and information services*, 6th edn, Facet Publishing.

Creative Commons (2009), History, https://creativecommons.org/about/history [accessed 6 April 2016].

Crews, K. D. (2015) *Study on Copyright Limitations and Exceptions for Libraries and Archives*, updated and revised, World Intellectual Property Organization, www.wipo.int/meetings/en/doc_details.jsp?doc_id=306216 [accessed 6 April 2016].

DfES (2005) *Harnessing Technology: transforming learning and children's services*, Department for Education and Skills, http://webarchive.nationalarchives.gov.uk/20130401151715/ www.education.gov.uk/publications/eOrderingDownload/ 1296-2005PDF-EN-01.pdf [accessed 6 April 2016].

European Commission (2016) Digital Single Market,
    http://ec.europa.eu/priorities/digital-single-market/ [accessed 6 April
    2016].
Hargreaves, I. (2011) *Digital Opportunity: a review of intellectual property
    and growth*, Intellectual Property Office,
    https://www.gov.uk/government/uploads/system/uploads/
    attachment_data/file/32563/ipreview-finalreport.pdf [accessed
    6 April 2016].
HM Treasury (2006) *Report on Gowers Review*,
    http://webarchive.nationalarchives.gov.uk/+/www.hmtreasury.
    gov.uk/d/pbr06_gowers_report_755.pdf [accessed 6 April 2016].
IPO (2014) *Protecting your UK Intellectual Property Abroad*, Intellectual
    Property Office,
    www.ipo.gov.uk/types/copy/c-abroad.htm [accessed 6 April 2016].
Jisc (2015) Intellectual Property Rights in the Digital World,
    https://www.jisc.ac.uk/guides/intellectual-property-rights-in-a-
    digital-world [accessed 6 April 2016].
Jisc (2016) Implementing the FELTAG Agenda,
    https://www.jisc.ac.uk/rd/projects/implementing-the-feltag-agenda.
Jones, C., Ramanau, R., Cross, S. J. and Healing, G. (2010) Net Generation
    or Digital Natives: is there a distinct new generation entering
    university?, *Computers & Education*, **54** (3), 722–32.
Kretschmer, M., Derclaye, E., Favale, M. and Watt, R. (2010) *The
    Relationship Between Copyright and Contract Law*, Strategic Advisory
    Board for Intellectual Property Policy,
    http://eprints.bournemouth.ac.uk/16091/1/_contractlaw-report.pdf
    [accessed 6 April 2016].
National Archives (2015) Open Government Licence for Public Sector
    Information, www.nationalarchives.gov.uk/doc/open-government-
    licence/version/3/ [accessed 6 April 2016].
NUS (2012) *Student Attitudes Towards Intellectual Property*, National Union
    of Students, www.nus.org.uk/PageFiles/12238/IP%20report.pdf
    [accessed 6 April 2016].
OECD (2007) *Giving Knowledge for Free: the emergence of open educational
    resources*, Organisation for Economic Co-operation and
    Development,
    www.oecd.org/edu/ceri/38654317.pdf [accessed 6 April 2016].

Open Source Initiative (2009) *The Open Source Definition*,
www.opensource.org/docs/osd [accessed 6 April 2016].

Padfield, T. (2015) *Copyright for Archivists and Records Managers*, 5th edn,
Facet Publishing.

Pedley, P. (2012) *The E-Copyright Handbook*, Facet Publishing.

Pedley, P. (2015) *Practical Copyright for Library and Information
Professionals*, Facet Publishing.

Prensky, M. (2001) Digital Natives, Digital Immigrants, *On the Horizon*,
9 (5), www.marcprensky.com/writing/Prensky%20-%20
Digital%20Natives,%20Digital%20Immigrants%20-%20Part1.pdf
[accessed 6 April 2016].

Research Information Network (2007) *Researchers' Use of Academic
Libraries and their Services*,
www.rin.ac.uk/system/files/attachments/Researchers-libraries-
services-report.pdf [accessed 6 April 2016].

Rowlands, I., Nicholas, D., Williams, P., Huntington, P., Fieldhouse, M.,
Gunter, B., Withey, R., Jamali, H. R., Dobrowolski, T. and Tenopir, C.
(2008) The Google Generation: the information behaviour of the
researcher of the future, *Aslib Proceedings*, **60** (4), 290–310.

Rusbridge, C. (1998) Towards the Hybrid Library, *D-Lib Magazine*
(July/Aug),
www.dlib.org/dlib/july98/rusbridge/07rusbridge.html [accessed
6 April 2016].

Secker, J. (2004) *Electronic Resources in the Virtual Learning Environment:
a guide for librarians*, Chandos Publishing.

Suber, P. (2015) *Open Access Overview*,
www.earlham.edu/~peters/fos/overview.htm [accessed 6 April 2016].

UCISA (2014) *2014 Survey of Technology Enhanced Learning for Higher
Education in the UK*, Universities and Colleges Information Systems
Association,
www.ucisa.ac.uk/~/media/groups/dsdg/TEL%20Survey%202014_
29Sep2014.ashx [accessed 6 April 2016].

UNESCO (2002) *UNESCO Promotes New Initiative for Free Educational
Resources on the Internet*,
www.unesco.org/education/news_en/080702_free_edu_ress.shtml
[accessed 6 April 2016].

Universities Canada (2015) Fair Dealing Policy for Universities, www.univcan.ca/fair-dealing-policy-for-universities/ [accessed 6 April 2016].

Universities UK (2014) *Patterns and Trends in UK Higher Education 2014*, www.universitiesuk.ac.uk/highereducation/Pages/ PatternsAndTrendsInUKHigherEducation2014.aspx [accessed 6 April 2016].

Universities UK (2015) *International Higher Education in Facts and Figures*, www.international.ac.uk/media/3636975/International-Higher-Education-in-Facts-and-Figures-2015.pdf [accessed 6 April 2016].

University of Nottingham (2015) *SHERPA/RoMEO: publisher copyright policies and self-archiving*, www.sherpa.ac.uk/romeo [accessed 6 April 2016].

White, D. and Le Cornu, A. (2011) Visitors and Residents: a new typology for online engagement, *First Monday*, **16** (9), http://firstmonday.org/ojs/index.php/fm/article/view/3171/3049 [accessed 6 April 2016].

2

Digitizing text-based content for delivery in a VLE

Introduction

This chapter is concerned with the copyright issues associated with digitizing or scanning text-based works held in paper form for use in online learning. This includes both published material such as books and academic journals (what the CDPA defines as literary works), the images and illustrations that they contain, and potentially unpublished content such as personal correspondence and manuscripts. This chapter only considers images embedded in literary works, and standalone images are discussed in Chapter 3. Digitizing traditional paper resources for online delivery allows distance learners to access the content easily, from the convenience of their chosen digital device. There has also been a growing demand from campus-based students to have access to core readings in electronic format. Library statistics from groups such as SCONUL (Society of College, National and University Libraries) demonstrate that while campus-based students visit academic libraries just as frequently as they traditionally have, they are increasingly accessing readings in digital format (SCONUL, 2015). Library visits are often driven by the growing use of the space for learning and group work. However, significant numbers of students in the UK study part-time, with over 600,000 students in 2013–14 registered as part-time according to the Higher Education Statistics Agency (HESA, 2015) and far more working while they study and requiring flexible access to learning resources. The trend for electronic access is also related to the different expectations of young people about how they access information, as discussed in Chapter 1. Libraries are responding to increased demands for digital readings and find it relatively easy to produce digital readings in-house, with scanners and multi-functional devices now being inexpensive to purchase. Some libraries are also motivated by a desire to reduce the physical size of the library collection. While many institutions have addressed this by adopting 'e-first' policies (if an electronic version is available they will purchase this rather than the print version) when purchasing new content, there is still a place in many libraries for digitization. This is largely an interim reaction to the fact that many publishers have still not digitized their back catalogues.

In the UK, the provision of core readings in scanned format has escalated in the past ten years, largely facilitated by the inclusion of scanning rights in the CLA blanket licences. All three of the CLA education licences – covering schools, further and higher education – allow institutions to digitize copyright material in addition to photocopying (see Chapter 4 for more information on using 'born digital' material under licences). The CLA first introduced scanning rights into the business and further education sectors in 2004, and in 2005 it added these to the higher education licence. The CLA currently requires licensed HEIs to report details of all the scanning annually, which has led to an increased administrative burden, and is therefore something CLA has been attempting to address. Despite the administrative overheads of reporting scans, HEIs in the UK have been scanning high numbers of readings largely for delivery via e-learning systems. The CLA is responding to this by developing a cloud-based content hosting platform called the Digital Content Store (DCS), which is intended to remove reporting requirements by collecting usage data at the point of use. This chapter presents further details of this activity against the backdrop of changing technologies and licensing models, by comparing data from recent surveys against a survey completed for this book's first edition. It explores how scanned readings are being used to support e-learning and how copyright issues have affected the administrative processes in higher education libraries.

As we saw in Chapter 1, in various other countries around the world the reprographic rights organizations are also issuing licences to cover scanning copyright materials. For example, New Zealand, Canada, Australia and Ireland all have similar licences. However, currently only in the UK have rights holders required full data reporting to monitor every reading that is scanned for use in higher education. This chapter will briefly consider how universities in the USA digitize published content under either copyright exceptions or licences. This chapter does not seek to be comprehensive in examining other countries in the world. The focus instead is on how legislation and licences regulate activity in this area and shape e-learning in a selection of English-speaking countries.

Finally this chapter also briefly focuses on the digitization of unpublished materials, including historical or archival materials where direct permissions usually need to be obtained from rights holders. It also considers how to deal with items where rights holders cannot be traced. These are frequently referred to as 'orphan works'. For reasons of clarity, the use of existing digital resources (sometimes called 'born digital content' or digital originals) such as articles from electronic journals or e-books is discussed in Chapter 4, along with the use of digital content obtained from websites, repositories or colleagues.

The chapter includes two case studies, from Middlesex University and a US university, describing how staff digitize course readings.

Using published materials in e-learning

Copyright issues inevitably arise when teachers want to scan or digitize content for use in an online course. Although the copyright in many resources that teachers upload into e-learning systems will be owned by the teachers themselves, or their respective institution, it is common for teachers to want to use materials whose rights are owned by an author or publisher. This type of content is often called 'third-party material' as it is not owned by the teacher, institution nor students but by a 'third party'. While some teachers, particularly in higher education, might be keen to create all their content from scratch, this is rarely practical or desirable all the time. Moreover, in a college or university, while teaching materials (such as PowerPoint presentations, class handouts and lecture notes) are usually created by lecturers, they often want to include content from external authoritative sources such as books and journals. However, because of the nature of scholarly publishing, the copyright of journal articles is usually assigned, or transferred, from the author to a publisher through a publishing contract. Even when publishing a monograph, academic authors frequently share copyright with their publisher and are required as a courtesy to notify their publisher if they want to make the final published content available to their students. While the open access movement, discussed in Chapter 1, has done much to highlight this issue, many academic authors are still signing contracts with publishers that stop their content from being used in e-learning in its final published version without permission. In the past, negotiating permissions for published content was commonplace when building an e-learning course that relied on third-party content. In recent years blanket licences issued by reprographic rights organizations such as the CLA have been helpful so there is less of a need to secure permissions by negotiating with individual publishers. This process can be time consuming and very few educational establishments have designated staff to obtain copyright permissions. Therefore blanket licences have enabled an increasing number of educational establishments to include published content in the VLE.

By far the most common type of content that educators wish to include in the VLE is published content from books, journals, magazines or newspapers. It is standard practice to expect someone following a course of study to undertake 'further reading' and to provide them with a reading list. In a digital environment it is the logical next step not just to suggest what the student should read, but actually provide them with a digital copy of the text. In the case of distance learning, the teacher may feel some of the resources will be difficult to obtain for students who may not have easy access to an academic library. Meanwhile in some subject disciplines, such as history or English literature, the teacher may wish students to consult archival sources and so digitization can provide access to otherwise unobtainable material. For some teachers (and students) e-learning has become synonymous with digital access to content, and while many learning technologists try to encourage academics to make their courses more interactive, VLEs are still frequently used as an online document store for a range of course materials.

Scanning technology is now extremely cheap to purchase and the production of a digital copy of a printed document is often as straightforward as photocopying an item. Multi-functional devices, which combine printing, photocopying and scanning functionality, are largely ubiquitous in educational establishments and have the facility to produce a digital file with great ease. However, scanning or digitizing a copyright work and distributing a digital file such as a PDF via a network is a restricted act under most copyright laws and the exclusive right of the copyright owner. Only in the USA, where 'fair use' covers educational copying, an institution might undertake this practice, but specific guidelines govern what is permitted. Yet, many educators wrongly believe that they are exempt from such laws if they place the content on a secure network, restricted to students on a course of study or protected with a password. This is rarely the case, as we shall see later in this chapter.

Scanning published content in the UK

This chapter examines scanning activities that support e-learning in the UK higher education sector in some detail. It includes results from a recent, updated survey that highlight how the CLA Licence has affected the support for e-learning that institutions can now provide. While third-party content is not vital to the success of e-learning, in an increasingly global education market, differences in copyright law make it easier for some countries to provide their students with published content. It is also inevitable that confusion and misunderstandings can occur, particularly when teachers move to different countries to teach and find that the law is not the same from one country to the next. This chapter provides a useful overview for teachers in higher education in the UK to help them stay within the law and licensing guidelines. It also highlights how the legal framework is influencing the nature of e-learning and impacting on higher education.

Since the legal reforms referred to in Chapter 1, the UK's copyright laws have become relatively more liberal following the exceptions that apply under the Copyright, Designs and Patents Act 1988. Before 2014, provisions for making copies of copyright works for educational purposes were limited to 1% per quarter of a published literary, dramatic or musical work per institution. The updates to Section 36 of the CDPA that took place in 2014 allowed making of multiple copies of up to 5% of any published work (with the exception of a broadcast or a standalone artistic work) within an educational establishment. However, in reality most scans distributed via VLEs are made under the terms of the CLA Licence. This is largely because the law requires educational establishments to take out licences where they are available rather than rely on the provisions in Section 36, and because the legal requirements for scanning content where licences are not available (e.g. CLA-excluded content) are not consistent with the CLA Licence conditions. For example s.36 allows only one 5% extract to be made from any one publication throughout an entire establishment within the course of the year, whereas the CLA Licence permits the same extract to be used on different courses of study within the same establishment. Some educational establishments have incorporated the copying allowed under Section 36 into their standard scanning processes.

As described in Chapter 1, UK law includes a provision known as 'fair dealing' (frequently confused by many people as being the same as 'fair use' – see the Glossary, page xxx). Copying of a work under fair dealing can be undertaken for private study and non-commercial research, but also for the purposes of quotation and/or criticism and review. However, in reality very few educational establishments would rely on fair dealing as a defence for putting material on a network, because generally only single copies are permitted. Therefore, much educational copying is undertaken under a CLA Licence and all universities and most schools and colleges take out such a licence to cover their staff.

Background and context

The CLA is the UK's reprographic rights organization, representing publishers, authors and other rights owners of published books and journals. Since 1983 it has issued licences to facilitate copying beyond the provisions in UK law and issued its first blanket licences for the education sector in 1986 (CLA, 2015a).

Digitization of copyright materials was first explored in some detail by Jisc, which funded several projects under its e-Lib programme in the mid to late 1990s to explore copyright issues associated with digitizing core readings for students. Projects such as Access to Course Readings via Networks (ACORN) and Scottish Collaborative On-demand Publishing Enterprise (SCOPE) had looked at the feasibility of setting up electronic short loan services, but every item had to be cleared directly with a publisher. In 1998 Jisc and Blackwells set up a project that led to the creation of a service known as Higher Education Resources On-demand (Heron), which offered copyright clearance and digitization services for the sector. The work of Heron was greatly facilitated in 1999 when the CLA became the world's first reprographic rights organization to issue a digitization licence, albeit as a transactional licence. Items covered by the CLA Licence could be cleared via a service known as CLA Rapid Clearance

Service (CLARCS) and then made available in digital format to students.

The Heron service is at the time of writing in the process of being retired as it has been acquired by the CLA, which intends to provide a digitization and extract storage solution with the DCS. However, between 1999 and 2005 approximately 80 universities used Heron services, which provided a clearing house for permissions, and digitized materials on behalf of the institutions. Heron operated as a commercial service after 2002, following the withdrawal of Jisc funding, and it was run first by the digital content suppliers, Ingenta and latterly by Publishing Technology Ltd. Under the first CLA digitization licence, prices for copyright clearance were based on the numbers of pages of an article or chapter and the number of students on a course of study. Despite an agreement between the Publishers Association and Jisc that recommended the rate should be set at 5 pence per page per student, in reality the costs were far higher. Many universities were unable or unwilling to pay for clearances of a transactional nature and never took out the CLA digitization licence. However, of those that did, quite a number used Heron to process the requests and digitize material, while a few carried out this work in-house.

In addition to obtaining permission for digital copies, universities had been using the CLARCS service to clear paper course packs since 1998. The need to clear permissions was causing problems for many universities and in 2000 Universities UK (which convenes a Copyright Working Group[1] with GuildHE to negotiate the CLA Licence on behalf of the higher education sector) referred the terms of the higher education licence to the Copyright Tribunal. The subsequent ruling in 2002 led to the abolishment of the CLARCS service for paper course packs and a less than favourable view of transactional licences within the sector.

Negotiations towards a blanket digitization licence were time con-suming, and after lengthy debates between the Universities UK / GuildHE Copyright Working Group and the CLA, the trial scanning licence was initially launched in 2005. The licence was an optional addition to the CLA higher education photocopying licence and, priced at an additional 50 pence per student, was considered by many institutions to be expensive. At this time CLA and publishers insisted on the full reporting of items that were digitized for those that took up the trial. In 2008, again following lengthy negotiations, the CLA and Universities UK agreed a Blanket Scanning and Photocopying licence that ran until August 2011, with two years where a 'roll-over' of the existing licence terms were agreed. At that point the licence took two forms: the basic licence, which covered photocopying and scanning, and the comprehensive licence, which included photocopying, scanning and the use of digital originals. The comprehensive licence was more expensive and only ever taken out by a minority of institutions. For example, in 2010 only 38 institutions had signed the comprehensive licence while 122 had the basic licence. However, in 2013 Universities UK and GuildHE agreed with the CLA that the two licences would be rolled into one single licence, which gave the comprehensive level of cover. The fee negotiated by Universities UK was a minimal increase and this licence continues until August 2016. Further details of the CLA higher education licence are available from the CLA website (CLA, 2015b). In essence the licence allows copies to be made within the limit of one chapter from a book, one article from a journal issue or 5% of a work (whichever is greater) per course of study. It is calculated based on a price per full-time-equivalent student and issued annually. It has a number of other terms and conditions, so for example scanned items must have a cover sheet with specified wording. Institutions must also participate in periodic surveys to collect data on the levels of photocopying in their institution and provide full returns of all the scanning they undertake. Finally, the CLA undertakes periodic audits (CLA, 2016a) to ensure universities are complying with the licence terms and conditions for scanning and digital copying.

One aspect of the CLA Licence which changed after the 2013 agreement was that only newly scanned items and digital originals needed to be reported annually, with full reporting of all readings used required every three years. Despite this change in reporting requirements, many institutions have been dissatisfied with the administrative burden they feel that this places on their staff, a burden which has largely been shouldered by academic libraries, rather than e-learning teams. This is because libraries hold the published works, usually have greater staff numbers and are responsible for providing access to this type of content. However, as previously mentioned, from 2016 the CLA intends to launch the DCS, which is designed to remove or greatly reduce the burden of reporting.

As part of a recent strategy to provide additional services over and above the rights to make copies, the CLA has acquired the Heron services from Publishing Technology Ltd including the rights management system,

PackTracker, which Heron developed to speed up the reporting of scanned items to the CLA. Heron also provided services to clear material which was excluded from the CLA Licence and the CLA intends to move Heron users and other libraries on to its Second Extract Permissions Service (SEPS). SEPS is a brokerage service which launched in August 2015 that allows universities to acquire permissions directly from publishers using the CLA as a clearing house. Similarly the CLA's intention is for all PackTracker users to have moved to using the DCS by the summer of 2016.

Another organization that has developed services to manage the creation and reporting of CLA-licensed content is Talis Education Ltd, creator of the Talis Aspire reading lists system. Their Talis Aspire Digitised Content (TADC) product, launched in 2013, provides similar functionality to PackTracker and the upcoming CLA DCS, but is designed to integrate with the Talis reading list system which is used by a significant number of UK universities. The use of TADC is described in the case studies from Middlesex University (Case Study 2) and the University of Auckland (Case Study 5).

Newspapers

At this stage it is worth briefly mentioning that CLA does not license the copying of newspaper content, although since 2014 it has administered an education establishment licence on behalf of NLA Media Access. NLA Media Access is a reprographic rights organization (a type of collective management organization that licenses the reproduction of copyright works, primarily text and images, on behalf of a large number of individual rights holders) owned by newspaper publishers that license copying of newspaper clippings to UK organizations. The NLA education establishment licence (NLA Media Access, 2016) has a provision for scanning and delivery of digital newspaper clippings to a VLE. However, the licence imposes a limit of 28 days making it impractical in the context of most institutional online learning services. In addition, the licence fee matrix combines 'corporate' use of press clippings for public relations purposes with educational use, which presents considerable confusion to institutions determining licence costs and agreeing who should bear them. As a result many institutions rely on only the basic photocopying component of the NLA licence, and use subscriptions to newspaper databases for teaching purposes.

Music

As with newspapers, use of sheet music in the UK is not included within the CLA higher education licence, although CLA has an arrangement with Printed Music Licensing Limited (PMLL; www.printmusiclicensing.co.uk) to license schools to make copies of limited extracts from sheet music (CLA, 2016c). At the time of writing CLA and PMLL are still in discussion about extending this licence coverage to the higher education sector. Therefore for many educational establishments, digitizing sheet music and making it available via a VLE involves getting permission from the music publisher. Alternatively the exception to make multiple copies of published editions (Section 36 – see Chapter 1) can be used to copy and communicate up to 5% of a musical work where no licence is available. As discussed in Chapter 3, the digitization of sound recordings usually requires permission, although it might be possible to rely on the exception for illustration for instruction to make limited, fair dealing copies of musical recordings. For more information visit the International Association of Music Libraries, Archives and Documentation Centres, UK & Ireland (IAML, UK & Irl; http://uk-irl.iaml.info/).

Case Study 2   Digitizing course readings at Middlesex University

Kate Vasili

Middlesex University is a culturally diverse institution, which currently has 3000 staff members and 40,000 students enrolled worldwide; 25,000 of those students are based in London. The University has overseas campuses in Dubai, Mauritius and Malta, and collaborative partnerships with 180 leading educational institutions from the UK and around the world.

Resource provision

Middlesex University academics have always retained full autonomy in the creation and provision of course teaching materials, initially including handbooks, reading lists, and course readers containing print copies of required reading material, and continued to do so even after the introduction of the VLE in 2001 and the CLA Higher Education Trial Blanket Scanning Licence in 2005. Despite their freedom to populate learning spaces on the VLE, it became apparent over the years that academics were not taking full advantage of the scanning or the later digital copying provisions in the licence. Although extensive copyright guidelines and training were available, the reasons given for this were confusion or a lack of confidence in the understanding of copyright law and the requirements and limitations of the CLA Licence, but also the burdensome administrative and reporting requirements of the licence. Even where academics were scanning, many were not fully aware of, or misunderstood the licence requirements and omitted to check the CLA repertoire, add the requisite copyright notice or report the scanning. The scans were frequently of poor quality and inaccessible to students relying on assistive technology.

Because of the low use of this costly licence and the increasing expectations of students to be able to access resources electronically and online, it was decided that the Library would introduce a digitization service to support academics in the creation of digital resources and copyright compliance.

The Digitization Team

The team was initially set up in April 2012 within the Library's Teaching and Research Support Directorate (since renamed Library and Learning Enhancement), with two full-time members of staff, managed by the university copyright officer. A flatbed book scanner was purchased, which would protect the spines of books by scanning to the edge of the glass. A generic copyright mailbox was set up to receive and send requests and correspondence. A scanning database was created using Microsoft Excel, to record each request received by the Digitization Team as well as the process, copyright status and outcome with detailed notes. The spreadsheet was designed primarily around the CLA scanning record spreadsheet, with additional columns and criteria added for completeness. Excel was used rather than Access because it was considered more flexible to manipulate the data and to search, sort and create reports of any criteria. This spreadsheet is still maintained to date as the primary database of all scanning and digitization requests, and backed up regularly.

Dealing with requests

Requests are currently received from the subject liaison librarians or the academics via the Talis Aspire Reading Lists where they are actioned automatically by the Talis Aspire Digitised Content Module as described below.

Step 1 Source checks

The library catalogue and e-resources are searched for university holdings:

◆ If held in electronic format, a link is relayed to the requestor.
◆ The internet is searched for a legitimate, freely available copy that can be linked to or copied depending on the terms of use or licensing, e.g. publishers' open archive collections, institutional repositories, open access or Creative Commons licensed copies.
◆ If an electronic copy is not held or found but available for purchase, the subject liaison librarians are advised and it is purchased wherever possible and within budgetary constraints.
◆ If only available in print format within the university or to purchase, or it is not viable to purchase an e-copy and no available digital version is found elsewhere, the digitization procedure begins (Step 2).
◆ If the item is not held by the Library or department at all and no suitable copy found online:
 ◆ a digital copy is purchased wherever possible or a print copy of a book is purchased to scan from unless not available or viable
 ◆ journal articles and book extracts the Library is unable to purchase are ordered via the British Library Document Supply Service (after consulting the CLA repertoire), paying the copyright fee to enable re-use. Costs for BL orders are borne by the Library from the resources budget.
◆ If no copy can be sourced at all, the request is referred back to the academic to consider an alternative reading.

Step 2 CLA Licence checks

The CLA repertoire is checked to ensure the publication is mandated and the item length is calculated to ensure the quantity requested falls within the licence limits:

◆ Items mandated and within limits are approved for scanning (Step 4)
◆ If items fall outside the licence mandate and/or limits, application of the s.36 legal exception is considered or they are referred back to the academic to determine:
 ◆ if an alternative will suffice

- if the quantity can be reduced to fall within the licence
- if they require rights owner copyright permission to be sought, advising that additional costs will be incurred.

Step 3 Permissions requests

If the requested item falls outside the criteria of the CLA Scanning Licence, rights owner permission may be sought either by the academic or the copyright officer if the item is absolutely crucial to the course. The costs for copyright clearance were initially recharged to the schools. However, following the announcement by the CLA of the exclusion of many US publications from the CLA repertoire, the library executive agreed to bear the costs of copyright clearance to reduce the impact on student access.

Academics usually refrain from requesting direct permissions and prefer to explore alternative content to avoid the costs incurred in fees and staff time, but also because the timescales involved in receiving replies or permissions from rights owners often exceed the date the item is required.

Step 4 Scanning

Unless rejected, the item is then scanned to PDF, redacted and converted into machine-encoded text through optical character recognition for accessibility and searchability; the file is uploaded to the Talis Aspire Digitised Content module where the CLA copyright notice is attached and the file is uploaded to Springshare LibGuides.

Step 5 Link provided

A live link to the digitized reading appears on the reading list, enabling online access to students registered on the course or module. Occasionally a PDF file is forwarded to the requesting academic, for provision via e-mail to students experiencing difficulty accessing it online.

Analysis

Turnaround times from the point of receiving a request to fulfilment vary from same day to two working days if the publication is held by the Library and the request is licensed by the CLA, to up to eight weeks if not held and the source or permissions needed to be acquired. The turnaround times obviously increase with the number of requests received, and during term time when the required items may be on loan to students, but requestors are notified of any known delays or issues.

The number of digitization requests received by the Digitization Team reached approximately 482 in the first year, an increase of over 800% and increasing the number of scans previously reported in the annual CLA scanning return from 63 to 1029.

Because the readings were relatively new to the course content, none required weeding in the subsequent years, but the re-checking and weeding process required by the CLA Licence was still necessary, which proved time consuming.

Middlesex University introduced the Talis Aspire Reading List software in the summer of 2012. The reading lists were initially created and administered by the 15 full-time-equivalent subject liaison librarians, which ensured that all resources that students were being directed or advised to read would be available via the Library and in digital format wherever possible. This resulted in a further increase in digitization requests and was closely followed by a trial and subsequent subscription to the TADC Module in September 2013, which automated the digitization process, particularly around the source and licence compliance checking.

Requests received up to the next cut-off date for the CLA scanning return, 31 May 2014, had now reached almost 1500, and 1030 of these were fulfilled and reported to the CLA. The total has since climbed to a total of 3333 as at 31 December 2015, with very positive feedback received from academics and students.

During this period, Middlesex also signed up to the CLA higher education comprehensive licence to cover copying from born digital publications, effective from 1 February 2013, just six months before this licence was to become compulsory to all HEIs. This was to alleviate the licensing problems in making copies from born digital content, for distance learning students studying in remote locations with internet access issues, and from born digital content automatically supplied by the British Library. The Photocopying and Scanning Licence specifically excluded any copying from born digital publications, but changes within the British Library Document Supply Service had resulted in requests being fulfilled automatically from born digital, with no option for HEIs to request a copy specifically scanned from print. The comprehensive licence was not an outright solution as the CLA mandates for copying from digital resources were not as extensive as the print repertoire, so fewer extracts were available.

Overseas students

In 2013 it was discovered that details of the University's overseas campus-based students were no longer captured in the main body of student numbers in the HESA return and therefore they were not covered by the CLA Licence to receive copies. Following requests from Middlesex and other interested HEIs, the CLA launched a trial licence to cover overseas campus and collaborative partnership students who are registered with a UK HEI. The optional Overseas Campus Based Student Trial Licence was launched on 1 August 2014, initially intended to run for one year, but it was extended for an additional year in order to collect sufficient data on demand and usage, and to determine a fair rate. Participants in the trial are required to report the numbers and geographical location of students requiring cover to receive digital copies of course readings. The copies can only be created and provided within the UK and must be reported to the CLA in the annual digital copying return. This licence, in addition to individually negotiated e-resource subscription licences, has enabled Middlesex to ensure it meets its obligation to provide a mirrored learning experience to overseas students, in line with that received by their UK counterparts (within local legal and cultural constraints).

Copyright guidance

The increased use of the VLE and online reading lists led to increased interest in the inclusion of a variety of copyright-protected materials, e.g. images, films, broadcasts and music, and the accompanying legal implications – copyright infringement in particular. Therefore, support by way of copyright training and guidelines had become more important to ensure that all resources provided to students were legal and the University was free from possible infringement claims.

Copyright and intellectual property queries on the re-use of staff members' own materials produced for teaching, through research or for publication, also increased. Many were unaware of the terms of their own publishing contracts, such as transfers of ownership or restrictions on re-use, or about open access publishing agreements.

Conclusion

Despite recent legislative changes, copyright law and licensing continues to be opaque and confusing for many in higher education; it often requires a comprehensive knowledge and understanding of statute, case law, court decisions, licence terms and mutual interpretations of all the aforementioned. Although technology has been implemented to assist with the digitization processes – source and copyright checking, licence compliance and accessibility – the frequent referrals and queries have highlighted the ever increasing requirement for manual intervention, copyright guidance and support. However, as a result of the continuous financial constraints on higher education and library budgets, the University Digitization Team has since been reduced to 1.5 full-time-equivalent staff members in addition to the copyright officer.

The CLA is currently exploring a solution to alleviate the onerous administrative requirements of the higher education licence, although there are some concerns about future implications for the sector.

Scanning in the UK: results of a survey

In the first edition of this book findings from a survey that provided an overview of scanning service in UK academic libraries, the Survey of Digitisation of Core Readings in UK Higher Education, were presented (Hedges and Secker, 2009). The survey provided a snapshot of activity relating to the digitization of core readings in higher education in the UK at this point. Some previous research had been carried out (Delasalle, 2007) but there was relatively little written about this topic. The first survey was launched in March 2009 shortly after the introduction of the CLA's comprehensive licence, which permitted HEIs to photocopy and scan from print published materials. This licence also permitted the copying of digital content, for example from e-books, e-journals or databases, if institutions had taken out the full licence. In order to update the data and to provide a comparison, a follow up survey was undertaken in December 2015 (Secker and Morrison, 2016). As with the first survey, the 2015 survey was publicized widely on mailing lists such as LIS-Copyseek for university librarians and it was also circulated on the SCONUL mailing list, which goes to heads of library services. Both surveys were made available using online survey tools. The 2015 survey included fewer questions than the earlier survey as some questions were considered redundant, particularly where the data could be obtained elsewhere. Additional data included in this chapter was drawn from the UK Copyright Literacy Survey (Morrison and Secker, 2015) and from sources such as the HESA and an LIS-Copyseek workshop held in July 2015.

Survey topics and response rate

The UK Higher Education Scanning Survey originated as the Survey of Digitisation of Core Reading. Both were designed to collect information about scanning under the CLA Licence in the UK and about operational decisions that were being made in university libraries to support this work. It covered the following areas:

- the number of digital readings made available at the institution and staffing levels to carry out this work
- procedural issues including promotion of the service, scanning processes, management and delivery of readings
- wider matters such as collection management and motivations for scanning, and how these activities related to other support for e-learning.

In 2009 respondents from 44 institutions completed the survey, with some notable gaps from larger universities, and in 2015 the survey received 72 valid responses. In the interests of clarity in the analysis below comparisons are provided as percentages rather than total responses.

A range of people completed the surveys, most of whom worked in the university library. One of the first questions asked about the scanning and digitization services used in the institution. In 2009, 57% of the respondents were members of the Heron service and just 7% used the Heron software PackTracker to manage their digital readings. The contrast in 2015 was marked, with only 11% of respondents using Heron services (a significant decrease) and 33% using PackTracker (a significant increase). Services used by institutions in 2015 included digitization services such as the Higher Education Scanning Service, a British Library service used by 76% of respondents, and the CLA SEPS, which was launched in June 2015 and 56% of institutions reported using it.

Digitization activities

The results of the Survey of Digitisation of Core Reading demonstrate a clear increase in digitization activities in higher education in the UK in the ten years from 2005 to 2015. The blanket licence has clear advantages over the transactional licence that had operated until 2005, as this had been expensive, difficult to budget for and time consuming to process. However, the launch of SEPS in June 2015 reintroduced a transactional element to the licensing of scanned readings. Very few libraries have a dedicated budget for copyright permissions, so permission fees are usually passed to academic departments or faculties. As with the old transactional licence, clearances obtained via SEPS are based on a 'per page per student' model, so the courses where there might be the greatest benefit in digitizing material (where there are high student numbers) can be extremely costly. Therefore, it will be interesting to see in the future the extent to which UK universities choose to use the SEPS service and who in the institutions pays the permission fees. The findings from our survey were unclear as to whether the institutions had simply signed up to the SEPS service or if they were actively using it.

Data from 2009 showed there was a huge variation across higher education in the number of items that are scanned each year under the CLA Licence. For example the survey showed anywhere between 20 and 2844 readings were scanned per institution in 2008–9, with a mean result of 515 scans. This variation has continued; in the 2015 survey institutions reported scanning between 6 and 9871 readings per institution in 2014–15. The mean number of scans in 2015 was 1769. In both surveys the results are skewed by the small number of institutions carrying out large amounts of scanning; consequently in 2009 the median number of scans was 300, and in 2015 the median was 940. In 2009 most institutions were anticipating a growth in the number of items they would scan in the next year. Data obtained from the survey in 2015 showed this growth to be significant with the mean number of scans being more than three times greater than in 2009. Data was obtained from the CLA for the period 2007–8, which shows the mean number of scans across all institutions to be 341 digitized items per institution, suggesting the group that responded to the survey was more actively involved in scanning. Compared with previous years, the mean number of scans had grown year on year since the licence was first launched in 2005. In 2005–6 just 46 scans were reported per institution and in 2006–7 the figure had increased to 146. The CLA supplied updated data for this edition of this book, covering the period 2013–15: the mean number of scans for each state funded HEI for 2013–14 was 1449. This figure was based on full census reporting across all the institutions, although the data collection exercise methodology was amended in 2014–15 so that only a third of HEIs supplied a full return. The mean for 2014–15 was 1320 scans, which again suggests that institutions that responded to the survey were those more heavily involved in scanning.

Staffing

Increasing numbers of UK libraries have established services to digitize core readings, so this work is carried out centrally rather than devolved to academic departments. Early adopters of the approach to establish a centralized unit based in the library were UCL, the University of Sheffield, the London School of Economics (LSE) and the University of Derby. Dedicated teams have been set up in some institutions as part of the library's role in supporting teaching and to ensure that records for the CLA can be managed centrally. The Survey of Digitisation of Core Reading found that there were variations in the number of staff involved in this work, with some institutions having no dedicated team and others having more than three full-time-equivalent staff members. Of the respondents to the survey in 2009, 48% had a dedicated team while 52% did not. This compares with 59% of institutions having a dedicated team in 2015, while 41% did not. In 2009 24% of respondents reported an increase in staffing to cope with workload but the majority (76%) had not and were redeploying staff from other areas to cope with the work at peak times of year. This trend seemed to be continuing in 2015 where those institutions without a dedicated digitization team used library staff such as subject librarians, library assistants working in interlibrary loans or document delivery services staff to carry out scanning. In three instances (4% of responses) academic staff carried out scanning themselves, although records were usually kept by a member of library staff or the copyright officer.

Scanning readings

Scanning has become a relatively straightforward process now that the equipment required to make and prepare copies suitable for distribution on the web is so readily available. The Survey of Digitisation of Core Reading therefore asked who undertook the scanning to establish if this was carried out in-house or outsourced. In 2009, 44% of institutions in the UK carried out scanning in-house, with 15% saying that they would always outsource this work. Meanwhile 41% of institutions engaged in a mixture of both in-house and outsourced scanning (presumably dependent on timing, and the particular quality requirements). The evidence from the most recent survey shows that the trend for scanning in-house has increased, with 64% of institutions scanning material in-house and only one entirely outsourcing this work. However, 34% of institutions still carried out a combination of in-house and outsourced scanning work.

In 2009 scanning was mainly outsourced to the Higher Education Scanning Service provided by the British Library (37% of institutions used this service). The service was launched in 2008 as a solution for institutions that wanted to scan items under the CLA Licence but did not have internal facilities. Meanwhile 29% of respondents used Heron to provide digitization services in 2009. By 2015 the picture was somewhat different, with 76% of institutions using the Higher Education Scanning Service and just 11% using Heron for scanning purposes. The management of the scanning process has been facilitated by two commercial systems: PackTracker, developed by Heron, which was used by 25% of institutions responding to the 2015 survey, and TADC, which was used by another 25% of institutions. Nearly one-quarter (23%) have developed their own in-house system to manage the digitization process and another 23% did not have a system. Of the remaining three institutions (4%), two were migrating systems at the time of completing the survey and one was using PackTracker but also part of the pilot group using the CLA's DCS.

Scanned files are almost always provided to students in Adobe PDF format, but in 2009, 33% of respondents reported that they create text files using some form of optical character recognition process. By 2015, 49% of institutions reported that they routinely provided text files to students, although 38% did not and 13% did not know. Optical character recognition technologies have also improved in quality significantly in recent years, becoming cheaper as well. In order to comply with disability discrim-ination legislation, educational establishments in the UK must make appropriate adjustments for students with a disability. This could include providing readings in an accessible format that can be read by screen-reader software. The survey found that in 2009 just over half (51%) of institutions provided text files for visually impaired students, 27% did not and 22% were unsure. Interestingly, by 2015 just under half (49%) of institutions said they provided accessible files for students with a disability and 33% did not, with one institution not knowing. In the comments the data suggested that this service operated quite separately from the scanning undertaken by the library, often by a specialist disability unit.

Managing demand for the service

In 2009 the results of the Survey of Digitisation of Core Readings suggested that managing demand for digitization services was a key issue for academic libraries in the UK. For example, the question on whether library staff digitized all readings they were asked to by teaching staff generated the largest number of free text comments. These comments from 2009 revealed that very few libraries had the capacity to digitize all of the items that were requested by teaching staff. Material that fell outside the CLA Licence was particularly problematic and a large proportion of libraries only scanned items covered by the Licence and did not undertake copyright clearance work. However, some took a case-by-case approach, as this respondent stated: 'If the request falls outside the CLA Licence then a discussion is held with the academics as to whether we progress their request to the Heron service (at a cost to the department).'

In 2009, 84% of respondents did not have a limit on the number of readings that could be requested and in 2015 the figure was very similar (83%). Only 4% of institutions said they had a limit on the number of readings they would digitize for a course in 2015. The comments revealed that in many cases there was no need to have a limit or that it would not be practical. However, many libraries still do not have a budget to pay for copyright permissions, and in 2015, 47% of institutions said they did not arrange transactional clearances for material outside the CLA Licence. The remainder (53%) did: 39% of institutions obtained permissions direct from publishers, 24% used the Copyright Clearance Centre in the USA and 13% used Heron to obtain permission. Demand for the service seemed to be managed in other ways; for example in 2009, 20% of respondents did not actively promote their digitization services, relying instead on word of mouth. One respondent reported: 'We have been resistant to this [greater publicity] as we are unsure of demand and how we would cope.' This situation was similar in 2015, with 22% of respondents not promoting the digitization services. However, 88% did promote the service via a variety of channels, including web pages and online guides, via subject librarians who did this either in meetings, or e-mail and in a smaller number of instances through guides, posters, training sessions and social media.

Delivery of readings: the role of e-learning

The CLA Licence requires that scanned readings are prepared for students on a course of study and are password protected rather than placed on the internet. However, the Survey of Digitisation of Core Readings wanted to discover more about how electronic readings are delivered to students across higher education in the UK. The licence mentions the use of VLEs but is not prescriptive about the method that a university uses to manage access to the material. VLEs are now widely used in UK universities so the survey wanted to establish how extensively they were used to deliver digitized readings and whether other tools were used instead or in combination. Since 2009 there has been a growth in the use of commercial online reading list systems, such as Talis Aspire and Rebus. In 2009 the majority of universities (92%) used the VLE to deliver readings to students, but by 2015 the picture was a little different. The question on the delivery of readings allowed respondents to select all answers that applied and the results suggest that several institutions have more than one way of delivering readings to students: 59% of institutions used a reading list system to deliver digitized readings to students; 75% used the VLE; four institutions (6%) used another method, including the library catalogue, a USB stick or disk; and one had an in-house system. An additional explanation for respondents selecting more than one option is that many reading list systems are integrated with the VLE so the responses are likely to reflect that. To contrast with the 2009 data, only 28% of the respondents used a reading list system then. In 2015, we asked which reading list system was being used and 66% of the institutions that answered this question used Talis Aspire, 18% used Rebus and 16% used another system, which in most instances was an in-house reading list system.

In some instances library staff do not have access to the VLE, with 23%

of respondents making this point in 2009. However, access to the VLE for library staff has become more common since then, perhaps driven in part by the reporting element in the CLA Licence that has encouraged e-learning and library staff to work together more closely. By 2015, 38% of respondents said library staff had routine access to the VLE, and 49% had access on request. Only 12% of respondents said library staff did not have access to the VLE.

While readings are delivered via the VLE, they were not always stored in the same place and the 2009 survey revealed that readings tend to be stored either on a separate library server or in the VLE, although some institutions store scans in more than one place. The findings from 2015 were broadly similar, with 46% of institutions storing readings in the VLE, 51% storing them on a secure server, and 25% using the TADC system. In four cases (6%) the files were stored in other locations, including a digital asset management system or repository, a desktop PC and one institution was transitioning to using TADC. The location of the scans is interesting as arguably material that is uploaded directly into the VLE may become more difficult to track and manage from a copyright perspective, without standardized procedures.

In 2009 the survey asked if copyright permissions were managed by library staff for other types of content, such as images, video or audio. At that time only 10% of respondents said that copyright permissions for other materials were managed by the library. In 2015, while 80% of respondents said that other types of content were available in the VLE (such as images, links to online content and recordings carried out under the ERA licence), again in only 6% of cases was this digital media managed by the library staff. Clearly content uploaded to the VLE is often managed by different groups of staff in the institution. Eight respondents specifically stated that only reading list material was managed by the library.

Usage statistics

Libraries are often keen to collect statistics on the services they provide, but in 2009 usage statistics about digitized readings were only collected by around a quarter of the respondents to the Survey of Digitisation of Core Readings. By 2015, 38% of institutions were collecting usage statistics, but 57% were not and 4% did not know if they were. Of those that did collect usage statistics, only 13% of institutions actually acted on them: for example not renewing requests if material was not used by students, or following up with a lecturer if the usage statistics far exceeded the number of students on a course. In 2015, 10% of universities were planning to use this data in the future and many that used TADC had become aware of this functionality recently.

Motivations for scanning

The Survey of Digitisation of Core Reading asked institutions about the motives behind scanning core readings, providing them with several choices that they could rank and an 'other' option. The results from 2015 showed that improving access to course readings was the most compelling reason for scanning a copyright work, cited by 54 of the 70 respondents and 94% ranking it first, second or third. This corresponds to the data collected in 2009, but meeting student expectations was cited far more frequently in 2015 (73% of respondents ranked it first, second or third). Support for e-learning was the third most cited reason for scanning a copyright work, whereas in 2009, this had been listed second. Meanwhile, in 2015 the fourth most common reason given for scanning a copyright work was 'to comply with the CLA Licence or copyright law', a reason which had not been mentioned in 2009.

In line with the data collected in 2009, space and cost efficiencies were unimportant reasons for scanning in 2015, as was raising the profile of the library. These findings are unsurprising and demonstrate that easy access to full-text readings, often as part of the online support provided in the VLE, is a common expectation among students in higher education. With increasing numbers of e-books to supplement widespread availability of e-journals, the need to visit the library to access core readings is becoming less pressing. Therefore, the CLA Licence is in many ways ensuring that copyright content not yet available in electronic format is accessible at the point of need to students. Since 2009 and the introduction of fees in the higher education sector, UK universities are mindful of growing student expectations. Academic libraries are also keen to ensure that their institution obtains a favourable score in annual National Student Survey (www.thestudentsurvey.com), which is completed by final year UK undergraduates. The student survey has a question that addresses respondents' satisfaction with the availability of learning resources. Libraries often provide digital readings and reading list systems in an attempt to give students reading material at the point of need in order to improve student satisfaction with the library service.

One further point is that the data supplied by universities to the CLA could also be used by publishers to inform their digitization programmes and the decisions they make about e-book availability. To date there is no real evidence that this has happened and so the number of readings that UK universities digitize is currently still growing. This is partly to meet the demand from teaching staff for content that is not available in electronic format, but also because some born digital content is not offered at a suitable price or delivered via a suitable platform to meet the needs of universities. The development of the DCS provides an opportunity for publishers and institutions to understand more about what types of content at article and chapter level are actually needed for teaching.

Collection management and e-resources

The Survey of Digitisation of Core Reading explored the impact that digitization might be having on collection management policies in academic libraries and the acquisition of electronic resources. In 2009, 74% of respondents said that their collection management policy took into account the availability of e-books and they would also check e-book availability before scanning an item. At the time of carrying out the survey in 2009, the CLA Licence stipulated that institutions should check whether an electronic version of a published work was available before scanning. Publishers were anxious that the Licence should not be used to substitute primary sales, and if a university decided to scan an e-book or e-journal they had to indicate why they did this on the CLA data return. This requirement has been removed from the licence so in the 2015 survey the question was reworded to find out what an institution would do if they received a request to scan an item available in electronic format. Many academic libraries have adopted e-first policies – they seek to purchase titles in electronic format in preference to paper. The survey found that 59% of institutions would purchase content in electronic format where possible, but cost was clearly a factor: 52% said that they would do this where it was affordable and only 12% of institutions would digitize an item regardless of electronic availability. This finding suggests that the CLA Licence is not being used to replace primary sales of material, but the comments from this question reveal that decisions are often made on an ad hoc basis. Factors such as student numbers, the accessibility of the e-resource platform and the cost of e-resources all influence the decisions made in many instances by subject librarians. Clearly if a resource was available to purchase at a suitable cost, or a journal article was available through a subscription, few academic libraries would digitize this material.

The relationship with the CLA

The CLA website is an important source of information for those wishing to copy material under the Licence. Since 2014 the CLA has had an online Check Permissions tool to allow institutions to establish whether a specific title is included in the Licence (CLA, 2016b). In 2009 more than three-quarters (76%) of respondents to the Survey of Digitisation of Core Readings reported that they regularly consult the CLA website, and by 2015 this figure had grown to 96%. Respondents were asked about the usefulness of this CLA website: 56% said it was very useful and 42% found it useful, a sharp contrast with the data collected in 2009 when 65% of respondents said it was 'quite useful' and only four institutions (13%) said it was very useful. The CLA has invested considerably in its customer services and developed a dedicated website for higher education in the past five years, and the value of these additional services is reflected in the findings from the survey.

The CLA Licence has specific reporting requirements for the higher education sector: bibliographic details of every item that is either scanned or used in digital format must be submitted on a spreadsheet to the CLA annually, along with details of the course of study and the student numbers. The survey had already collected data about the software used to help manage the digitization process, and also investigated how institutions managed the data reporting to the CLA and any specific issues involved. In 2009 the survey found that 39% of institutions used PackTracker to manage data reporting and 53% used the CLA spreadsheet. In one institution academic departments were asked to complete the record sheet and another method was used in two institutions. The picture was a little different in 2015: 30% of respondents used the spreadsheet from the CLA, 26% used PackTracker, 21% used TADC and the remainder (23%)

used a variety of other methods such as an in-house system.

In late 2008 the CLA established two working groups to help them better understand the needs of higher education. The working groups reflected the CLA's desire to resolve issues of concern for publishers and HEIs, and the groups report to the parent body, the Universities UK / GuildHE Copyright Working Group. The Data Collection Working Group, made up of representatives from a range of UK universities, has undertaken a lot of work on data reporting and agreed with the CLA to remove fields from the data return and streamline the reporting process. The DCS, which is being piloted in 2015–16 and planned for launch in August 2016, is an attempt by the CLA to find a solution to the problems associated with the data reporting process. The survey conducted in 2015 revealed that data reporting remains a considerable administrative burden for universities. The time consuming nature of completing the return, the need to check the data (even when a system such as PackTracker or TADC was used) and problems completing the return accurately were all cited by respondents in the survey. Responses suggested that many librarians believed that managing scanning through a central service was the most effective way to ensure compliance with the CLA Licence.

Licence coverage

When the CLA Scanning Licence was launched in 2008 the repertoire included only UK publishers, with a separate list of excluded works. Since this date the licence has been extended to include some US publishers and a number of countries such as South Africa, Canada and Spain. At the time of the 2009 Survey of Digitisation of Core Readings almost all respondents (31 out of 34) said they would like to see the repertoire increased further. In order of frequency, the countries suggested include all European countries, Australia, the Netherlands, Germany, Ireland, Canada and Scandinavian countries. Countries or regions that were mentioned just once each included the Far East, Japan, France, Spain and South Africa, and one respondent asked for 'All English-speaking countries'. The CLA has made significant progress in extending the repertoire of its licence and obtaining mandates from international publishers. However, difficulties remain, with US publishers needing to opt into the licence and this causing particular difficulties for universities.

One particularly problematic aspect of the UK licence is that the repertoire for photocopying is different from that for scanning and using existing digital content. When material is only available for photocopying it can be challenging to explain this to academic staff, who prefer to use the VLE as their default method of distributing content. However, the ease with which a title can be checked using the Check Permissions tool does add a greater clarity into the licence.

Handling copyright issues

In 2009 the Survey of Digitisation of Core Readings explored how copyright was dealt with internally in universities and found that 63% of the responding institutions had a copyright officer, 34% did not and one respondent (3%) was not sure. The data is broadly similar to findings from the 2014 Copyright Literacy Survey (Morrison and Secker, 2015, 88), which found that across the cultural heritage sector in the UK, 64% of institutions had a person with responsibility for copyright. Within higher education the figure was higher and the survey found 74% of institutions had such a post. This research found that while levels of 'copyright literacy' were generally high among UK librarians, copyright was often a source of anxiety and that new technology and changes to the law were particular areas where librarians wanted to improve their knowledge. In 2009 the survey found that the JISCmail list LIS-Copyseek was used most frequently for copyright queries, by 92% of institutions. To a lesser degree the CLA was consulted with queries (76%), colleagues at respondents' institutions were also a good source of advice (68%) and, where they existed, institutional copyright officers (32%) were of course important. In 2014, the sources of advice cited in the Copyright Literacy Survey revealed that websites and colleagues were the most valuable sources of advice (cited by 76% and 70% of respondents). The next most important sources were book or articles (62%), professional associations (59%) and discussions lists such as LIS-Copyseek (47%) (Morrison and Secker, 2015, 85–6). The need to keep up to date in this field was clearly important for many librarians and the research suggested a wide range of topics for inclusion in the professional education of librarians and continuing professional education. Education and training is discussed in more detail in Chapter 6.

Further issues

In 2009 a variety of other subjects than those discussed above were raised in response to an open ended question at the end of the survey, but this question was not included in the 2015 survey, because the authors had been able to collect feedback from institutions in a number of other ways. In particular, a workshop was held in July 2015 with university librarians, institutional CLA Licence co-ordinators and copyright officers to help inform the negotiations for a new CLA Licence. This workshop provided valuable feedback on the impact of the Licence on UK academic libraries, including what was working, what was not, what the sector wanted to see for a new licence and attendees' opinions of the CLA. Priorities specified by the sector are currently being used to inform negotiations towards a new licence from August 2016. Respondents to the 2009 survey had complained about the increase in workload for library staff as more scanning was requested by teachers. For example, one respondent said: 'Managing digital readings is demanding, and requires extra staffing to do it properly.' Another commented: 'The issues of time, ongoing funding, difficulty of CLA reporting and problems of copyright compliance come up time and again.' In 2009 an important concern was the addition of the US publishers to the CLA Licence repertoire (in August 2008), which had had a major impact on workload. However, in 2015, the exclusion of some US publishers and titles from the licence in 2013 was causing problems. Many institutions remained concerned that managing the licence and renewing readings each year was generating additional work, as this respondent said: 'All these problems are exacerbated by up-scaling of each library's digitization service – even if there is not a concerted effort to increase through-put, just re-using items year on year means the time, reporting and staffing burdens are always increasing.' It remains to be seen if the CLA's DCS will resolve many of these issues and how the Licence might operate after August 2016, as negotiations are still ongoing at the time of writing this book.

Using published content outside the UK

The results from the surveys on the digitization of core readings in 2009 and 2015 demonstrate that licensing agreements and copyright issues in the UK have shaped the services offered by libraries to support learning.

Digitization of core readings has gone from being a niche activity undertaken by larger institutions with established copyright clearance units, to a mainstream activity in many academic libraries. Yet copyright and digitization work is still not always supported by a dedicated team and the work sometimes falls between the remit of subject librarians and those in teaching support roles. The requirement to provide full census reporting of all the materials digitized under the CLA Licence is regarded by many as an administrative burden; the CLA recognizes this and is seeking to address the matter with the launch of the DCS later in 2016. Copyright remains an important concern that most university libraries have taken responsibility for and processes such as the CLA audit remind institutions that VLEs need to be copyright compliant. In the UK many librarians have been able to make extensive use of the blanket licence to meet student demands for digitized readings, despite the administrative burdens. Many librarians in the UK are also working hard to ensure that lecturers are aware of copyright issues and that copyright is not a barrier to e-learning.

Chapter 1 showed how many of the English-speaking countries of the world have followed the UK's example and the reprographic reproduction agencies in Australia, New Zealand and Ireland (to name but a few) now offer digitization licences. We have also seen that many countries in the world are attempting to reform their copyright laws, yet in most of the world using published content for education and specifically for online learning requires either negotiating individual permissions or taking out a blanket licence of some form. At times lecturers cannot add the resources that their students need to the VLE.

The USA

We have seen in Chapter 1 how the copyright laws in the USA are different from those in the UK and that this has affected the way in which published content is used in online learning. The 'fair use' concept covers the copying of material for educational purposes so educational establishments have been able to make paper and digital copies for students for teaching purposes without seeking permissions from rights holders. Some institutions choose to seek copyright permission to digitize material for teaching purposes and subsequently make it available, but many do not.

However, in 2007 the US CCC offered universities the option to take out a blanket licence. Opinions have been divided over the value of purchasing such a licence, with some institutions seeing it as security and others feeling that it compromises the fair use provision. The following case study from a US university (where the term for this type of service is electronic reserves) illustrates how the situation compares with that in the UK.

Case Study 3　Electronic reserves and copyright in a US university

Introduction and background

This case study is from a medium-sized liberal arts university in the eastern USA enrolling approximately 5500 undergraduate and 2100 graduate students. Undergraduates fulfil general education requirements, choose a variety of elective courses, and pursue departmental concentrations and interdisciplinary certificate programs. At the graduate level students may earn advanced degrees in the humanities, social sciences, natural sciences and engineering.

To support the educational curriculum the Library has always offered a course reserve service to faculty. Faculty members submitted their requests for materials in all formats to be placed on reserve for their courses and staff made them available to students, either in tangible or digital form, through our closed reserve stack operation. Although library staff were certainly mindful of the copyright implications of duplicating journal articles, it was rare that they had more than two or three copies of the same article on reserve at any given time. The number of copies on reserve was determined by the number of students enrolled in the course. Most of the articles were from the Library's own collection to which the students had access and could make their own copies. Faculty members also had – and used – the option of having course packs created. These packs were created by an independent agency (for example, Kinko's), which would seek copyright permission to create the packs and pass any associated costs on to the students via the fee they charged. Because of the expense of these packs, faculty members often supplied one copy of the pack to be placed on reserve for student use.

The electronic reserves service

The Library began an electronic reserve service in 2001 as a pilot programme using courses in the humanities and social sciences. At that time they agreed to scan only journal articles and book chapters and adhered to the guidelines that were set at the CONFU. These guidelines suggested that scans should be limited to no more than 10% of a book or a single article from a journal issue. A small number of faculty members agreed to use the services in their courses during this pilot phase.

Over time, however, the electronic reserve service blossomed, and became the norm for course reserve services. In recent years, very few faculty members continue to request print material be placed on reserve. The service grew not only for print material, but also for audio and video resources.

Working with the faculty and the IT department, library staff devised a system to record the audio material required, place it on a streaming server, which is locally hosted, and make it available to the students from the Library and from off-site through a password-protected mechanism. As with the digitized printed items, the digitized audio items are available only to students enrolled in the courses for which those materials are needed.

Members of some disciplines, such as a film studies department, used these resources extensively in the past, but faculty members in other departments now see the value in emphasizing points, making comparisons, or demonstrating effects of events through the use of video – both documentary and feature films. As a result, the size of the collection in the Library, which until recently had a very small video collection, has grown exponentially. Because of their positive experiences with digitized print and audio resources, faculty members using video resources also want a way to make them available electronically. Having had the experience with the audio reserves we used a similar model to present the digitized videos. As with the audio the Library digitize only content that they own in physical form (in this case either in video, DVD, or Blu-ray) and it is made available only in streaming format, at select locations (in classrooms and the library), and restricted to students enrolled on the courses for which the resources have been requested.

The Library's integrated library system, Voyager, has an e-reserve component but lacks many features including perhaps most importantly one that would restrict access to e-reserve readings to students enrolled on a particular course. The locally developed system includes an online request service for faculty members to submit the citations, as well as a complex database structure on the backend to manage those requests and to make the readings available. In addition to providing access via the Library's website using course-specific IDs and passwords, working with the University's IT department, staff were able to make the readings, audio and video available through our course management system or VLE – Blackboard. Library staff encourage all faculty members who use the service to instruct students to access the e-reserve content exclusively through Blackboard; access through the Library's website should be secondary and only if Blackboard was unavailable for some reason, or if someone in the course, such as an auditor, was unable to log in via Blackboard.

Copyright compliance

Although library staff were fairly certain that they maintained copyright compliance by offering the electronic reserve service in a manner similar to our traditional reserve services, they consulted extensively with the campus' Office of General Counsel, which provided legal advice to ensure this compliance. Because they adhere to the CONFU guidelines, the Office felt that there was no need for further action at that time. For any item exceeding the guidelines set by CONFU the Library would seek permission from the copyright holder before making the item available to the students. As the electronic reserve service expanded, so did the requests for larger and larger portions of copyrighted works. It was not uncommon for the Library to receive requests for more than half of a book – or even an entire book – to be scanned. The trade-off for the popularity and effectiveness of this service is that copyright costs began to skyrocket as the Library believed many of the requests could not be scanned under the terms of 'fair use'.

In one year, the cost of copyright fees totalled more than $50,000. At that point, something had to be done! The library had also been purchasing many e-books (standalone and packages). It was also fairly common for the e-books to be purchased using the multiple simultaneous user option, enabling more than one person to read the content at a time. In conducting an analysis of the cost of e-books to the cost of copyright fees, we decided to pursue e-book purchases more actively, when feasible. Our analysis also found that even for e-books where there is a single-user-only option available, the cost of purchasing multiple 'copies' of the e-book was often less expensive than the copyright fees required. Although much more labour intensive, it is now practice for library staff who receive an electronic reserve request to consult the availability of an e-book and compare the cost of the e-book with the cost of copyright fees, and then choose the best option based on the cost savings to the Library.

Conclusion

Library staff believe that our electronic reserve service continues to be successful, as demonstrated by the feedback it has received from faculty and students and by the increasing number of requests for electronic reserve materials from the faculty members. We consulted extensively with our Office of General Counsel to ensure copyright compliance. Although the Office of General Counsel believes that the institution – and other libraries – should push the limits of fair use in order to protect those rights, we must also do so in a fiscally responsible manner. For several years, the Library pushed the limits of the fair use statutes with strength sufficient to ensure that the resources that the faculty and students need are available to them in a format which is easy to access. However, as we continued to push those limits, so did the faculty in their requests. We continue to be concerned about the number of court cases that involve the use of digitized content for electronic reserve – irrespective of the original format (print, audio, video, etc.). For our audio and video collections, our Office of General Counsel believes that because of the restrictions that the institution has in place (restricting access to certain locations, only to students enrolled on courses, and only to material that is physically owned) we are in good stead. We believe we have found, also, a solution for the print material by increasing our purchase and use of e-books. The landscape for e-reserves continues to change either in response to challenges, or in anticipation of them. It is imperative that we keep abreast of the changes in higher education, publishing and the courts, in order to determine how best to continue meeting the needs of our faculty and students.

Using unpublished content

Unpublished content can include all manner of materials, such as theses, archival materials including letters, files and other historical materials. While this content may seem very different from published material there are some similarities to the copyright clearance process for published material. In the case of unpublished content the author needs to be traced before a work can be digitized, which is similar in theory (if not always in practice) to identifying the publisher of a published work. However, unlike published content, unpublished materials are rarely covered by blanket licences and therefore direct permissions need to be sought. Where the copyright owner can be traced it is sensible to keep records of any permission fees and the terms and conditions that the owner might have stipulated. Further details about requesting copyright permission for materials is available in Chapter 3 (see pages 97–8). When requesting copyright permission, always specify what you intend to do with the material, and include details such as:

◆ who will have access to the material; if specific students on a course, specific student numbers and duration of permission are required
◆ what file format the material will be made available in, for example, PDF
◆ whether any password protection will be in place or if the material is going to be made available in an open access repository.

If a work is out of copyright (which for unpublished literary, artistic, dramatic and musical works in the UK is either 70 years after the death of the author or, for certain works, 31 December 2039) it can be digitized. In the USA some recently created works, such as material produced by the Federal Government, pass immediately into the public domain and unrestricted copying and communication can be undertaken. It is more problematic when a rights holder cannot be traced despite reasonable endeavours. Works by a rights holder who cannot be traced are often called orphan works; if a teacher wants to go ahead and use an orphan work the institution needs to consider a number of options when deciding how to manage their institutional risk.

Since November 2014 UK law has provided educational institutions with two routes to making legitimate copies of 'orphan works', both of which need to be considered carefully, as more than one option might apply in any given situation:

◆ The IPO's Orphan Works Licensing Scheme, which is time limited to seven years, only covers usage within the UK and involves a licensing fee and administration charge. Licensees apply to the IPO for a licence from the Government, which provides them with protection should the rights holder make themselves known and object to the use, or ask for a fee.

◆ Rely on the EU Directive (2012/28/EU), which provides educational and cultural institutions with an exception to preserve and make orphan works available for non-commercial purposes. The exception is not limited by time or territorial boundaries, but does not allow use of standalone images such as photographs.

Both options require a 'diligent search' for the rights holder for each work to be digitized, the details of which are provided on the IPO's website (IPO 2015a). There has been criticism from some in the cultural and education sector that the orphan works solutions available in the UK are confused and only offer a partial solution to the problem. They certainly do not facilitate mass digitization programmes of in-copyright content held in many collections, because of the requirement to carry out diligent searches on all content, but institutions might decide to use them for individual course readings.

Before these solutions were available any institution or individual intending to digitize orphan works and make them available was forced to take a risk-managed approach. Effectively this means that while formal clearance has not been obtained, the institution doing the digitization has done a full risk assessment of the situation and taken measures to mitigate potential legal action. As previously mentioned, this is still the only option for those wanting to undertake mass digitization of in-copyright content.

These are some questions to ask when considering the risk involved in digitizing orphan works:

◆ Is the owner likely to find out and object to the use of the material?
◆ Is the owner likely to be financially affected by the decision to digitize?
◆ Is the material sensitive in any way – are there any privacy or data protection issues?
◆ What would the institution be prepared to pay if the owner came forward?

Many UK universities have adopted a risk-averse approach to digitizing content without permission, concentrating on special collections that are either owned by an institution or material that is clearly out of copyright. Other material, which perhaps might be more useful for teachers, has tended to remain in archives in its original format. Many still hope that the new solutions for orphan works will have a positive effect on the availability of archive content, but at the time of writing (September 2015) only 287 items have been cleared through the IPO scheme in the ten months since launch (IPO, 2015b). Similarly the UK Copyright Literacy Survey (Morrison and Secker, 2015) suggested that awareness of orphan works solutions among librarians and information professionals was significantly lower than digitization of published content under blanket licence schemes (only 34% were extremely or moderately familiar with orphan works, compared with 49% extremely or moderately familiar with general digitization issues).

Conclusion

Many online courses require the inclusion of scanned text or images from third parties, so using licences, obtaining permission or relying on relevant copyright exceptions is inevitable. Staff then need to take advice, often from a librarian or copyright officer, to ensure that they are familiar with the law and any licensing schemes in operation in their own country. There may be exceptions that allow published material to be scanned, but more often than not permission fees will need to be paid. This chapter has looked in detail at one country, the UK, where a licensing scheme has allowed limited extracts of published content to be used in online learning. However, the Survey of Digitisation of Core Readings in UK Higher Education carried out in 2009 and 2015 showed that universities in the UK were not entirely satisfied with the terms of the CLA Licence, in particular the reporting requirements that it placed on them. The Copyright Literacy Survey carried out in 2014 also suggests that librarians have many concerns about keeping up to date with copyright issues. Meanwhile in the USA 'fair use' allows limited amounts of published content to be scanned for educational purposes, but publishers are extremely sensitive to any allegations of copyright infringement, or activities that may impact on their primary sales. Therefore, caution is advised when using any published content in e-learning. Course managers should ideally ensure that they have an adequate budget to pay for any necessary permissions if published content is required. Even using unpublished material is not without pitfalls and is likely to require permission from the copyright holder. As a response to the increasingly competitive education market many universities are investing heavily in online learning courses. This is seen as an essential part of a compelling 'student experience' and traditionally publicly funded institutions are now competing with commercial providers in markets such as 'Executive Education', which is designed to make a profit for the university. Consequently, if there is money to be made, many publishers would like to see some form of remuneration. Those involved in designing online courses need to be mindful of this when deciding what content they wish to include. Educational establishments also need robust copyright procedures, policies and compliance strategies in place to operate in this increasingly complex environment. As we shall see in Chapter 6, it is essential that these policies are understood and practised by employees through appropriate education and staff engagement.

Note

1   This group negotiates licences for the higher education sector and offers advice to Universities UK and GuildHE on EU and UK copyright initiatives and draft legislation. Details and current membership of the Universities UK / GuildHE Copyright Working Group are available at www.universitiesuk.ac.uk/aboutus/whatwedo/PolicyAnalysis/ Regulation/Pages/CopyrightintheHigherEducationSector.aspx.

References

CLA (2015a) Who We Are, Copyright Licensing Agency, www.cla.co.uk/about/who_we_are [accessed 6 April 2016].
CLA (2015b) CLA Higher Education Licence, Copyright Licensing Agency, http://he.cla.co.uk/your-he-licence/your-he-licence/ about-the-cla-higher-education-licence [accessed 6 April 2016].
CLA (2016a) Audit Materials, Copyright Licensing Agency,

http://he.cla.co.uk/complying-with-your-licence/audit-materials [accessed 6 April 2016].

CLA (2016b) Check Permissions, Copyright Licensing Agency, http://he.cla.co.uk/check-permissions [accessed 6 April 2016].

CLA (2016c) Schools Printed Music Licence, Copyright Licensing Agency, http://schools.cla.co.uk/about-your-licences/schools-printed-music-licence [accessed 6 April 2016].

Delasalle, J. (2007) The CLA HE Trial Scanning Licence – how we're using it, *Library and Information Research*, **31** (98), www.lirg.org.uk/lir/ojs/index.php/lir/article/view/39/46 [accessed 6 April 2016].

Hedges, J. and Secker, J. (2009) Survey of Digitisation of Core Readings in UK Higher Education: final report, http://discovery.ucl.ac.uk/1400635/2/Survey_finalreport.pdf [accessed 6 April 2016].

HESA (2015) Free Online Statistics – students & qualifiers, Higher Education Statistical Agency, www.hesa.ac.uk/stats [accessed 6 April 2016].

IPO (2015a) *Orphan Works Diligent Search Guidance for Applicants*, Intellectual Property Office, https://www.gov.uk/government/publications/orphan-works-diligent-search-guidance-for-applicants [accessed 6 April 2016].

IPO (2015b) *Orphan Works Licensing Scheme Register*, Intellectual Property Office, https://www.orphanworkslicensing.service.gov.uk/view-register [accessed 6 April 2016].

Morrison, C. and Secker, J. (2015) Copyright Literacy in the UK: a survey of librarians and other cultural heritage sector professionals, *Library and Information Research*, **39** (121), 75–97.

NLA Media Access (2016) Education Establishment Licence, www.nlamediaaccess.com/default.aspx?tabid=142 [accessed 6 April 2016].

SCONUL (2015) Changing Trends in Loans, Visits and the Use of E-books, extract from SCONUL data 2013–14, www.sconul.ac.uk/sites/default/files/documents/Analysis%20_Loans%20ebooks%20visits%20June%202015.pdf [accessed 6 April 2016].

Secker, J. and Morrison, C. (2016) UK Higher Education Scanning Survey

Report, https://ukcopyrightliteracy.files.wordpress.com/2016/03/
uk-he-scanning-survey-2015-final-report-for-open-access1.pdf
[accessed 6 April 2016].

3 Using digital media: video, images, sound and software

Introduction

There is a growing demand for non-text-based digital media content, such as images, video and sound recordings, to provide engaging materials for use in both traditional and online learning. However, copyright questions become increasingly complex when education professionals wish to digitize existing analogue content, as it is usually necessary to obtain permission from several rights holders. Meanwhile, producing digital media content in-house is now technically straightforward but can raise a host of copyright and IPR issues. In both cases delivering this type of content using a VLE highlights, but also exacerbates, the copyright issues. This chapter explores the copyright issues associated with the digitization of non-text-based digital media content, starting with using images in education. It goes on to explore using recordings of broadcast material. In the UK, the ERA licence permits broadcasts to be recorded off-air and digitized for educational use. Although a number of restrictions apply, the ERA licence allows subscribing institutions to deliver free-to-air broadcast content via secure digital networks within the UK. This chapter will also consider digitization of commercially available non-text-based material (including recordings that can be purchased specifically for educational use). Often in these situations permission is required from the rights holder and therefore the procedures for identifying the owner and for securing copyright permission are outlined.

Many educational institutions are now producing digital media content in-house and there are many copyright issues that need to be considered. For example, semi-automated lecture capture systems are now available in many universities in the USA, the UK and other countries (UCISA, 2014). These offer institutions the ability to record and deliver lecture material asynchronously (e.g. after the event for revision purposes) via a computer network. However, copyright issues become a much bigger area of concern when classroom teaching is recorded and made available online. Aside from the need to get permission to include third-party content, the ownership of the resulting video also raises wider IPR concerns in institutions. In some institutions teaching staff have raised concerns over their lectures being recorded and have cited IPR issues (such as their rights as a performer and responsibility for clearing third-party rights) as reasons for objecting. This chapter explores some of these topics, and gives advice for dealing with third-party content and guidance for resolving the ownership of the resulting material. Finally the chapter includes a list of visual, audio and audiovisual resources (sound, video and image collections) for teachers, including some that can be used for educational purposes without the payment of fees. Arguably, directing teachers to openly licensed collections, or those licensed for educational use, is an important role for e-learning professionals. In doing this, an understanding of copyright issues can become embedded as good practice in finding and using resources for teaching. Sources of advice for resolving queries related to digital media content are also included in this chapter; the case study comes from UCL and covers some of the complexities of negotiating rights to deliver content worldwide in an open way.

Why use sound, images and video in teaching?

Non-text-based content is increasingly used in the classroom as a way of engaging students. Many authors have written about the way that young people spend less time reading and more time consuming visual and audio content. Arguably this may be changing the way they want to learn. The notion of the 'Google Generation' or 'Net Generation' was discussed briefly in Chapter 1 (see pages 8–9). Although Prensky's (2001) idea of young people being 'digital natives' as opposed to 'digital immigrants' has been found to be over-simplistic (Jones et al., 2010), it is fair to say that many people have become increasingly visual learners with a shorter attention span. The digitally connected student has a tendency to switch focus from their phone, laptop and face-to-face interactions rapidly, with relative ease.

We are all bombarded with music, moving and still images and consequently audio and video resources are being used as an addition to traditional text-based teaching resources. In the 21st century these resources are a valuable way of conveying information to students who tend to spend more time online, using social media, playing video games and using their smartphones than they do reading books, newspapers or listening to the radio. For example, a study from 2015 called *Adults' Media Use and Attitudes* (Ofcom, 2015) found young adults are now spending just over 27 hours a week online, compared with around ten hours in 2005, and are more likely to use their mobiles, computers and games consoles every day than older respondents. The evidence that using multiple media (known as 'multimodal learning') helps students retain information is still not concrete, but in one study (Sankey, Birch and Gardiner, 2010) students reported favourably on this approach as it engages both aural and visual senses and caters to those with different learning styles. Sankey, Birch and Gardiner cite several studies that show how audio and visual material can engage students better than traditional material does and how it has particular benefits for low achieving students (Moreno and Mayer, 2007); therefore it is unsurprising that there is a growing demand from teachers to use this type of content in online learning.

In the past five years there has also been a growth in the number of digitally enabled interactive teaching methods, such as the 'flipped classroom', which was made popular by Harvard physics Professor Eric Mazur. This approach maximizes face-to-face teaching time by getting students to watch a pre-recorded video covering the key concepts of a lesson before attending class. Class time is spent in discussions, with peer and teacher-led instruction. Recording short videos to replace a lecture or screencasts is relatively easy, with many lecture recording systems having a facility to record using most digital devices. Given the ease with which video recordings can now be made, some teachers have also chosen to respond to questions from students by producing supplementary material in video format and uploading it to the VLE.

Copyright and non-text-based works: an introduction

Images, audio and audiovisual material present a whole set of copyright challenges for the e-learning professional and the copyright adviser. They might not only have to obtain permission for the re-use of content, but also need to advise on ownership of resulting materials and determine appropriate re-use terms. Establishing copyright ownership and obtaining permission to re-use printed materials such as books and journals are relatively well established processes, with many larger publishers having dedicated rights and permissions departments to handle requests. However, managing rights in non-text material is inherently complicated by the multiple layers of rights involved. Audio and audiovisual material in particular is often produced by more than one person and there could be a whole range of rights holders pertaining to each of the rights involved (e.g. the script, the film, the sound recording, the music). In addition there is no obvious single body such as the CLA that can grant permission or act as a broker for handling permissions.

Copyright laws protect the various types of work incorporated in a single piece of content (e.g. the film, the sound recording, the script as literary work, etc.) and determine the duration of copyright protection that applies to the material. In the UK sound recordings are now protected for 70 years from the year of creation,[1] while films are protected for 70 years after the last to die of the principal director, the author of the screenplay, the author of the dialogue or the composer of the music. As a result, in reality very few films are out of copyright. Moreover film companies have been quick to extend copyright protection by re-mastering and re-issuing films, as the copyright in the re-mastered versions is calculated from the date of the new version, not the original. In the USA, sound recordings produced before 1978 are protected for 50 years but those published after 1978 qualify for 70 years' protection.

Copyright can easily become complicated when dealing with dramatic works, film and sound recordings. For example, performing a work such as a play or a piece of music is the exclusive right of the copyright holder and the cast or group's performances qualify for performance rights, which become significant if the work is recorded. Performances qualify for protection for 50 years, as do broadcasts. However, under Section 34 of the CDPA films and sound recordings can be shown in the classroom for educational purposes, and musical and dramatic works can also be performed. In October 2014 the law in the UK was changed so that the fair dealing exceptions apply to sound recordings, film and broadcasts, but establishing what is 'fair' when copying films, broadcasts, images and sounds recordings is less easy to define than it is for literary works. In order to deliver this type of content online, it needs to be copied.

Using images in education

The use of images presents a unique challenge to those considering the copyright implications of teaching in the digital environment. As previously mentioned, images are a hugely important component of almost all teaching, but for the use of an image to have any value it almost invariably must be reproduced in its entirety. This clearly provides a challenge to those who wish to use images either under licence or exception. In the case of acquiring a licence, a rights holder's expectations as to the value of their artistic work being reproduced in full may be at odds with a teacher's need to use a wide range of images for illustrative and genuine pedagogic reasons. Similarly, a key aspect of applying a fair dealing test to consider whether exceptions such as illustration for instruction or quotation apply is whether the amount of copying is excessive. In a situation where almost all use of images in education requires the reproduction of entire copyright works, the focus then turns to the other aspects of fair dealing, particularly whether the use of the work disadvantages the rights holder or interferes with the normal exploitation of the work. For example, making available a low resolution image may be less likely to disrupt the normal exploitation of the work and be considered fair dealing. However, as mentioned later in the section on digital images collections on pages 93–5, it is important to check that any amendments made to images, such as cropping, distorting or re-contextualizing the image, do not breach the creators' moral rights.

Another key challenge to having an appropriate approach to the use of images is that there are many different types of image, created by different people (or even by computers) for different reasons, under widely varying commercial models (including those made with no commercial end in mind). This makes it virtually impossible to have a one-size-fits-all approach. The value associated with graphs, charts and diagrams published in academic textbooks is likely to be different from that associated with works of fine art, historical photographs, illustrations from children's books, cartoons or iconic imagery from popular culture. The reproduction of charts from textbooks in a teaching environment is likely to be accepted without an expectation of payment from most rights holders particularly if they do not constitute a substantial part of the book. A publisher might also expect further sales of the textbook to the students on the course so the reproduction of the image in the teaching would have little to no negative impact on the normal exploitation of the work if it was properly attributed (or perhaps even a positive impact). However, there are many images, such as photographs controlled by picture libraries (see below), where there are established market rates and norms of use. The issue here is that these market rates and licensing mechanisms do not translate to an educational environment where the use of the images is likely be extensive, but often only available to small groups of people (students on a course of study). The situation is further complicated if an educational establishment wishes to teach in a more open way, such as by launching a massive open online course (MOOC) – see Chapter 5, page 199, for more on this.

It is widely accepted that the copying of images in to a digital document (such as a PowerPoint slide deck) for presentation to a room of students is now defensible in the UK under the illustration for instruction exception, as long as the teaching is for non-commercial purposes.[2] However, whether it is also defensible to post the presentation slides including those images to a VLE, or indeed record the teacher giving the presentation and upload the video file, is less clear. From a rights holder's perspective the use of the work in this way involves the making of multiple copies of entire copyright works and they may well expect teachers or institutions to obtain permission. From a teacher's perspective the ability to show a range of images (most of which may well be easily accessible to anyone via a Google image search) in a classroom, but not to be allowed to share the file digitally with their students afterwards, suggests there is a contradiction in copyright law. The pressure on teachers to carry out their own rights clearance or consider whether fair dealing applies can cause considerable anxiety, particularly when under pressure to deliver high volumes of teaching with limited support. This is why it is very important that educational establishments develop clear guidance and procedures to support teachers in the legal and ethical use of images. As discussed later in Chapter 6, it is important to focus on the positives – the types of images that teachers *can* use easily (such as Creative Commons licensed images). It is also important to liaise with those from particular subject areas and disciplines to identify collections of content which are either licensed by the institution or available for re-use under appropriate terms. A selection of these types of collections is included later in this chapter. As mentioned in Chapter 1, it is also helpful to encourage teachers to consider open practices when creating their own visual resources (e.g. taking photographs to create a collection associated with a particular area of study) and if appropriate make them available for re-use by others. This can have the benefit of raising the profile of the teacher and the institution and providing a common resource for other teachers.

The use of content from digital image libraries is described in further detail in the next section along with an explanation of the licensing body, the Design and Artists Copyright Society (DACS; www.dacs.org.uk), which primarily represents commercial visual artists. Many in education might be tempted to decry the lack of a blanket licence or exception that allows use of any images for teaching purposes. However, given the wide range of images and artistic works that exist, this type of licence is not practical nor would it be welcomed by many artists or photographers. In the same way that a blanket licence cannot allow the use of all written (literary) works, a blanket licence or exception for all artistic works is not realistic. For this reason educational establishments need to build a clear approach to encouraging and supporting the ethical use of images in digital education. The most fundamental element of this is that all images, whether used under licence or exception, need to be attributed appropriately to the creator and the rights holder (where practical).

Digital images collections

This section concentrates on dedicated image collections rather than incidental or illustrative images found on websites. As mentioned previously, images are particularly useful in many educational subjects from science to art, history to medicine. They add interest to text-based content and in some cases may be a more appropriate way of conveying information than using text-based material. For this reason, there are a wide range of digital images collections available and these fall into several categories including:

◆ Commercial or subscription collections that are available either on a pay per item basis or as a subscription for the collection. Examples of these include the Getty Image Archive, the Jisc Media Hub, private image collections either from photographers, artists or art galleries and museums such as the Bridgeman Art Gallery.

◆ Image collections where the content is considered to be out of copyright or in the public domain. These are often made available by libraries, museums or other charitable bodies. Examples of these include collections from the University of Virginia Library and Images of America.

◆ Image collections that have been licensed under Creative Commons licences and so can be re-used under the terms of these licences. The photo-sharing website Flickr is the largest example of this type of collection and it is discussed in more detail in Chapter 4. Wikipedia now uses Creative Commons licences on all its images and Wikimedia is a good source of openly licensed images.

◆ Other image collections which can be used for educational purposes, for example, FreeFoto (www.freefoto.com) or OpenClipArt (https://openclipart.org/).

One of the issues of making digital images available in any online collection is that they are technically very easy to copy. It is also easy to reproduce only a part of an image, although in most cases this may be of little value. In fact by cropping an image it is also easy to change its meaning considerably, therefore misrepresenting the original intention of the artist or photographer and possibly breaching their moral rights. Professional photographers and organizations such as art galleries which rely on their images for a revenue stream tend to protect their images, for example by using watermarking, so the details of the copyright owners are clearly visible across a photo, limiting its use. Other rights protection techniques include making only low resolution files available online, with the higher resolution copies sold commercially via an online store. For example, many museums and galleries such as the National Portrait Gallery (www.npg.uk) offer high resolution images for sale, but allow lower resolution copies to be downloaded for non-commercial purposes.

Many subscription or commercial image collections tend to be governed by either licence agreements or terms and conditions. These set out how the images can be used and usually specify how the images must be credited. In the UK DACS provides a range of licences for those wishing to copy artistic works. One-off licences for copying specific material can be obtained and the pricing structure is fixed. This includes 'free' permissions for use of content in learning materials, although this involves paying a fee of £42 per reproduction. In the past many universities teaching fine art used the DACS slide licence scheme to allow them to reproduce artistic works in lectures. Although DACS has not issued a blanket digital licence to replace the slide licence, it has a reciprocal agreement with the CLA that allows artistic works within published works (e.g. illustrations) to be digitized under the CLA higher education licence. Currently dis-embedded images (those that are not reproduced along with accompanying text) need to be recorded on the CLA record sheet so that payments can be returned to the artists in question. However, images included within an extract of text-based material do not need to be recorded separately. If DACS issued a digitization licence of its own it would benefit those developing e-learning content, as it would allow universities to digitize their slide collections and integrate the materials into the VLE.

Where licences are not available, UK copyright law is clear about copyright ownership of images. The CDPA states that:

◆ Images are protected as artistic works and copyright lies with the artist.
◆ Copyright in photographs taken after 1989 is owned by the person taking the photograph, even if the photograph is commissioned by another person.
◆ Commissioned artistic works pre-1989 are owned by the person commissioning the work.
◆ Copyright restricts taking photographs of in-copyright artistic works unless they are on permanent display and open to members of the public.

Institutions that hold collections of artistic works (such as galleries and museums) may still charge a copying fee for a work in their possession, despite the work being out of copyright. Anyone seeking permission to reproduce an artistic work may wish to consult DACS for further advice.

Digitization of analogue recordings

In the same way that print resources are digitized to improve access in the online environment, many institutions have started to invest in digitizing audio and video collections that were traditionally available in an analogue format. In the home entertainment market, video recordings on analogue formats such as VHS have largely been superseded by digital formats like DVD, Blu-ray and digital downloads and streams. In the past many libraries might have built up significant analogue collections either on video or audio cassette. These collections are now rarely used even though they can be borrowed by individuals or shown in classrooms. Access to this material can be significantly improved if the content is digitized and placed onto a streaming server that would allow delivery over a network. Digitization also facilitates the material being used online either for face-to-face students or distance learners.

Format shifting to convert material from analogue to digital has become a relatively straightforward technical process but raises several copyright issues, particularly if the intention is to place the digital file onto a network for educational use. Even when audio or video material exists in digital format (on CD or on DVD) the file format is often not suitable for delivery over a network without some processing (this is particularly true for video material). In addition, recordings such as videos, DVDs and audio CDs tend to be licensed for personal use only. Following the Hargreaves Review in the UK (discussed in some detail in Chapter 1), copying of films, sound recordings and broadcasts in the permanent collection for preservation purposes is now permitted under Section 42 of the CDPA when undertaken by libraries. However, further copying or distribution via a network requires negotiating a separate permission.

The Survey of Digitisation of Core Readings in UK Higher Education discussed in Chapter 2 showed that few libraries responsible for digitization of text resources also deal with audiovisual material. This suggests that it is relatively uncommon in the UK higher education sector for permissions to be sought to digitize content such as film or sound recordings. The perception among staff is that the process is both time consuming and expensive, and the authors' experience suggests that this is the case. It is frequently difficult to know who to approach to get permission to use an excerpt from a film because the copyright often lies with several different individuals and permissions are usually handled by a large multinational organization such as a film distributor using a commercial licence model. Getting permission from smaller educational companies can often be more straightforward, and surprisingly inexpensive. However, without a dedicated copyright clearance person it is often unclear who in an educational establishment should be negotiating the permission (the academic, the learning technology team or perhaps library staff) and who should retain the documentation relating to any permissions received. Few universities are in the fortunate situation of the Open University to have a well resourced rights and permissions department that is well versed in negotiating permissions to use text, images and audiovisual materials in teaching.

Identifying rights holders and getting permission

If a film or sound recording is to be screened for clearly educational purposes, permission is not required. Additionally if you wish to use broadcast content from television and radio, the ERA licence (see below) covers most teaching activities, including making copies to support teaching. However, permission usually needs to be sought when films or sound recordings are copied so they can be made available online. The following guidelines can be used to help speed up the process and improve the chances of obtaining a positive response. This advice also applies to permission requests for other types of content, not just films and sound recordings. In order to obtain copyright permission take the following steps:

◆ First establish exactly what the teacher wants to do with the material, how much they wish to include (including exact timings of frames) and for what purpose. This will help establish if permission is required. For example, it may be that they only wish to show an extract from a film in class.

◆ Check what sort of budget might be in place to pay for any permission – is there a limit the teacher is prepared to pay?

◆ Spend some time establishing who owns copyright in the material – check the copyright statement on any packaging or in the credits on a recording.

◆ Spend some time researching the organization or person that owns the copyright, in order to find contact details. If they have a rights and permissions department, approach them first.

◆ Send permission requests in written format (either by letter or e-mail) or by following any specific instructions on the rights owners' web pages.

◆ Provide as much detail as possible about what you want to do with the material – for example, what file format you will distribute the material in, what sort of password protection will be in place and most importantly who wants to access the material (student numbers) and for how long (is it for one academic year or for several years?).

◆ You may well need to send several reminders if you do not get a response to your message. Do not assume if you do not receive a response that you can go ahead.

◆ Ensure you keep teaching staff informed about the progress of their request.

◆ If permission is granted to use the material, ensure that records are kept to manage the permission from year to year. If a licence is for a limited period of time ensure that teachers are aware of this restriction.

Copying broadcasts: the ERA Licence

In the UK the CDPA permits recording of TV and radio broadcasts for educational use under Section 35, but states that if a licensing scheme is available copying must be done in accordance with this. Licences from the Educational Recording Agency (ERA; www.era.org.uk) are available to educational establishments in the UK, with a separate licence available for schools, further education and higher education establishments (ERA, 2016). The licences cover scheduled, free-to-air broadcasts from ERA members, and cover the following channels:

◆ BBC television and radio (including content made by Open University Worldwide Limited)

◆ ITV Network services (including ITV2, ITV3 and ITV4)

◆ Channel 4, E4, More 4 and Film 4

◆ Channel Five and its subsidiaries

◆ S4C.

A full list of ERA members is available in the Licence Schedule (ERA, 2014). Any recording of free-to-air broadcasts by educational establishments in the UK must be undertaken in accordance with the terms of these licensing schemes, rather than under any exceptions in UK copyright law. However, as an example, the ERA Plus higher education licence[3] is relatively permissive and it allows educational establishments not only to record broadcast output, but also to copy this material, use extracts from a broadcast and digitize analogue recordings. Recordings can take place within the establishment or off the premises, for example they can be made by a lecturer at home. Recordings can be shown in the classroom or elsewhere on the premises of the educational establishment, and they can also be deposited in the library to facilitate access to the material by students. Furthermore, since 2014 ERA explicitly allows off-site streamed access to recordings by all students in a class or on a course through a secure service such as a VLE. The caveat to this is that the jurisdiction of this licence does not extend beyond the UK, so broadcasts cannot be delivered legally to students outside the UK.

There are further conditions and limits to the ERA licences; for example, it specifies that recordings on physical media must be labelled appropriately to include the name, time and date of the broadcast. Recordings stored digitally on a server should include this information as a written opening credit or web page which must be viewed or listened to before access to the recording is permitted. A recently added benefit of the licence is that it now allows educational establishments to access and download content from on-demand services in a similar way to personal private users.

Finally, satellite and cable broadcasts are not covered by the ERA licence. However, because a licensing scheme for this material is not available, educational establishments are currently free to copy this material under Section 35 of the CDPA provided the material is free-to-air and not from an encrypted or subscription service. Therefore premium rate satellite and cable channels such as Sky Movies are not covered by this exception, but Freeview and Freesat channels are.

There a number of additional services provided to universities by the British Universities Film & Video Council (BUFVC; http://bufvc.ac.uk) to support teaching and learning. These include the recording back-up service, where using a database known as the Television and Radio Index for Learning and Teaching (http://bufvc.ac.uk/tvandradio/trilt) you can find out when a programme was broadcast and request an off-air recording, and the BoB National (http://bobnational.net) service, see below. BUFVC also runs numerous training courses on digital media production and a one-day course focusing on obtaining copyright for multimedia resources. Further details are listed in the section 'Further resources'.

Box of Broadcasts

Box of Broadcasts (BoB National; http://bobnational.net) is a service available to UK further and higher education, which provides off-air recordings and a media archive for educational purposes. BoB is only available to institutions that are members of the BUFVC and hold an ERA licence. It is a shared online service for UK higher and further education institutions, which allows staff and students to record any broadcast programme from more than 60 TV and radio channels. The recorded programmes are kept indefinitely and added to an archive which contains (as of October 2015) over 1 million programmes. All content is available to users across the subscribing institutions. The service is particularly valuable for features such as the ability for users to edit programmes to create clips, playlists, embed clips into the VLE and share what they are watching with others. A number of enhanced features were launched as part of this service in January 2014; however, a key issue for those delivering online learning is that because of the limitations of Section 35 and the ERA licence, the service is only available to students in the UK. Therefore, its value to institutions providing distance learning for students outside the UK is limited.

Catch-up TV services and television on demand

Many radio and television broadcasters use internet technologies to provide catch-up or 'listen again' services on their websites or via apps on Smart TVs. However, with these on-demand TV services, television and radio programmes are not archived on the web in perpetuity and are only available for a relatively short period of time after the original broadcast (often less than one month) . Some programmes are available for streaming, others can be downloaded to a device such as a laptop, tablet or smartphone, but the downloaded files usually expire after a set period of time. Since 2014, the ERA has clarified that on-demand TV services such as the BBC iPlayer (www.bbc.co.uk/iplayer) or the ITV Player (www.itv.com/itvplayer) can be used by educational establishments under the terms of the ERA licences.

BBC iPlayer

The iPlayer service for the BBC generally makes programmes available for 30 days after they have been broadcast within the UK. Not all TV and radio broadcasts are available on the iPlayer because of rights issues, but the broadcasts can be watched via a streaming service, or downloaded via an iPlayer application onto a computer, tablet or other mobile device. The download service is only available in the UK, and downloaded files are encrypted with DRM software that deletes them from your device after their expiry date. Any attempt to remove the DRM protection from a downloaded file would be illegal under UK (and other) laws.

The use of the BBC iPlayer is governed by terms of use that state that in general educational establishments cannot use BBC Online Services unless they have taken out a licence with the ERA. So, for example, programmes (be they radio or TV broadcasts) can be added as a link from the VLE, or shown in the classroom. Because of the DRM protection, copies cannot be made of streamed programmes.

Frequently asked questions and help are available about the BBC iPlayer at http://iplayerhelp.external.bbc.co.uk/tv.

Creating audio and video content in-house: copyright issues

A number of educational establishments now create audio and video content in-house, partly to avoid the copyright issues associated with using commercial recordings or other third-party materials. While this requires an investment in equipment and staff expertise to produce professional recordings, the technologies are now increasingly sophisticated and inexpensive. Many universities are keen to capitalize on the expertise and knowledge of their teaching staff and make promotional videos as well as those that can be used in teaching. Some academic staff have considerable press and broadcasting experience and are regularly interviewed by newspaper, television and radio journalists when expert opinions are required. It therefore makes sense to use internal expertise to produce video and audio content. Most universities now have a YouTube channel and some use these sites to host recordings of public events or inaugural lectures that might have wider appeal. It is also increasingly common for high profile lectures to be live streamed, to enable those outside the university to participate online. While the costs associated with producing this type of content are not insignificant, the price of digital recording and streaming equipment has fallen dramatically in recent years and highly professional broadcasts and recordings can be made at a relatively low cost.

Aside from the technical skills and equipment requirements, legal questions – specifically copyright and other IPR issues – need to be considered when producing this material in-house. When recording individuals it is good practice to ensure that they sign a release form to make certain that they have given their consent for the resulting recording to be re-used. This applies whether the presenters work for the institution making the recording or not. In addition, it is important to be mindful of any third-party content that might be included to ensure it is either covered by exceptions (see Chapter 1), removed from the video or that appropriate permission is sought for its inclusion. For example, if a speaker is making significant use of images, clips from videos or audio recordings in a lecture, permission is usually required if the resulting material is going to be hosted on a network. A release form can be a useful way to remind people that permission may be needed for some of their content, if it is not entirely their own.

Institutions should use a release form if they wish to claim copyright in the resulting production or to obtain a license for their own re-use. Under UK employment law, if teachers or lecturers are recorded under the terms of their employment it would be standard practice that the institution would own this resulting material. However, academic lectures are often seen as performances and thus the recordings of the lecturer's teaching qualifies for performance rights, which are not automatically assigned to their employing institution. There is a certain degree of sensitivity around these issues and in 2006 Jisc recommended that all universities should have an IPR policy to clarify these types of concerns (Jisc, 2006). IPR policies of several universities are listed in the section 'Further resources', for institutions seeking to develop such a document.

Sound recordings

Creating sound recordings (or podcasts) of lectures or public events is technically more straightforward than producing a video. It also avoids the copyright issues associated with recording visual material, where it could be easy to include images or other media content from third parties inadvertently. Care still needs to be taken to ensure that re-use of any third-party content played during a lecture (for example, musical sound recordings or performances) is either covered by statutory exceptions or that copyright clearance has been obtained through existing licences or negotiated permissions. A variety of equipment is now available to facilitate the creation of audio recording such as digital recorders, radio microphones and audio tools embedded in the VLE. Commercial and open-source products are available; for example Wimba Voice (www.wimba.com/products/wimba_voice) offer a suite of tools including voice-recording facilities and online classrooms tools. Big Blue Button (www.bigbluebutton.org) is an open-source plug-in to Moodle which offers similar functionality. As previously mentioned the recording of the lecture creates performance rights, which are automatically owned by the speaker. For the sake of clarity a release form can be used, and this is particularly important when an external speaker is being recorded. Some institutions have an explicit statement to indicate that they (rather than the individual) will own the rights in the resulting podcast (an assignment of rights). Other institutions ask lecturers to grant them a licence to distribute the content, but allow the speaker to retain the rights in their work and performance. As with video, a release form can clarify issues such as what the recording will be used for, who will own the resulting copy and where it will be placed.

Lecture capture and intellectual property rights issues

Lecture capture is the term used to describe the semi-automated recording of a lecture. The US not-for-profit educational organization EDUCAUSE defines 'lecture capture' as 'any technology that allows instructors to record what happens in their classroom and deliver it digitally' (EDUCAUSE, 2008). In the past, lecture capture was usually restricted to an audio recording of the event, which might enable students to either revise or catch up on a missed lecture. Some universities used to record the audio of lectures, for example if there was a clash in the timetable that might prevent groups of students from attending. However, many universities have invested in large-scale lecture capture technology, which once installed in the classroom or lecture theatre enables the entire lecture (audio, video and screen capture) to be recorded with fairly minimal intervention by staff. Chapter 1 highlighted how over 50% of universities in the UK have now invested in these systems. The value of recording lectures has been recognized since the 1970s, but until recently video-recording equipment has usually been expensive and complex to use. The development of complete automated lecture capture systems such as Panopto (http://panopto.com/uses/lecture-capture), Echo360 (www.echo360.com) and Sonic Foundry's MediaSite (www.sonicfoundry.com) are transforming the lecture experience, allowing students to review the content after the lecture in their own time, or choose to watch a recording rather than attend a live lecture.

Lecture capture or video recording of lectures raises several interesting copyright issues, including:

◆ who owns the resulting recorded lecture
◆ whether it can be shown if a lecturer subsequently leaves an institution
◆ how to deal with any third-party content that might be included in the lecture
◆ who might be responsible for any copyright infringement if third-party content is shown in the lecture
◆ how far the copyright exceptions for 'illustration for instruction' and 'quotation' can be relied on for showing third-party content in lectures
◆ what to do about students' intellectual property issues if they are recorded during a lecture – for example when they ask a question.

The ownership of teaching materials in higher education has for many years relied on an unwritten agreement that respects academic and intellectual freedom. While universities as employers might legally own the materials produced by their teaching staff under employment law, they would rarely assert this ownership. This is very different from a commercial organization that would regard the intellectual output of their staff as the employer's property. However, classroom technologies such as lecture capture do concern some members of academic staff, and institutions have taken a range of approaches from 'opt out' to 'opt in' and all points in between. Some institutions routinely archive recordings and use them in subsequent years whereas others do not. Staff are advised to seek permission or remove substantial use of third-party content from the recordings of their lectures. Those institutions investing in such technologies would be advised to ensure that they address IPR questions early on to avoid any potential misunderstandings or problems in this area, though in many instances rights issues are only considered after such a technology is installed.

Screen recording

There are a number of free and commercial screen-recording tools that allow instructors to make a video recording of their computer displays to create educational videos for their students. Commercial products with this functionality include Camtasia Studio and Adobe Captivate. Meanwhile free or open-source tools include CamStudio, ScreenToaster, Jing, Screenr and Webinaria.

There are several copyright issues to be aware of when creating screen recordings, particularly if you wish to create demonstrations of other software. However, in general the same advice applies to creating any digital media in-house and, where possible, to avoid using any third-party materials without clearing the rights. It is also advisable to check the licence of specific software if you wish to make a screen recording that includes a named product. For example, if you were creating a screen recording to demonstrate how to use the reference management software Endnote you should check the Endnote licence to ensure that this is permitted.[4]

iTunes U

Mobile digital devices have revolutionized the way in which many people access audio and audiovisual content. The Apple iPod was launched in 2002 and although it only played audio and needed to be synced with another computer it brought home to many the power of mobile digital technology. In recognition of the growing demand for 'mobile learning' Apple launched iTunes U (www.apple.com/uk/education/ipad/itunes-u) in

May 2007 in partnership with Stanford University, UC Berkeley, Duke University and MIT. The service manages, distributes and controls access to educational audio and video content for students within a university as well as on the wider internet. Content is free to users, although password restrictions may apply to manage access to certain content within an institution. It is used by universities in countries throughout the world, including the USA, the UK, Australia, Canada, Ireland and New Zealand. Member institutions have their own iTunes U site that uses Apple's iTunes Store infrastructure. The University of Oxford was the first university outside the USA to go into partnership with Apple to make audio and video recordings available via the iTunes platform. Although today's internet-connected smartphones and tablets have powerful processors and high definition screens, which allow development of sophisticated interactive apps and services, iTunes U remains a popular platform for accessing educational content.

Case Study 4   Supporting open course creation at UCL

June Hedges

This case study presents UCL's evolving programme of online courses delivered to non-traditional[5] learners. It focuses primarily on how free, open courses[6] have been developed at UCL and how issues around IPR and third-party copyright have been handled with input from UCL Library Services.

Developing intellectual property right and copyright support for open courses
CPD4HE Project

CPD4HE was a small-scale project sponsored by Jisc and the Higher Education Academy under its Open Education Resources Programme 2009–12 (Jisc, 2009), which created open educational resources equivalent to 300 study hours in the priority areas of digital and information literacies and discipline-specific teaching and learning. The project included input from UCL Library Services' copyright support officer, who gave advice and guidance on IPR and copyright issues. This involved working with course designers to ensure that appropriate permissions were in place for any third-party content in the materials they wished to convert to open educational resources, and helping them to understand Creative Commons licensing. The copyright support officer created templates for recording any third-party content in their teaching materials, worked with each course designer to identify rights owners, provided templates for sending requests to rights owners for re-use, assisted in identifying 'free-to-use' alternatives, and ensured that course designers understood how to use Creative Commons licences to publish the materials. Ultimately, the responsibility for ensuring third-party materials were used correctly lay with the course designers so the project provided the blueprint for supporting the development of open courses or MOOCs at UCL.

UCL eXtend

UCL eXtend, UCL's public-facing online learning platform, was developed as a vehicle to deliver free, open courses to a wider audience (UCL, n.d.). It has since evolved to deliver a mixture of open (free) courses alongside paid-for short course and CPD provision. In addition to developing eXtend, UCL has in recent years entered into partnerships to develop and deliver courses via FutureLearn, the Digital Business Academy and Coursera[7] with a view to delivering more free, open courses to a much wider audience.

Work on UCL eXtend began in 2012 with the collection of pathfinder courses and offline development. This pilot period enabled colleagues supporting the project to develop processes and support systems that were flexible and scalable. The outcome of this was an online resource, built in the UCL wiki, which takes course designers through the process of creating an online, open course (see Figure 3.1 on the next page). Intellectual property rights and copyright support largely takes the form of written guidance and documentation that signposts issues around the re-use of third-party content and points course designers to alternatives.

Before going live the creation of an open course in UCL eXtend typically involves the following four points of contact with the UCL eXtend team and other support staff:

◆ The course proposal form is submitted online to the eXtend Team.
◆ The team member assesses the proposal and provides feedback (at this stage they put the course proposer in contact with the copyright support officer if they feel that third-party content will be an issue).

◆ The course is developed in an online test area (the copyright support officer can be granted access to the course in the test area if copyright concerns have been identified, so that they can assist with reviewing material).

◆ The course is submitted for approval by the Course Approval Team – copyright queries may still crop up at this stage so the copyright support officer may be contacted. The timescale for this stage is tight – typically three weeks.

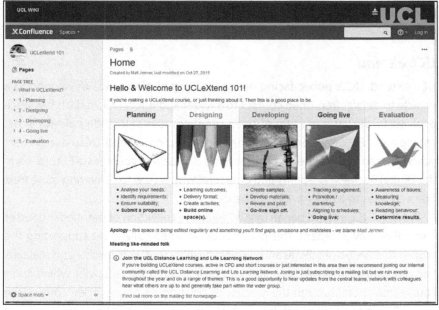

Figure 3.1 *UCL eXtend 101*

Dealing with third-party content issues

The onus for ensuring that content is being used legally within UCL's open courses rests with course designers. As a result they are strongly encouraged to generate their own content and avoid using third-party content wherever possible. Guidance on locating appropriate open resources (for example using Creative Commons filters in Google) and re-using them is provided within the UCL eXtend 101 resource. A process of critical appraisal developed in the CPD4HE project is also encouraged to weed out third-party content that is not essential: course designers must ask themselves 'does leaving this resource out impact on the learning experience of those following the course?'. More often than not the answer is 'no' and the content can be dropped. Finally, as part of the course approval process contributors must confirm that all content contained in the course has appropriate copyright clearance.

Perhaps as a result of the effectiveness of briefing course designers during the planning stages, the copyright support officer has not been asked to clear copyright on any content to be used in open online courses to date. They have, very occasionally, been asked to review content in courses during the development stage. Where this support has been provided the focus has been in identifying alternative versions of essential materials or assisting with making a request for re-use where there is no clear licence associated with a resource. For instance, open access versions of published articles located in institutional repositories have been a valuable resource as alternatives to papers in published, licensed journals; where papers have not been available colleagues have helped course designers make contact with researchers elsewhere to request they deposit a paper in their local repository.

After a few years of developing open courses, the UCL eXtend team refers relatively few courses to the Library's copyright support officer for additional support. This is mainly because course designers are not simply opting to repurpose components of existing modules, but are using the free, open environment to develop modules that are more skills-based[8] and therefore less dependent on third-party content, or they focus more on learner participation (e.g. discussion) and depend less on learning from secondary sources. Only one course proposal has been rejected outright by the eXtend team because of the level of third-party content.

The future

As UCL plans to expand its portfolio of free, open courses via partnerships with FutureLearn and other MOOC providers and to increase its life learning offering, the issue of access to learning resources, particularly licensed content, continues. Discussions on how to avoid inequality in learner experience, particularly for the fee-paying life learning cohort, are currently underway at UCL. Meanwhile, the model of support developed for UCL eXtend provides a basis for working with course designers who want to engage with both open and life learning courses.

With this in mind, UCL Library Services has started a project to enhance the support provided for course designers working on open and life learning courses. To ensure the continued scalability of this support, the primary vehicle for this will be a new web-based resource that brings together the issues and options for accessing and re-using content that draws on the experiences of our existing free, open courses.

References

Jisc (2009) *Open Educational Resources Programme*, https://openeducationalresources.pbworks.com/w/page/24838291/ Open%20Educational%20Resources%20Programme [accessed 6 April 2016].

UCL (n.d.) UCL eXtend, https://extend.ucl.ac.uk/ [accessed 5 January 2016]. Find out more about the service at https://www.ucl.ac.uk/isd/services/learning-teaching/elearning-staff/ opportunities/pelp [accessed 6 April 2016].

Managing digital media content

While it is not strictly a copyright issue, managing digital media content is increasingly important for institutions who are building up collections of digital 'assets' that they either own or have permission to distribute. In the past five years many academic libraries have replaced their traditional library catalogue with an integrated search service that can manage all their print and digital assets, such as Ex-Libris Primo or Serials Solutions Summon. This makes it possible to include metadata about multimedia content alongside traditional bibliographic records. Encouraged by funding bodies such as Jisc, some universities in the UK have an in-house 'learning object repository', which can manage storage of and access to multimedia content. Several commercial and open-source solutions are also available, such as:

◆   intraLibrary (www.intrallect.com)
◆   Drupal (http://drupal.org)
◆   DSpace (www.dspace.org)
◆   EPrints (www.eprints.org).

In many instances the physical storage of digital media files remains an issue because of the relatively large file size. In addition, many institutions are keen to provide this content in streamed format to facilitate access, rather than requiring individuals to download files in order to listen to or watch the content. Streamed files in general require storage on specialist servers and increasingly institutions require metadata to manage access to the material and storage space for the files. Metadata schema, such as Dublin Core, include fields for describing rights information and it is vital that rights information is stored alongside digital media. So, for example, if material has been digitized with the permission of a commercial publisher, or is available under a licence, this information needs to be retained alongside the digital object. While many large educational institutions have resolved this issue by using a repository or specialist digital library tool, in small organizations where resources are more limited this is unlikely to be the case. Therefore, it is vital that records are retained and that a system is devised for managing licence or rights information alongside the digital assets. This could take the form of a simple spreadsheet or database, which would then also facilitate re-use of the content. Whatever system is used staff should ensure that if copyright permissions need to be renewed, alerts or reports can indicate this in good time, so that they are not overlooked.

Software

Although software is protected by copyright as a type of literary work, in practice the use of software is rarely if ever allowable under a copyright exception and therefore requires appropriate licences. The concept of using only a limited proportion of computer code does not translate to the normal usage of software, which needs to be available in its entirety to work properly. Most educational establishments have people and teams responsible for acquiring and managing software licences, which are often available at an educational discount. One area of caution for those wanting to use software provided at no charge such as 'freeware', is that 'freely available' does not necessarily mean free of licensing restrictions. It may be that a software application is free for download for personal use, but an educational institution would be required to pay licensing fees. Commercial software vendors can be very protective of their products and have audit programmes aimed at educational establishments to ensure they are not under-licensed and are providing software only to authorized users. It is important that educational establishments have appropriate procedures in place to minimize the likelihood of software licence infringement, and measures in place to respond to audit requests. However, much free software is open source and can be used throughout an institution without incurring any costs.

Finding digital media content for use in e-learning

There are many different collections of images, video and audio that are available for use in an educational context, some of which are free at the point of use. Other collections are subscription resources, where a licence fee is paid by the institution. In most cases institutional licences allow unlimited use of the material in the collection for teaching purposes. A selection of resources is provided in the next section, although this list is not comprehensive and is intended only to provide a starting point. It can be helpful to maintain a list of 'free' or approved resources in-house for teachers, to direct them to suitable multimedia and image collections. At the London School of Economics and Political Science (LSE), Learning Technology and Innovation maintains such a list for teaching staff, which is illustrated in Figure 3.2.

It is important to educate teachers and lecturers about Creative Commons licences that allow them to re-use an increasing number of copyright works without having to ask for further permission. Staff can be encouraged to use the Creative Commons website, which can be searched to find resources. The Creative Commons Search is available at http://search.creativecommons.org.

The site does not describe itself as a search engine but rather links to the search engines of other websites, to which it applies a licence filter. For example it searches the photo-sharing website Flickr for images, pulling back results where the person uploading the image has applied a Creative Commons licence to it. Creative Commons Search also can help locate royalty-free music and provides a link to a wide variety of sources (https://creativecommons.org/legalmusicforvideos). It is also possible to search Google to find images and other content licensed under Creative Commons, using an advanced search and amending the usage rights.

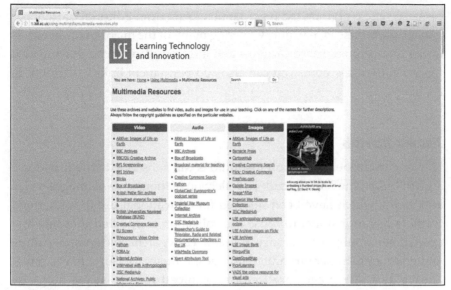

Figure 3.2 *Multimedia resources page of LSE Learning Technology and Innovation,*
http://lti.lse.ac.uk/using-multimedia/multimedia-resources.php (4 April 2016)

Those who wish to re-use resources they find through regular search engines need to obtain copyright permission (or determine if an exception applies to their proposed activity) unless the material is licensed under a Creative Commons or similar open licence.

Example sources for still images
British Cartoon Archive

The British Cartoon Archive (https://www.cartoons.ac.uk) is the UK's leading collection of political and satirical cartoons and is held at the University of Kent's Templeman Library. The collection includes work by many famous cartoonists such as Ralph Steadman, Martin Rowson, Steve Bell and Carl Giles and over 170,000 items from the collection have been digitized and are available to view on the Archive's website. In some cases images can be downloaded for educational use where licences permit.

Cartoons for the Classroom

A selection of cartoons called Cartoons for the Classroom (http://nieonline.

com/aaec/cftc.cfm) from the Association of American Editorial Cartoonists is available for use in teaching. Covering many of the major political events of the 20th century, these cartoons and a lesson plan can be downloaded for use in the classroom. You can also add permanent links to cartoons in a VLE.

Jisc Media Hub

Higher and further education institutions can subscribe to the Jisc Media Hub (http://jiscmediahub.ac.uk), a collection of thousands of images, video and audio, which have been selected for educational use in higher and further educational institutions. The collection is updated monthly and spans diverse subject areas such as architecture, archaeology, arts, culture and entertainment, environmental issues, industry, leisure, news, music and politics. All images are free to download for use in teaching and research and can be displayed online via a secure network, such as an e-learning system. The collection now includes a number of previously separate services such as NewsFilm Online, which offers access to news clips from ITN and Reuters ranging from 1910 onwards, and the Education Image Gallery, which includes Wellcome Images and a Getty Images collection of still and moving images. It also includes a collection of openly licensed materials that can be used by anyone without a subscription.

MorgueFile

MorgueFile (www.morguefile.com) is a free 'stock photo' site. Registration is only required if you want to submit photos; downloading and redistribution is allowed 'for . . . ordinary personal and/or commercial purposes'. You should include credits with any photos that you use. It is not clear how many images are available. The unusual name is a publishing term for a place to keep reference material.

Pics4Learning

Pics4Learning (www.pics4learning.com) is a 'copyright-friendly' image library for teachers and students. There are approximately 28,000 images in the collection all of which are donated by students, teachers and amateur photographers. Permission is granted for teachers and students to use the images in print, multimedia and video productions within an educational setting.

FreeFoto.com

FreeFoto (www.freefoto.com/index.jsp) is an archive of over 130,000 photos that are 'free to private non-commercial users'. Some images are licensed under Creative Commons licences, others are available for anyone to use provided you attribute them to freefoto.com. The website allows images to be used for educational purposes and to be used online, including on social media websites provided users give credit and a link to the website.

Google image search

Google now offers a 'licensing filter' for its image search (http://images. google.com/advanced_image_search), so you can search for images that you will be able to re-use in your teaching without needing to ask for permission. Note, however, that you may still need to attribute the work – check the specific licence that applies in each case to find out whether this is necessary. You should also amend the 'usage rights' field if you wish to search for images that are openly licensed. You should also use caution and consider whether any Creative Commons licences you find assigned to images have actually been applied by the creator themselves.

Example sources for moving images
BFI InView

The British Film Institute's InView (www.bfi.org.uk/inview) is a collection of diverse and rarely seen moving image titles focusing on the changing social, political and economic landscape of Britain in the 20th and into the early 21st century. The content is searchable and also comprehensively catalogued and organized under six main historical categories (education; health; environment; immigration, race and equality; industry and economy; and law and order). Sources include television documentaries, party political broadcasts, parliamentary debates and newsreels. This is a subscription resource for higher and further educational institutions.

BFI Player

BFI Player (http://player.bfi.org.uk/search) is a video on-demand service offering a wide variety of modern and classic British films from the British Film Institute. A collection that may be of interest to teachers is called Britain on Film (http://player.bfi.org.uk/britain-on-film), which has over 1000 films from around the UK accessible from an interactive map of the UK. Most of the collection is free to watch using the free BFI Player app. Owing to geo-blocking, the collection is only available in the UK; where films can be watched by international audiences the BFI has made them available on its YouTube channel.

Blinkx

Blinkx (www.blinkx.com) is a video search engine that uses speech recognition and video analysis to filter its results. The video content comes from a wide range of providers including national broadcasters and commercial media producers such as the British Broadcasting Corporation (BBC), Home Box Office (HBO) and Music Television (MTV). The videos available are for the most part streamed, so they may be linked to, but not downloaded.

The British Pathé film archive

The British Pathé film archive (www.britishpathe.com) contains over 3500 hours of British Pathé film footage, covering news, sport, social history and entertainment from 1896 to 1970. The still and moving image files are available to schools and educational establishments through a subscription service.

iTunes U

iTunes U (www.apple.com/uk/education/ipad/itunes-u) is a subset of the iTunes store that manages, distributes and controls access to educational audio and video content for students within a university and on the wider internet. Content is free to users, although password restrictions may apply to manage access to certain content within an institution. It is used by universities around the world and you can download lectures and a variety of course content in almost every academic discipline. Some universities (e.g. Oxford University) make some content available under a Creative Commons licence.

Open Culture

The Open Culture website (www.openculture.com) contains a wide range of educational media including free movies, courses, books and audio books. Its mission is to curate 'high quality cultural & educational media for the worldwide lifelong learning community'.

TeacherTube

TeacherTube (www.teachertube.com) was launched in 2007 by a US teacher and is modelled on the popular video-sharing service YouTube, but has the aim of providing educational video content. It contains images, audio and teaching resources, has a search function, and you can browse the extensive list of channels. The content comes largely from school teachers, although some university level material is also available. Resources can be linked to, or embedded into, online materials, but remain copyright of the contributor and are not available for download.

YouTube EDU

Launched in March 2009, the popular video-sharing service YouTube EDU (www.youtube.com/edu) has an educational channel, which has allowed some of the world's leading universities to share audiovisual content. It contains an eclectic mix of lectures, interviews with vice chancellors and promotional materials. Universities need to apply to have their content available on this channel so there is some form of quality control.

Example sources for audio
British Library Sounds

British Library Sounds (http://sounds.bl.uk) is a collection of 50,000 sound recordings available for use by staff and students in further and higher educational institutions under a free licence. The collection contains many different types of materials including classical music, sounds from nature, spoken word and world and traditional music. Recordings can be downloaded in MP3 format for use in education.

Creative Commons Legal Music for videos

The Creative Commons Legal Music for videos (https://creativecommons. org/legalmusicforvideos) web page provides advice and a list of search engines to find Creative Commons licensed music that can be incorporated into films and videos. It suggests a way of crediting the music and warns users not to re-use any music with a 'no derivative' licence component because incorporating this into a new work would breach the licence terms.

The Internet Archive

The Internet Archive (www.archive.org/index.php) is wide ranging and contains all sorts of online resources, with specific sections for moving images and audio. There is an enormous range of different types of content, including millions of free books, movies, software, music and archived web pages. Most content is in the public domain and therefore freely available for use in teaching.

Royalty Free Music

The Royalty Free Music (www.royaltyfreemusic.com/free.html) website contains a selection of stock music that is free for download and use in education. Royalty free means that the content can be used without further payment to the rights holder; this is not the same as copyright-free, which means something is not protected by copyright or the copyright in it has expired. In addition to music, the site also contains royalty-free stock footage, royalty-free sound effects, royalty-free clip art, royalty-free images and royalty-free photos.

Partners in Rhyme

The Partners in Rhyme website (www.partnersinrhyme.com) contains royalty-free music and sound effects, some for free and others at a very low cost. The site is aimed at amateur and professional multimedia producers, film makers, musicians and students. It provides music, sound effects and audio tools. A selection of music loops and sound effects are available for free download, provided that they are not used for commercial purposes.

Conclusion

Films, sound recordings and images are rich sources of content that many teachers want to use in e-learning, but it is all too easy to infringe copyright laws when embedding this type of content into an online course. Advice for teachers is needed early on in the course design process to help them identify copyright cleared sources, and to ensure that if permission is required it is sought in good time. Teachers also need to be educated about open licences such as Creative Commons licences, which can help them find digital media that can be re-used. Sources of advice for training and support specifically related to using non-text-based digital media content are listed in the section 'Further resources'.

Notes

1   This change came into law in 2013. Previously sound recordings had been protected for 50 years but after heavy lobbying from the recorded music industry the duration was extended by an additional 20 years.

2   For clarity most traditional education providers such as schools, colleges and universities regard their activities as fundamentally non-commercial, even if they charge fees. This is in contrast to companies providing training courses at commercial rates, whose activities are unlikely to be regarded as non-commercial.

3   From 2007 to 2014 the ERA had a two tier licensing scheme – ERA and ERA Plus – with the latter providing rights to copy and access content digitally. Since 2014 the ERA Licence Plus is the single scheme open to HEIs.

4   Contact your software licensing team for this information, but many higher and further education institutions in the UK license software through the Eduserv Chest consortium agreements

(www.eduserv.org.uk/services/Chest-Agreements).

5   The term 'non-traditional' is used to describe any learners who do not form part of a university's enrolled student body, and are therefore not entitled to access their licensed resources.

6   UCL has produced a number of free, open courses, but these have been quite specialist and/or niche. Its first official MOOC was launched in January 2016 via the FutureLearn platform (UCL News, 2016).

7   This course is delivered via the University of London's International Programme.

8   For example, the series of seven urban graphics courses developed by the Bartlett Faculty of the Built Environment, which develop skills via a number of exercises using licensed software or open-source alternatives. See Urban Skills Portal in UCL eXtend for more information: https://extendstore.ucl.ac.uk/catalog?pagename=urbanskillsportal.

References

EDUCAUSE (2008) *7 Things You Should Know About Lecture Capture*, http://net.educause.edu/ir/library/pdf/ELI7044.pdf [accessed 6 April 2016].

ERA (2014) *ERA Licensing Schedule*, Educational Recording Agency, www.era.org.uk/the-licence/details-rates/licence-archive/era-licence-scheme-2014 [accessed 6 April 2016].

ERA (2016) *ERA Rates and Agreements*, Educational Recording Agency, www.era.org.uk/the-licence/details-rates/rates-agreements [accessed 6 April 2016].

Jisc (2006) *Intellectual Property Rights (IPR) in Networked E-Learning*, www.jisclegal.ac.uk/Portals/12/Documents/PDFs/johncasey.pdf [accessed 6 April 2016].

Jones, C., Ramanau, R., Cross, S. J. and Healing, G. (2010) Net Generation or Digital Natives: is there a distinct new generation entering university?, *Computers & Education*, **54** (3), 722–32.

Moreno, R., and Mayer, R. (2007) Interactive Multimodal Learning Environments, *Educational Psychological Review*, **19**, 309–26.

Ofcom (2015) *Adults' Media Use and Attitudes: report 2015*, http://stakeholders.ofcom.org.uk/binaries/research/media-literacy/media-lit-10years/2015_Adults_media_use_and_attitudes_report.pdf [accessed 6 April 2016].

Prensky, M. (2001) Digital Natives, Digital Immigrants, *On the Horizon*, **9** (5), www.marcprensky.com/writing/Prensky%20-%20Digital%20Natives,%20Digital%20Immigrants%20-%20Part1.pdf [accessed 6 April 2016].

Sankey, M., Birch, D. and Gardiner, M. (2010) Engaging Students Through Multimodal Learning Environments: the journey continues, ASCILITE Conference, Sydney, http://eprints.usq.edu.au/9100/2/Sankey_Birch_Gardiner_Ascilite_2010_PV.pdf [accessed 6 April 2016].

UCISA (2014) *2014 Survey of Technology Enhanced Learning for Higher Education in the UK*, Universities and Colleges Information Systems Association, www.ucisa.ac.uk/~/media/groups/dsdg/TEL%20Survey%202014_29Sep2014.ashx [accessed 6 April 2016].

UCL News (2016) UCL Launches Free Online Course Examining Global Social Media Impact, UCL News, 12 January, www.ucl.ac.uk/news/news-articles/0116/120115-ucl-launches-free-online-course-social-media#sthash.FoxXo7SQ.dpuf [accesssed 6 April 2016].

4 Copyright issues and born digital resources

Introduction

This chapter focuses on what is sometimes called 'born digital' content. The term is used to refer to content that is both created and made available in digital format, such as web pages, word-processed documents, academic journals and e-books. It includes content available through subscription databases (behind a paywall) and content made freely available on the open web, but is in contrast with material that is digitized from print (analogue) format for either preservation or access reasons. This chapter will also discuss the copyright and IPR issues associated with institutionally owned digital resources, for example teaching materials that are created specifically for use in online learning, such as online tutorials, online quizzes and other 'learning objects', and digital content created by students as part of their course.

In reality a lot of content produced today such as music, images and video is born digital, but this chapter focuses largely on text-based content. While the law does not distinguish between material created in digital or analogue format, the use of born digital content is usually subject to licences that govern what those in educational establishments can do with the content. Those wishing to make the best use of the content for teaching purposes need to understand the relationship between licence agreements and copyright exceptions. In several countries around the world (including the UK) the law now states that copyright exceptions, such as copying for the purposes of non-commercial research and private study, cannot be overridden by licence agreements. The interaction between copyright exceptions and licences makes it more important that teachers understand what they are permitted to do with digital content as they come to use it for their teaching. It is often technically straightforward to incorporate the material into an online course, either through linking to it, or uploading it into the VLE. However, the ease with which people can copy or re-use digital content is not necessarily reflected by a corresponding awareness or comfort with the copyright or licence implications of doing so. The situation may be further complicated as some subscription resources use DRM technology to restrict how the content can be used. The case study in this chapter is from the copyright officer at the University of Auckland. It highlights the Course Reading List Service at the University of Auckland and how this helps to manage copyright compliance.

How is born digital content different?

Digital content, whether it is a word document, a PDF, a video or audio file, can often be easily downloaded and copied. Distribution of the content is also relatively straightforward if the file is placed online, either on a VLE or cloud-based service such as Dropbox, or sent via e-mail to multiple recipients. In the UK the CDPA 1988 (as amended) refers to this as 'communication to the public', which is a restricted act only permitted by the rights holder. Digital copies are exact copies of the original file, so unlike a scan or a photocopy there is no degradation of quality when digital files are copied or distributed. For these reasons and others, those who produce digital content for commercial purposes are usually keen to ensure that they retain control over their material, often using DRM technology to try to protect their content. Where content is sold commercially on the internet (such as via a subscription database or website), the use or re-use of that content is usually governed by a licence agreement or terms and conditions. Therefore contract law rather than copyright law is the primary legal framework because the licence terms constitute a legal contract between the rights holder and the end user. Some contracts can limit the rights (exceptions to copyright) provided by the copyright laws of a country, so those in institutions responsible for acquiring digital resources should consult the small print carefully before signing licences. In Chapter 1 we saw that following changes to UK law in 2014 contracts now cannot override some exceptions provided by the CDPA. The same is true in Ireland where the Copyright Act has been amended to ensure that copyright exceptions cannot be limited by the terms of electronic resource licences. Elsewhere in the world this is not necessarily the case and regardless of the relationship between copyright and contract law, the use of DRM often makes it difficult to use digital resources even when a copyright exception applies.

Although a huge amount of digital content is now free at the point of access via the world wide web, access to much scholarly content produced by academic publishers is restricted because of its commercial value and the financial investment associated with its production and communication via the traditional academic publishing model. The two key ways that copyright owners protect their content in a digital environment are through licence agreements and through DRM. Many companies that make digital content available use a combination of these techniques in order to protect their content. This chapter first examines DRM technologies, which are usually a technical solution to preventing copyright infringement, and then explores the terms and conditions and licences associated with several different types of digital resources and how they govern what a teacher or academic can do with the content. Several examples are included to show how website content is protected by both commercial and not-for-profit organizations. A number of other examples are included from subscription databases that academic institutions frequently purchase, to illustrate the ways that these commercial organizations protect their copyright but might allow it to be re-used in an educational context.

Digital rights management

DRM as a concept covers any way of encoding rights information within digital content, but the term is frequently given to several different technologies that are used to control access to digital content or devices, to protect copyright in those works or the works used on the devices. Various methods have been developed which can prevent a user from either accessing or copying material in digital format, for example using encryption techniques or preventing material being printed or downloaded. Many of these methods are referred to as technological protection measures. The terms are sometimes used interchangeably, but in essence DRM is a broader term and technological protection measures constitute a subset describing technologies that put digital 'locks' on content. DRM and its impact on libraries is discussed in Pedley (2015, 126–9). Most significant for readers of this book is the stipulation in copyright laws around the world that DRM technologies must be respected and that anyone who tries to disable or 'circumvent' such a system can be charged with copyright infringement. In the USA the DMCA (1998) was hugely controversial because of the provision that made it illegal to 'circumvent any DRM technologies'. European copyright legislation has also been amended to make illegal any attempts to tamper with or remove DRM technologies. There is similar legislation in Australia and Canada and the legislation and technologies can cause problems to the education community because of the way they inhibit innovative use of content.

In the UK, bodies representing libraries, archives and the education community, such as the Library and Archives Copyright Alliance (LACA), are concerned that DRM technologies make it is difficult to re-use electronic content for educational or research purposes. Many publishers have taken to defining their services such as e-book collections as databases, thus giving the material protection under copyright and database rights legislation. The use of the material in these collections is then governed by licences or contracts. By putting DRM protection mechanisms in place it can in some instances be extremely difficult to take advantage of copyright exceptions and fair dealing provisions. Currently an individual or organization in the UK needs to make a complaint to the IPO if they believe DRM is preventing them from taking advantage of a copyright exception, and they want to circumvent this legally. Further guidance about this process is set out on the IPO website (IPO, 2014). However, this process is not straightforward and complaints are only considered after considerable effort has been made by the potential user to secure permission from the rights holder to remove the DRM technology.

One example of the impact of DRM on the education community is the way it is used by e-book suppliers to protect their content from being copied. For example, ProQuest delivers e-books through the MyiLibrary platform, which is used by many academic, medical, professional and public libraries around the world. This platform is popular with libraries as individual titles can be purchased from a collection of over 750,000 books; other e-books suppliers often sell titles in bundled deals. However, MyiLibrary has DRM in place that restricts how teachers and students can use the content, and the number of pages that can be printed varies from publisher to publisher. So, for example, with some titles only a maximum of ten pages can be printed from an e-book, whereas for others it may be 5% or 10% of the work. As is common with several other e-book providers, the titles from MyiLibrary cannot be downloaded by users onto their own personal e-reader or mobile device. Although the platform allows tutors to share direct links to books (or specific chapters) with their students, the material must remain on the MyiLibrary platform and cannot be placed into the VLE. The licence is discussed in more detail later in this chapter (see page 149).

In 2009 Jisc undertook a comparison of e-book platforms and of the seven platforms they compared, only Credo Reference did not use DRM. DRM technologies are also common in the music and film industries to protect material and to try to prevent illegal copying. However, in educational settings DRM can restrict the way in which teachers are able to use content. Copying the work, even in small quantities, can be difficult or technically impossible, and circumventing the DRM that puts the restriction in place is illegal. This is because the Copyright and Related Rights Regulations 2003, which were implemented following the EU Information Society Directive (2001/29/EC) in the UK, added six new sections (296ZA–ZF) to the law, all under the new heading 'Circumvention of protection measures' (Caddick, Davies and Harbottle, 2016, section 15-07). Consequently librarians, learning technologists and teaching staff are well advised not to tamper with any DRM mechanism that restricts the copying or use of a copyright work, even if they believe there is a valid copyright exception. Where DRM prevents copying, the institution or individual can appeal to the rights holder to have this removed and if unsuccessful make a complaint. The process to complain about a technological protection measure is set out by the Intellectual Property Office (IPO, 2014).

Using content from websites

There is a huge amount of educational material available on the web and this overarching category of resources includes not only text-based websites, but also digital images, sound and video collections (which are discussed in some detail in Chapter 3). When content was first made available on the web many individuals and organizations did not consider the copyright implications. Few early websites had copyright statements that made it clear to those accessing the information what they were allowed to do with the content. For a number of years many people who accessed information on the web had misconceptions about what they were able to do with that material. People equated 'free to view' as 'free to copy' and while the advice and support about copyright issues is arguably now more developed in the education community than elsewhere, misconceptions still remain. Most large organizations now include a clear copyright statement on their website and provide further information, for example in terms and conditions, about what can be done with their content. Nevertheless, it seems that relatively few people look at these statements or understand what they might mean. It is also common for these statements to claim that all the content on the website belongs to the organization despite the inclusion of material created by third parties.

In general, if you wish to use content from the web in your online course, and want to minimize your exposure to legal risk, it is advisable to link to this material rather than to copy or download it. The matter of hyperlinking to online content has been the subject of several cases in the European courts recently. For example in 2014 the Court of Justice of the European Union dealt with the case *Svensson and Others vs. Retriever Sverige AB* (C466/12). This case found that a website that redirects internet users through hyperlinks to protected works which are already freely available online does not infringe copyright in those works.[1] Hyperlinking from the VLE therefore largely avoids any copyright issues as the content remains on the website and the teacher directs students to the page where it is hosted and they have legitimate access to the content. Some teachers claim that linking to the web can be problematic as links might change and this can result in a broken link from their course. While it is true that some organizations reorganize their websites fairly frequently, usually a check every six months to see if a link is in place should be sufficient. Teachers can also encourage students to report any broken links to them so they can be repaired quickly. If a teacher adds many links to the web from an online course it can be time consuming to check that they are still working, but they can use link-checking software to save time and there are several link-checking tools that work with popular VLE software such as Moodle and Blackboard. Social bookmarking tools such as diigo.com or delicious.com or other more visual tools such as Pinterest.com allow users to manage large numbers of web links, rather than adding them to a reading list or a web page in the VLE. These are discussed in Chapter 5 in more detail and may be an option for a teacher who wishes to provide students with an extended list of web links.

There can be instances when students are required to access web-based content and a link is insufficient. For example, a course on web design might wish to show several websites and perhaps compare how they looked at different periods in time. In other instances a teacher might have genuine concerns that the content on the site will be removed before the course finishes and so downloading the material is preferable to linking. To assist with advising teachers about using content from the web, this next section includes some examples of websites that make a specific provision for educational use of their site. It also provides some good practice guidelines for teachers who wish to download content from the web and upload it to the VLE.

Website terms and conditions

It is advisable to check the terms and conditions or the copyright statement on a website before using the content in teaching. The terms and conditions of websites generally state that they assume you have read and understood their terms of use and that in accessing their website you have agreed to be bound by them. Almost all websites where it is necessary to register or create some form of personal account require the user to agree to their terms and conditions, usually by checking a box. Commercial websites (such as Amazon, eBay and iTunes) where users purchase either a product or a service also require users to agree to their terms and conditions before allowing a user to place an order. It is common for copyright statements to be included and if you wish to use content from a commercial site for educational purposes you are well advised to check the statement in some detail. It is rare for a commercial website to mention exceptions for educational use of the site explicitly because the primary purpose of the website is for commercial gain. Most companies are anxious to safeguard their copyright and want to protect the use of their content and logo by others. Be aware that since 2014 in the UK a licence cannot override exceptions provided for in the law (see Chapter 1 for more details). Therefore, depending on what you wish to do and subject to whether 'fair dealing' applies, you may be able to copy limited amounts of content from a website under a copyright exception such as 'quotation, criticism and review' or 'illustration for instruction'.

Example of a commercial website terms and conditions: Amazon

In July 2015 it was reported that Amazon.com was the largest internet retailer in the world with a $92 million net income (Li, 2015). People commonly use Amazon's services to purchase all manner of products from books, DVDs and CDs to household goods, clothes and a wide variety of other products including born digital content. Amazon also has potential uses in education; for example teachers may wish to highlight to students the books they want them to buy, or to search inside a book to ascertain its relevance to a course. Thus it is not uncommon for teachers to ask about using Amazon content for educational purposes. Lecturers have been known to build online reading lists for their students with accompanying images of book jackets to make the lists more visually attractive. Although many users may be unaware of the terms under which they can access Amazon's site, the opening clause of the Amazon.co.uk website Conditions of Use & Sale (Amazon, 2015) states: 'Please read these conditions carefully before using the Amazon.co.uk website. By using the Amazon.co.uk website, you signify your agreement to be bound by these conditions' (Amazon, 2015).

These are the specific parts of the licence that relate to copyright:

- You may not extract and/or re-utilise parts of the content of any Amazon Service without our express written consent. In particular, you may not utilise any data-mining, robots, or similar data gathering and extraction tools to extract (whether once or many times) for re-utilisation any substantial parts of the content of any Amazon Service, without our express written consent.
- You may also not create and/or publish your own database that features substantial parts of any Amazon Service (e.g. our prices and product listings) without our express written consent.
- You may not frame or use framing techniques to enclose any trademark, logo or other proprietary information (including images, text, page layout, or form) of Amazon without our express written consent.

Amazon, 2015

Although it would be safe to assume that the primary reasons for these clauses is to protect Amazon from having their content re-used by a commercial competitor, as a teacher it would still be sensible to link to the Amazon home page, rather than to use a deep or frame link. Teachers should also not take images or any other content from the site, for example book jacket images, for use in an online reading list. The ownership of the copyright of the content on this site is clear; it states:

- All content included on the website, such as text, graphics, logos, button icons, images, audio clips, digital downloads, data compilations, and software, is the property of Amazon.co.uk, its affiliates or its content suppliers and is protected by Luxembourg and international copyright, authors' rights and database right laws.

Amazon, 2015

Anyone wishing to use substantial amounts of Amazon content for educational purposes would be advised to contact the company before proceeding. However, arguably there are a number of exceptions that subject to fair dealing might permit screenshots or small amounts of content to be used under certain circumstances. These should be judged on their individual merits and if there is any concern it is advisable to obtain permission.

Non-commercial and not-for-profit websites

In contrast to the above example, the websites of non-commercial organizations often have more liberal terms and conditions if you wish to use their content for educational purposes. You should still check the terms and conditions of a specific site carefully, but in doing so you may find that educational use is permitted. The owners of non-commercial websites are often well aware that the education community wishes to use their content.

Non-commercial or not-for-profit websites include:

- government or inter-government organizations
  - government departments
  - other public bodies such as the British Library, other national libraries and The National Archives

      ◆   international organizations such as the United Nations, the
            World Bank and UNESCO
◆   other educational institutions, for example, schools, universities and
    colleges
◆   educational funding bodies, such as Jisc and HEFCE
◆   non-governmental organizations, e.g. the Red Cross, Amnesty
    International
◆   charities
◆   special interest groups or professional bodies, for example, the
    American Library Association (ALA).

Several examples are now provided to illustrate how the terms and
conditions of use of online content published by these non-commercial
organizations might vary.

Example terms of use from the Department of Communities and Local Government, UK

The Department of Communities and Local Government (DCLG) is a UK
central government department and its website (see Figure 4.1) includes a
statement to indicate that the site (like most central government websites) is
licensed under the Open Government Licence (see Chapter 1, page 16 and
below) https://www. nationalarchives.gov.uk/doc/open-government-licence/
version/3.

As with all central government department websites in the UK the
content is subject to Crown Copyright but the Open Government licence
allows users to:

•   copy, publish, distribute and transmit the Information;
•   adapt the Information;
•   exploit the Information commercially and non-commercially for
    example, by combining it with other Information, or by
    including it in your own product or application.

                                        The National Archives, n.d

The licence also specifies that where you do any of the above, you must
'acknowledge the source of the information in your product or application

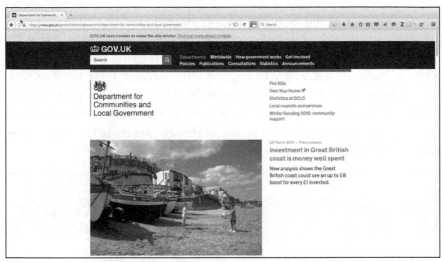

Figure 4.1 *The DCLG website (9 April 2016), www.communities.gov.uk*

by including or linking to any attribution statement specified by the Information Provider(s) and, where possible, provide a link to this licence.' This means that a teacher wishing to use this content in the classroom, or to reproduce the material in the online learning environment, would be able to do this without needing to request permission and without payment of a fee. This may be useful as government department websites tend to change fairly frequently and reports can sometimes be difficult to find. In general it is still advisable to link to content on this website rather than to download the material and host it on an institutional server, but the terms and conditions do allow the latter if required. The Open Government Licence states that content such as departmental or public sector organization logos should not to be reproduced without permission. The re-use of images and logos from many websites is often subject to a different set of terms and conditions, largely so that organizations can protect themselves from misrepresentation or perceived endorsement of other companies that could be potentially damaging.

Example of the terms and conditions of an international organization: UNESCO

UNESCO is the United Nations agency devoted to education, social and natural science, culture and communication. The terms and conditions of the UNESCO website (see Figure 4.2) show that this organization is relatively protective of its copyright. Its copyright statement (UNESCO, 2015a) is typical of many websites that permit copying for personal use, and the terms of use apply to anyone who accesses their website. The copyright statement says: 'All contents on this website are protected by copyright. UNESCO is pleased to allow those who may choose to access the site to download and copy the materials for their personal, non-commercial use.'

Figure 4.2 *The UNESCO website (9 April 2016), http://en.unesco.org*

Teachers wishing to use content from this site are advised to provide a link to this material rather than download it. Educational use is not explicitly mentioned and 'personal, non-commercial' is unlikely to extend to hosting the material on a VLE to allow access to multiple users.

The UNESCO site goes on to state:

Any copy made of the materials must retain all copyright and other proprietary legends and notices in the same form and manner as on the original. Any use of textual and multimedia information (sound, image, software, etc.) in the website shall be accompanied by an acknowledgement of the source, citing the uniform resource locator (URL) of the page (Title of the material, © UNESCO, URL).

No other use of the materials is authorised without prior written permission from UNESCO.

UNESCO, 2015a

Further details are provided in a terms of use statement, which includes information about hyperlinking to the UNESCO site and how to get permission (UNESCO, 2015b). Users are advised to link to the top level of the site, rather than to deep link,[2] as UNESCO cannot guarantee that deep links will persist. Again the logos are protected and must not be used without express permission.

Good practice guidelines

The following good practice guidelines may be helpful for anyone wishing to use website content in their teaching:

◆ Where possible direct users to content on the web via links rather than downloading it and ensure links open in a new browser window.

◆ Do not use frame links that open content within an e-learning system as it may be unclear that the content is coming from an external source. Framed links can also be difficult for students from a navigational and accessibility perspective.

◆ Check the website terms and conditions to see if deep links (links that bypass the home page and point to a page within a larger website) to a site are permitted – if they are, be aware that they may change if the website is reorganized.

◆ If the terms of use state that deep links are not permitted, any links you add to the site should go to the home page of an organization and students can be given navigational information to locate the specific part of the website you wish them to consult. If you wish to deep link and it is not permitted you should contact the website for permission or seek alternative content. However, note that deep links are more likely to break than links to the top level of the site and they need frequent updating, so aside from any legality, they tend to be less persistent.

◆ If you think it is essential to download material, check the terms and conditions or copyright notice on the site before any material is downloaded to see if educational use is permitted. If it is not you should contact the website to request permission or seek alternative content.

◆ If you include a screenshot of a website, include details of the organization, the uniform resource locator (URL) and the date that the screenshot was made. In general reproducing a screenshot of a website might be considered insubstantial copying or could be permitted under an educational exception, such as 'illustration for instruction'.

◆ If you are unsure if content from the site can be downloaded for educational use, check for any contact details and ask permission before downloading the material. If you do not receive permission you should not download or copy the material and instead seek alternative content.

◆ Retain any permissions received for website re-use in an appropriate rights management system (which may be a dedicated database, or could equally be a spreadsheet or a paper file depending on the organizational need) so that any subsequent teachers are clear that permission was obtained.

Content from publishers

There is an increasing range of scholarly resources available from publishers in digital format including electronic journals, electronic books and other subscription databases. These resources include material such as law reports, conference papers or other full-text documents. This section will examine e-journals and e-books in some detail before considering a selection of subscription databases, all of which are largely paid-for content, and not available freely on the internet. Their use is governed by licence agreements that individuals, or more commonly, institutions agree to. In the UK, Jisc has made considerable efforts through Jisc Collections to negotiate more favourable licences for the further and higher education sectors. The Jisc model licences such as the Model Licence for Journals (Jisc Collections, n.d.) are intended to help institutions make effective use of electronic resources in teaching, learning and research, saving time and money. They are also an attempt to provide a consistent approach to the access and use of online resources thereby allowing users to exploit the content to its fullest potential in support of their educational activities. These are some examples of some of the activities that the model licences permit:

◆ cutting, pasting, copying parts of the resource into electronic and print materials produced as part of their teaching, learning and research
◆ printing out or saving parts of the online resource, for example, journal articles, images, book chapters and search results.

More importantly for e-learning, model licences allow students and staff to incorporate parts of the resource in learning materials and objects in VLEs, as long as proper acknowledgement is given. For example you can:

◆ put together teaching and learning materials, such as reading lists, handouts, course packs and interactive tutorials, using extracts from the resource as required
◆ allow students to include extracts in their course work, projects, dissertations and assignments; for example, using a mix of text, images or sound to illustrate an argument in a new way
◆ allow staff and students to take a variety of materials from a range of resources, and create work that is much greater than the sum of its parts; they can use them at presentations, workshops, conferences and seminars.

The terms of the Jisc model licences are broad and cover many of the activities that staff might undertake for teaching online. One word of caution is that these licences are a starting point for negotiations with publishers. Some publisher agreements are modified to remove the more permissive activities specified in the model agreement and so institutional licences may vary from the model licences. This is why it is important for institutions to invest in keeping up-to-date records of licence terms as they relate to collections of electronic content. It is also worth noting that if the activity you wish to undertake is covered by a fair dealing exception, the terms of the licence contract cannot override what is permitted under that exception. For example, it is now permitted to carry out computational analysis (more commonly called text and data-mining) for non-commercial purposes using subscription resources such as journal databases, under Section 29a of the CDPA. This exception cannot be overridden by the terms of a licence agreement.

Journals

Almost all academic journals are now published in electronic format. Although print journals do still exist, in the last ten years the higher education community (lecturers, librarians and students alike) has embraced what is commonly called e-journal content. In fact many libraries have now disposed of their print back runs of journals where they have electronic access in order to free up physical space. In general teachers and academic staff have little need to purchase personal subscriptions to journal content but rely instead on institutional subscriptions. Journal subscriptions are usually purchased by the institutional library and a typical site licence allows staff and students to access the content without additional charges being made per article accessed. With improvements in authentication systems, access to titles for authorized users is routinely available both on and off campus, using authentication or access management systems such as OpenAthens and Shibboleth, or through a proxy server. E-journal licensing has become a complex area for academic libraries, with some titles sold in bundles from aggregators, such as EBSCO, Ingenta or Swetswise. Smaller journal publishers such as scholarly societies tend to use an aggregator service to host their content. Meanwhile large journal publishers such as Oxford University Press have a dedicated platform to host their e-journal content so when purchasing journal titles there is a variety of purchasing options and models. For example, some print journal subscriptions have complementary access to the electronic version while other electronic journals are licensed in bundled deals, which may lead to institutions subscribing to titles in electronic format that may fall outside the scope of their traditional collection policy. Because of this complex landscape institutions often have a large number of licence agreements, the varying terms of which might determine what a teacher can do with the content in a number of different ways.

In the UK, the Jisc Collections Model Licence for Journals attempted to provide some form of consistency for those in higher and further education, but invariably different institutions negotiate different agreements with publishers to meet their specific requirements and to try to get the best price. Consequently understanding how electronic journal content can be re-used in online learning often requires extensive consultation of multiple licences from individual journal publishers and aggregators. Where an institution has multiple subscriptions to large numbers of journals it makes sense for the licence agreements to be managed by specialist library staff, who have a good understanding of what can be done with e-journal content. However, it is still important that licensing information is conveyed to academic staff and teachers, who are unlikely ever to see these licences. For example, many journal licences do not permit PDF articles to be downloaded from their site and posted to the VLE. Yet, many teachers find this the simplest technical solution and may not recognize that this practice puts their institution in breach of the licence. In fact most licences permit teachers to provide students with a deep link to the article on the publisher's website. The use of links allows publishers and librarians to record journal usage accurately. Further, the PDF is available to students even if an institution cancels their subscription. It is therefore important for institutions to have a clear idea of the content they have licensed, and to be able to communicate this to users of their information services for all the reasons stated above. This presents a significant challenge given the number of agreements signed and the resources available in many libraries to do this work and keep the information current.

Since 2013 all universities with the CLA higher education licence have been able to copy what are termed 'digital originals' (PDF articles from participating journal publishers) and host them on their VLE. Before this the copying of digital originals was an optional add-on to the licence. However, for the licence to apply the articles must be covered by the licence (and the digital to digital coverage is more limited than paper to digital) and reported on the data return to the CLA. As a result of the reporting requirement many institutions still request that teaching staff link to journal content, but staff may still add journal articles to the VLE, because of the relative ease of doing so compared with the process of linking to the content.

Many publishers use digital object identifiers (DOIs) as a stable or persistent way of maintaining a link to journal articles, so the process of creating links has become far easier in recent years.

Digital object identifiers

Many e-journals are hosted on databases and creating stable links to material within these systems is not always straightforward. Some journal platforms have developed their own persistent links, which they display with the citation of a journal article, but many now use DOIs, which are governed by the Digital Object Identifier System (https://www.doi.org). DOIs are a standard way of identifying and managing digital content and a useful way of creating a stable link to content in e-journals. DOIs are a unique reference for identifying a piece of digital content, independent of the publisher or platform that might hold it. The system is managed by the International DOI Foundation, which is an open membership consortium and includes both commercial and non-commercial partners. It is not restricted to e-journals, but includes all types of digital content. Once a DOI is registered, it can be used to create a stable link to the item. The link can then be added to a reading list system or directly to the VLE; unless the article is in an open access journal, it is usually necessary to have a subscription to gain access to the full text.

E-journal licence agreements

Three examples of e-journal licences are examined below to highlight some of the approaches to licensing digital content. The specific clauses that cover how the material can be used in online learning are discussed.

Wiley Online Library

Wiley (http://olabout.wiley.com) is the international publisher of scientific, technical, medical and scholarly journals, owned by John Wiley & Sons. It has over 6 million journal articles from around 1500 titles in many academic disciplines and has partnerships with a range of leading professional societies. Many academic libraries in the UK have a subscription to the Wiley Online Library and they can choose whether to receive print and online titles or just online journals. This publisher offers a variety of open access journals and the collection includes around 16,000 e-books. Some of the features of the licence are:

◆ access to journals across multi-site campuses and global corporations

- course-pack use
- use in interlibrary loan
- walk-in user access for academic institutions.

The collection supports linking at article or chapter level using DOIs and their own linking system, and they offer guidance in how to construct these links. Teachers who wish to use these journals for teaching should add links to the articles. Some journal titles might be covered by the CLA Licence, but if journal articles are uploaded to the VLE under this licence they would need to be reported to the CLA.

Project MUSE

Project MUSE (https://muse.jhu.edu) is a collaboration between libraries and publishers and provides full-text access to over 600 journals mainly in the humanities and social sciences. Access to titles is comparatively inexpensive and titles are available from many of the world's leading university presses and scholarly societies. Project MUSE has a reasonably restrictive approach to how its content can be used in a subscribing institution. An example of the standard subscription licence is available from the Project MUSE website (https://muse.jhu.edu).

The licence includes a section of permitted acts that include allowing users to:

- distribute a copy of individual articles of items of the licensed materials in print or electronic form to authorized users, including the distribution of a copy for non-commercial educational purposes to each individual student (authorized user) in a class at a subscriber's institution
- use a persistent URL, or durable URL, for the licensed materials, including full-text articles, for courses of instruction offered by the subscribing institution, where access is restricted to students enrolled in the course, to instructors, and to library staff maintaining the link: such access is limited to the duration of the course; each item should carry an appropriate acknowledgement of the source, copyright and publisher, and the links to such items shall be deleted by the subscriber when they are no longer required for such purpose.

The JSTOR licence

JSTOR (www.jstor.org) is a not-for-profit organization that was founded in 1995 by the Andrew W. Mellon foundation as a solution to the storage problems academic libraries were facing in managing journal collections. Scholars often require access to historical journal material (particularly in the arts and humanities) and JSTOR has been a tremendous success story, extremely popular with researchers and students. In 2009 JSTOR merged with a company called Ithaka (www.ithaka.org), another not-for-profit organization, and in 2011 started offering the organization's first e-books. The JSTOR journal collection, however, focuses on preserving digitized back runs of journals covering the humanities, social sciences and sciences. In many instances the most up-to-date issues of a journal are hosted directly by a publisher or by an aggregator, so JSTOR has concentrated its efforts in digitizing historical material and ensuring that complete back runs of scholarly publications are available to subscribing institutions.

The following information comes from the general licence available on the JSTOR website and again subscribers will need to consult their institutional licence as this may differ. However the general licence covers licensees and authorizes users to: 'search, view, reproduce, display, download, print, perform, and distribute Licensed Content for the following Permitted Uses, provided they abide by the restrictions . . . and elsewhere in these Terms and Conditions of Use' (JSTOR, 2015a).

Permitted uses are then defined as research activities; classroom or organizational instruction; student assignments; as part of a scholarly, cultural, educational or organizational presentation or workshop; in research papers or dissertations; data for research and by linking. It also specifically mentions fair use (a US term) and the educational exceptions to other copyright laws. In addition, the licence includes sharing small amounts of the text with others for non-commercial gain and 'for purposes of collaboration, comment, or the scholarly exchange of ideas'.

Linking to content hosted by JSTOR is often the most efficient way of using this content in teaching. All JSTOR journals have title and article level stable links (which JSTOR calls stable URLs) clearly marked in their database. This enables teachers to use these links to provide direct access to reading materials. There is detailed information on the JSTOR website (JSTOR, 2015b) about how to create stable links to journal articles or titles. JSTOR does not use DOIs (see page 140), which have been adopted as a standard open-URL linking procedure by much of the publishing industry.

Case Study 5 The Course Reading List Service of the University of Auckland, New Zealand

Melanie Johnson

Introduction

This case study describes the Course Reading List Service (CRLS) of the Libraries and Learning Services (LLS) at the University of Auckland, which is New Zealand's leading university. The University has 41,953 students studying across eight faculties and two research institutes (University of Auckland, 2015).The collection expenditure of the LLS is ranked with the top five Australian university libraries (University of Auckland Library, 2015).

Background

New Zealand universities have held a licence to copy from hard copy print originals from Copyright Licensing New Zealand (CLNZ) since 1995. In 2013 CLNZ referred a significant increase in the licence fee and a new licence to the Copyright Tribunal naming all eight New Zealand universities as respondents (*Copyright Licensing Limited v Universities of NZ* (24 December 2013)). In December 2014 the court action was settled and New Zealand universities entered into a two year pilot licence with CLNZ to make it mandatory for all staff distributing content to students under the CLNZ licence to do so using e-reporting software (CLNZ, 2015b). As a consequence, the University entered into an agreement with the software service Talis Aspire (https://talisaspire. com) for its two products: Reading Lists, which allows teaching staff to create lists of course readings, and Digitised Content, which manages the digitization of hard copy books and journals. From the first semester in 2016, all university staff who offer students access to course readings through a digital platform, in print course books or through the LLS course pages are required to create a Talis reading list.

The Course Reading List Service

The CRLS was created to manage the digitization of print content under the CLNZ licence through Talis. The CRLS replaced the Electronic Course Material Service, which had operated since 2003. A digitization request made through the Talis digitized content module is submitted to a validation process known as the Concierge.

The Concierge has an in-built rule set which automatically checks that a request is compliant with the CLNZ licence. The CLNZ licence extends the amount that can be copied under Section 44(3) of the New Zealand Copyright Act 1994 from 3% or three pages to 10% or one chapter of a book, and one journal article from a periodical (CLNZ, 2015a). A lecturer requesting digitization receives an automated response indicating whether or not the item has copyright clearance.

If the request is rejected for any reason, the lecturer is informed by e-mail. Reasons for rejection include:

◆ detecting that a newer edition is available
◆ the copy limit being exceeded (although there is functionality which allows a manual override to cater for exceptions in the licence, allowing for five newspaper articles from the same edition, up to five journal articles if on the same subject matter, and whole works which are out of print)
◆ an electronic version of the item being available
◆ the request being a duplicate of an existing request in the system for that particular course.

If clearance is granted, the CRLS scans and uploads the material requested into the Talis cloud storage facility, the Vault. A lecturer who already has a PDF of the chapter or article requested can provide this to the Library for uploading. Once the digital copy has been uploaded to the Vault, a cover sheet is generated with the copyright warning notice required by CLNZ and the digital copy is automatically linked to the relevant reading list.

Talis can generate a report on all content stored in the Vault, as required by CLNZ, and replaces the previous time intensive manual survey that all teaching staff were required to complete.

The CRLS runs daily reports on published reading lists to identify any titles that require acquisition or additional access to meet student demand (Johnson, Garraway and Tollan, 2016).

Access

Once the lists of course readings are published, they can be accessed by students through the VLE, Canvas learning management system (https://www.canvaslms.com/about-us/), or students can search within Talis Aspire by keywords or course codes. Reading lists are freely available, but to view individual items held as electronic resources by LLS, or to view content stored in the Talis Vault, password authentication is required.

Lecturers are required to set the level of importance for each item in their reading lists:

◆ For readings marked as 'Textbook', LLS acquires an e-version if it is available wIth a multi-user licence to ensure concurrent access, or if an e-version is not available will provide one print copy per 40 students, up to a maximum of ten copies.
◆ For readings marked as 'Essential resources', the LLS ensures there is concurrent access to online resources, or provides one print copy on three day loan.
◆ Readings marked as 'Further resources' or with no importance applied are acquired for library collections but not placed in short loan collection.

This ensures that the LLS has sufficient resources to meet student need (University of Auckland, 2016).

Copyright compliance

The mandatory requirement to use Talis Aspire to generate course reading lists and manage digitization requests has allowed the distribution of course materials to be centrally managed by the Library ensuring that access to course materials is consistent across the University and course materials are copyright compliant. In particular:

◆ Citations can be imported with a click of a button and all course materials can be appropriately and correctly attributed.
◆ The reading list provides direct links to the full text of readings available online (e.g. subscription e-journals and databases, and openly available sites such as YouTube) removing the need to download content which may be infringing or in breach of the terms of licences.

◆ Access to course materials requires a student to be authenticated before access is provided to ensure that only those entitled to access the content can do so.

Conclusion

The LLS is still in the implementation phase of the project. Work flows are evolving as the CRLS is scaling up to meet the anticipated increase in demand for digitization. Subject librarians' focus is on supporting lecturers to ensure a successful implementation. With an assurance that universities are copyright compliant and more accurate and regular reporting of data on copying under the licence, it is hoped that some of the traditional tensions between publishers and universities can be avoided.

References

CLNZ (2015a) *A Guide to the CLNZ Education Licence*, Copyright Licensing New Zealand, www.copyright.co.nz/Downloads/Assets/2475/CLNZ-Education-License.pdf (accessed 6 April 2016).

CLNZ (2015b) *Our Story, 2014 Annual Report*, Copyright Licensing New Zealand, www.copyright.co.nz/downloads/assets/2722/FINAL%20PDF%20for%20WEB%20150366%20CLNZ%20Our%20Story%20Web.pdf (accessed 6 April 2016).

Copyright Licensing Limited v Universities of NZ [2013] NZCOP, 18 COP004/2013, www.justice.govt.nz/tribunals/copyright-tribunal/decisions/2013-nzcop-18-cll-v-universities-of-nz-24-december-2013 [accessed 6 April 2016].

Johnson, M., Garraway, J. and Tollan, E. (2016) *Taming the Lurking Beast: can mandatory e-reporting and the creation of course lists manage copyright in the digital space*, VALA 2016 (accepted for publication February 2016).

University of Auckland, *Talis Reading Lists for Staff*, www.library.auckland.ac.nz/services/teaching-support/talis/?ref=promo-talis-link2 (accessed 6 April 2016).

University of Auckland (2015) *Annual Report 2014*, https://cdn.auckland.ac.nz/assets/central/about/the-university/official-publications/documents/AR%202015%20web%20version%

20May%2026%202015.pdf (accessed 6 April 2016).
University of Auckland Library (2015) *Annual Report 2014*,
   www.library.auckland.ac.nz/sites/public/files/documents/annual-report.
   pdf (accessed 6 April 2016).

E-books

The e-book market in the higher and further education community continues to evolve as technology and user expectations change. E-book licensing is more complex than journals as the publishing community have been concerned about the impact that digital access might have on book sales, particularly in relation to textbooks. Whereas academic journals tend to be bought by libraries to allow institutional access, textbooks have traditionally been sold directly to students. Therefore, the pricing of digital versions of textbooks (as opposed to scholarly monographs) is often set to reflect the potential revenue from selling the book in large numbers. Many publishers have also been reluctant to offer institutional licences for their books, preferring to offer individual licences to students because of the income derived from textbook sales.

When e-books were first launched in the late 1990s publishers tried out different models for licensing this content. For example Net Library, launched in 1998, first started offering e-books for sale using a model that allowed for each title to be accessed by only one user at any one time. If a library wanted to allow multiple access, additional 'copies' of the e-book had to be purchased. From the perspective of teachers and students the concept of e-books clearly implies that access to titles should not be limited to one user, so many e-book publishers have now recognized that this model is not desirable. Institutional take-up of e-books was also slow because of the restrictive way that titles were sold in bundles, rather than individually. Libraries found that many bundled e-book collections did not contain enough titles that were on lecturers' reading lists to make them good value. MyiLibrary changed this model by allowing individual titles to be purchased. However, in 2007 Jisc Collections had become aware that the value and future of e-books was unclear, so the service negotiated free access to 36 titles from MyiLibrary for all HEIs (until August 2009) as part of the National E-book Observatory Consultation (Jisc Collections, 2010).

Jisc Collections launched a project which ran from 2007 to 2010 and gathered evidence from librarians, students and academic staff at over 120 universities to inform the future development of e-book licensing. This project used a technique known as 'deep log analysis' to assess the impact and use of e-books by the higher education community. Jisc Collections also carried out focus groups and user surveys and presented their final report in 2009 (Jisc Collections, 2009). The findings showed that academics were increasingly recommending e-books to students, for reasons of equity and access, and adding links from reading lists and VLEs. Librarians were in favour of e-books as a way of providing off-campus access to books, although they recognized that they were being used differently from hard copy books and noted that the lack of standardization in functionality and user experience was problematic. The report also considered the publisher perspective, and recognized that student expenditure on books was declining rapidly because of financial pressures. This research examined the impact on sales of the top ten titles that were part of the study and concluded that in only two cases had there been a decline in hard copy sales. The report advised that the key stakeholders (academics, librarians, publishers and aggregators) needed to work together and stated: 'Staying still is not an option. The pressure to find viable and sustainable business models for course text e-books is likely to intensify, as consumer expectations for immediate access to digital content continue to rise' (Jisc Collections, 2009, 32).

Since 2010, many academic libraries have purchased an increasing amount of e-books through the growing number of library e-book vendors. Nonetheless, concerns remain about licensing and DRM restrictions that prevent sharing and use of the content, the single-user licence models, proprietary file formats and poor functionality (Walters, 2014). Since the copyright reforms following the Hargreaves Review, the licence agreements for use of e-books in the UK cannot restrict fair dealing exceptions. However, many e-books are still available in proprietary formats, which discourage or prevent users from downloading or printing meaningful portions of the content. Where DRM exists that prevents copying, the user is unable to circumvent this technology legally and must apply first to the publisher to have it removed. Walters (2014, 93) argues that pressure to change e-books needs to come from the library and academic community, stating: 'As a group, librarians can decide whether barriers to e-book use and sharing remain in place, but only if we spend our money in ways that are consistent with our expectations and requirements.'

MyiLibrary

MyiLibrary (www.myilibrary.com) is a subscription e-book service provided by ProQuest that numerous academic and public libraries use. Like most e-book platforms the company uses DRM technologies to restrict copying and downloading from its site. However, the e-books are popular because they do not require users to install any specific reader software. Most titles are in PDF format, so can be read in the free Adobe Acrobat Reader. They can also be read by multiple users and be purchased as individual titles. The terms and conditions for the use of all ProQuest content are available on their website (ProQuest, n.d.). Content can only be downloaded for personal, non-commercial use, and the download limits vary depending on the publisher of the book, and typically set at ten pages per book. The terms of use have two relevant sections for teachers:

> Digital and Print Copies. Customer and its Authorized Users may download or create printouts of a reasonable portion of articles or other works represented in the [MyiLibrary] for its own internal or personal use as allowed under the doctrines of 'fair use' and 'fair dealing'. . . . All downloading, printing and/or electronic storage of materials retrieved through the Service must be retrieved directly from the online system for each and every print or digital copy.
>
> Electronic Reserves, Course packs, and Intranet Use. Provided that Customer does not circumvent any features or functionality of the Service, Customer may include durable links to articles or other works (or portions thereof) contained in the Service in electronic reserves systems, online course packs and/or intranet sites so long as access to such materials are limited to Authorized Users.
>
> ProQuest, n.d.

As MyiLibrary uses DRM, anyone wanting to use this content in teaching is best advised to link to the material rather than trying to download or print it. However, the licence permits what it terms 'scholarly sharing' where academic institutions, schools and public libraries

> may provide to a third party colleague minimal, insubstantial amounts of materials retrieved from the Service for personal use or scholarly, educational research use in hard copy or electronically, provided that in no case any such sharing is done in a manner or magnitude as to act as a replacement for the recipient's or recipient educational institution's own subscription to either the Service or the purchase of the underlying work.
>
> ProQuest, n.d.

Google Books

While not strictly an e-book platform, Google Books (http://books.google.co.uk) is worth considering in this chapter as it is one of the most ambitious book digitization projects in history. It started in 2004 as a joint venture between Google and several large academic libraries including Harvard, MIT, Yale and Oxford. The Google Book project has encountered many copyright issues over the years, which have given rise to a large-scale and widely publicized legal challenge by publishers and authors in the USA. In 2006 a class action copyright infringement lawsuit was brought against Google by the Association of American Publishers and the Authors Guild. As the case progressed, Google made frequent modifications to the service, and Google Books rarely looked or behaved the same from week to week. Limited previews of full text are now made available only with publishers' permission or when material is out of copyright, however, snippets of text are available for all books. This has remained a source of discontent for publishers and authors with Google claiming that this is fair use.

The Google Book settlement agreement was first reached in the US District Court for the Southern District of New York in 2008. There followed several more years of wrangling in the courts as Google promised to address publishers' and authors' concerns through establishing a system of payments to rights holders and an independent registry to regulate the usage of 'orphan works'. The Authors Guild rejected the settlement in 2011 although it was subsequently approved by a judge in late 2013 as falling under fair use. The Authors Guild appealed again in late 2014 but the issue finally seems to have been resolved in October 2015 in the appeal court (Reuters, 2015). UK publishers are included in the settlement brokered by their US counterparts, but the rest of the EU was dropped from the agreement several years ago. Google Books also faced legal challenges, from French publishers, again citing copyright infringement in 2009. This case is an example of the fact that scanning material under the fair use provision in US law is not always permitted under the laws of other countries. News reports (Reid, 2009) also demonstrated how European countries have been split over the issues.

While Google Books does not provide an e-book platform which directly replaces print core text collections, it does offer potential as a means of providing links to out-of-copyright book material. However, national libraries are also offering access to digitized cultural heritage resources through projects such as Europeana (www.europeana.eu/portal) and the Digital Public Library of America (http://dp.la). Additionally there are numerous collections of free or out-of-copyright books available, such as Project Gutenberg (www.gutenberg.org), so Google Books is just one (admittedly very influential) player in this increasingly diverse online environment.

Databases and other subscription resources

The distinction between electronic journals, e-books and databases is often not apparent to users although many e-book and e-journal providers define their product as a database to award it extra protection under intellectual property laws. The use of content from databases is usually governed by licence agreements, however, most licences and exceptions to database rights allow extraction of reasonable proportions of content, as long as the person accessing the database is doing so legitimately. Educational licences are available for a variety of high-value commercial databases used in professions such as law and business. For example, legal databases such as Westlaw (www.westlaw.co.uk), Lawtel (www.lawtel.com) and the legal and news database LexisNexis (www.lexisnexis.com) all offer special, cheaper licences for educational establishments. These licences specify that they are only to be used for educational, not-for-profit purposes by academic staff and students. The Westlaw licence states that students who are on internships, for example at law firms, are not permitted to use their Westlaw account for work purposes. Similarly, business schools might well subscribe to databases such as Thomson Reuters DataStream (www. datastream.com), Bloomberg (www.bloomberg.com) or one of the databases provided by Wharton Research Data Services (http://wrds. wharton.upenn.edu). These business databases are often only available on dedicated terminals in libraries, because of the licence restrictions and the high commercial value of the data they contain.

One of the problems with some of the professional databases listed above is that they are notoriously complex to search. Many are not primarily aimed at the education sector so the search interface is unfamiliar to students used to using simple search engines. Lecturers and tutors are often tempted to download this content and provide students with the material in an easy-to-use format in the VLE. However, teachers and lecturers need to be extremely careful if they wish to extract or copy content from these sources. The two legal databases Westlaw and LexisNexis have developed tools that allow teachers to create deep links to documents in their database, therefore removing the need to download content and place it on a network for students. However, because of the commercial nature of these particular databases, downloading content and posting it to an e-learning platform is rarely permitted under the licence agreement.

This next section will briefly examine two licences for databases. The Westlaw education licence has been chosen because it provides an example of a commercial database that has an educational licence. EBSCO online research databases (https://www.ebscohost.com) are then examined, as these resources hold an enormous variety of electronic content, including indexing and abstracting services such as Historical Abstracts, EconLit, PsychInfo, GREENFile, full-text electronic journals, e-books and a variety of services for the library community. They also offer licences to the higher education sector, schools, public libraries, healthcare organizations, government departments and other companies. In this instance, the general licence is used as an example and staff from institutions subscribing to either Westlaw or EBSCO databases should check their own licence agreement for variations.

The Westlaw UK subscriber agreement

Westlaw UK has a sample subscriber agreement available on its website (Thomson Reuters, 2015), which permits the downloading and temporary storage of 'insubstantial amounts' of the material and the creation of printouts of content. However, it seems unlikely that downloaded material could be stored within the VLE routinely without a separate agreement to permit this.

Nevertheless, Westlaw UK responded to requests from UK universities to allow stable links to content to be created by tutors. Westlaw representatives can provide lecturers and e-learning staff with personal accounts to access Westlaw, which in addition to the regular search function also include a 'build link' option when viewing any piece of content on the database. Clicking on this option gives the tutor a stable link, which can be inserted into the e-learning platform to direct students straight to the article. By using this tool users can stay within the terms of the Westlaw Subscriber Agreement but create direct links to full-text content from the VLE.

EBSCO online research databases

EBSCO online research databases can be accessed from https://www.ebscohost.com. The EBSCO licence states:

> The Licensee and Sites may not reproduce, distribute, display, modify, transfer or transmit, in any form, or by any means, any Database or Service or any portion thereof without the prior written consent of EBSCO, except as specifically authorized in this Agreement. . . . the Licensee and Authorized Users may download or print limited copies of citations, abstracts, full text or portions thereof provided the information is used solely in accordance with copyright law. Licensee and Authorized Users may not publish the information.
>
> EBSCO, 2015a

As with JSTOR, the electronic journal database discussed earlier, EBSCO makes provision for users to create stable links to items in their database. This allows lecturers to create online reading lists that link to content on the EBSCO platform, without requiring the material to be downloaded.

EBSCO provides advice about setting up database, title and article level links, called 'persistent links' on its training and support website (EBSCO, 2015b), which makes it easy to include content in an online course. In addition EBSCO allows subscribers to download logos, buttons and icons that can be used (subject to terms and conditions) in library guides, handouts and e-learning to promote the databases. It also has a Search Box Builder tool, which allows a customized EBSCO search box to be created and used as appropriate in your institution. This search box could also be made available to students through the VLE.

Lecturers' own digital content: teaching materials

This next section will consider the copyright issues associated with digital content created by lecturers, given that many teachers use the VLE to distribute their own teaching materials to students. This type of content includes course handbooks, reading lists, lecture notes and PowerPoint slides. The advantage for students is that they can access this material at a time and place convenient to them. Teaching materials for campus-based students are routinely distributed in this manner, in addition to using the VLE for delivering content to distance learning students who do not attend face-to-face teaching. The copyright on most of this material is relatively unproblematic if it has been authored by the lecturer or teacher in question. As an employee, copyright in teaching materials usually lies with the institution (see Section 11 of the CDPA). Some universities have attempted to formalize the IPR situation with regards to teaching materials, whereas others have not. In 2006, Jisc recommended that all universities in the UK should have a written IPR policy to make it clear with whom ownership of teaching materials resides. Institutions without such a policy (it is unlikely for example that many schools or colleges have one) may wish to develop an IPR policy to clarify the ownership of content. This is important when content is being developed collaboratively, for example for teaching staff working together with educational technologists or learning support staff. Rather than restricting academic freedom, the policies developed by many universities aim to strike a balance between ensuring that staff have the freedom to retain ownership of their teaching materials while giving the university the right to use teaching materials in the future, in any manner of teaching. However, there is inevitably a tension between lecturers wanting to use their teaching materials when they move to other institutions, and the institution wanting to be able to continue to exploit the content, potentially exclusively. A selection of university IPR and copyright policies are included in the section 'Further resources' for those requiring further guidance in this area (see pages 254–5). The WIPO also issued guidance for universities on developing IPR policies (WIPO, n.d.).

More complex copyright issues can arise when teachers include third-party content in teaching materials. For example, a lecturer may include images that they have downloaded from the internet in a PowerPoint slide, or lecture notes might include excerpts from a published work. Most lecturers have editing rights for the courses they teach in a VLE, and are therefore responsible for uploading their own teaching materials. This type of 'third-party content' can easily end up being available online, with little consideration of the copyright implications. In the classroom or lecture theatre, the inclusion of third-party content in teaching materials (for example, displaying an image on screen or on an interactive whiteboard, showing a film, or playing a sound recording) does not entail the ongoing storage of digital copies, which can be accessed at the time of an individual's choosing. Consequently it may be possible to use copyright material legitimately in a classroom setting under an exception to copyright, such as quotation, criticism or review, or illustration for instruction. However, where the material is uploaded to the VLE without permission this involves not just the restricted act of copying but also a 'communication to the public'. Therefore a rights holder could argue that this is an infringement of copyright to which no statutory defence (exception) applies. Currently in the UK there is no case law to determine what use of third-party content under the new exceptions might be acceptable on the VLE and therefore what can be considered 'fair'. Institutions need to devise a carefully considered, risk-managed approach to ensure that staff are given adequate support and training about copyright issues when creating teaching materials for use online. A risk-averse approach would involve clearing all content that is to be hosted on the VLE using existing licences (such as the CLA Licence), or sourcing content from openly licensed sources. A summary of the exceptions is provided in Chapter 1 and the use of third-party-owned images is discussed in Chapter 3. Training in order to enable staff to make informed decisions about copyright issues is discussed in Chapter 6.

Learning objects, online tutorials and other resources

Learning objects are digital assets created and arranged with specific learning objectives in mind. They may be relatively simple from a technical perspective, such as a series of web pages followed by quiz questions to test understanding, or could be more complex learning objects, which might also include video or other forms of multimedia. Typically they include some form of instructional content, an opportunity to practise or interact with the content and some form of assessment. Complex learning objects can be time consuming and expensive to produce, therefore the e-learning community has been keen to share these resources through dedicated collections, or learning object repositories. Some teachers have also invested in creating learning objects that can be re-purposed and re-used with new content, using proprietary tools such as Adobe Captivate (www.adobe.com/uk/products/captivate.html) or open-source tools such as Xerte (https://www.nottingham.ac.uk/xerte/index.aspx). There is now considerable overlap with the open educational resources movement and the term 'learning object' has largely been superseded by the term 'open educational resource'.

In 2006 Jisc established a learning object repository called Jorum (www.jorum.ac.uk) to facilitate the sharing of learning objects in further and higher education in the UK but this service will be retired in September 2016 to be replaced with a Jisc App and Content Store for those who wish to share educational resources. Other learning object repositories exist in other countries, for example Multimedia Educational Resource for Learning and Online Teaching (www.merlot.org/merlot/index.htm) in the USA, which contains peer-reviewed resources for faculty and students in higher education. In Australia LORN (http://toolboxes.flexiblelearning. net.au/index.htm) is a learning object repository, which contains materials for the vocational sector. In Europe the Learning Resource Exchange (http://lreforschools.eun.org/web/guest/for-cont-providers) is a repository containing materials for schools from 18 European countries. These online collections of learning resources are particularly popular with schools where teachers frequently share teaching materials. However, sites such as OER Commons (https://www.oercommons.org) are increasingly superseding the need for specific learning object repositories.

Copyright issues are particularly pertinent in the learning object or open educational resources world, particularly if any third-party content is being used in the resources. Anyone creating open educational resources must ensure that they own the copyright in the resource or have the appropriate permissions. Meanwhile, anyone wanting to use content they source from an open educational resources collection needs to familiarize themselves with the licence agreement and ensure that if they repurpose the material, they follow any specified terms and conditions. Most open educational resources are licensed under a Creative Commons licence and those re-using open educational resources shared under a 'ShareAlike' licence will need to release any derivative works under the same or equivalent licence terms. Further information about open education and the full range of Creative Commons licences is available in Chapter 1 on pages 37–9.

Student-created content

Another increasingly important issue that also needs to be considered is digital content created by students as part of their course of study. With innovative approaches to teaching and learning, student assignments in schools and universities can involve more than simply written content, as students are asked to use digital tools to create images, video and sound in a wide variety of subject disciplines. At the more basic level, most VLEs have a discussion board or online forum where students post messages or queries to their tutors and might, for example, be asked to write short reflections. Additionally, many universities require students to submit their written assignments such as essays or short pieces of writing via the university VLE for assessment purposes. In some universities tools such as wikis and blogs (either within the VLE, or on externally hosted sites) are used for collaborative writing projects. Where students are expected to participate in online activities and the creation of digital content, teachers, educational developers and e-learning professionals need to consider the copyright implications.

Students are likely to own the copyright to all of their work,[3] whether it is a contribution to a discussion board, an essay they submit as part of their coursework or their final dissertation. Therefore, if the teacher wishes to copy or re-use this work, they need to obtain permission from the student who created it. While many universities have modified student regulations to mandate that students use some form of e-learning (for example, for online submission of work) this does not usually mean that the institution owns the copyright in the students' work. It would be good practice to create a release form that students can complete if the institution wishes to retain and re-use student work, for example to compile a database of frequently asked questions, or to provide subsequent groups with access to example dissertations or essays. As students create their own digital content, particularly if it is being shared online, it also becomes important to teach them about copyright issues at undergraduate level, particularly the use of third-party content such as music, images and video. For example, at LSE students in some disciplines create video as part of their coursework, and the institution has created a guide to copyright for students making films. The guide (LSE, n.d.) covers topics such as third-party content and securing release from people appearing in the videos.

PhD theses

In UK universities, PhD theses are often now submitted by candidates in digital format and many existing theses are digitized as part of an open access and/or preservation strategy. As the theses are made available online through institutional repositories, copyright can present several problems. Some institutions require that doctoral students assign some of their rights to the institution awarding the degree, but in many instances copyright is retained by the student as the author of the thesis. Therefore the institution should not digitize or publish a thesis online without permission from the student. Before 2014, the examination exception in UK law (now replaced with 'illustration for instruction') allowed third-party content to be included in the thesis, albeit with permission required for any subsequent publication. Consequently, institutions publishing theses online need to decide how to handle any third-party content within the thesis. The type of content included might be artwork, graphics, diagrams, illustrations, tables, graphs, extracts from music, plays or poems or even company or market data derived from commercial products. In general institutions can publish the thesis containing third-party copyright material if they or the student has obtained the permission from the rights holders to include their content, removed the content in advance of publication or determined that the use of the material falls within 'fair dealing' under UK law. Fair dealing was discussed in some detail on pages 18–19; if material falls within fair dealing it is generally allowable to include excerpts from other published written works (short quotations or summaries) for the purposes of illustration for instruction, quotation or criticism or review, if properly attributed. However, long extracts or the inclusion of material which may be commercially valuable generally require permission or need to be removed from the online version of the thesis. Some libraries check a thesis for copyright before it is published and expect doctoral students to obtain permission for any third-party content. In addition, many universities now offer copyright training and advice for PhD students in recognition of the issues that placing theses online presents.

There are a number of areas where PhD students might require specific advice and support: whether to license the thesis, either under an open licence such as Creative Commons or with a publisher; when making decisions over whether to transfer the copyright to a publisher, or license the work either exclusively or non-exclusively; and when deciding whether to include third-party content in a thesis or whether to redact or restrict access to it. This needs to be clearly defined and communicated in institutional policies. Both the PhD student and the institution have a joint responsibility for getting this right because the student is the author and the institution is effectively a publisher if it makes theses available via its online academic repository.

Conclusions and general advice

This chapter has summarized the different ways that digital content from publishers, website owners, teachers and students can be used in e-learning. Born digital content by its very nature is often easy to copy or upload to the VLE, but in many cases if the content is available online then linking is a better option and avoids most copyright issues. Contracts and licence agreements need to be considered in conjunction with copyright laws and exceptions when determining how existing digital content can be used in teaching. In the UK, clauses in contracts that are more restrictive than the statutory copyright exceptions can be ignored. However, in practice some DRM technologies used by publishers can make it difficult to use the content in the way a teacher wishes. For example, some e-books restrict the number of pages that can be printed and some e-journal providers monitor the number of downloads and suspend access to a title if they suspect excessive copying might be taking place. Lecturers and teachers may need to seek advice from those who manage institutional subscriptions (often librarians), to check what specific activities are permitted with collections and databases. Institutions therefore need to invest in identifying the permitted uses of specific digital resources and communicating them clearly so that not only can they manage compliance, but their staff and students can also make full use of the resources the institution has paid for. Finally, teachers creating their own content, or asking students to create content, should consider the copyright issues that arise and these should ideally be addressed by an institutional IPR policy document. Further resources are suggested at the end of the book in addition to the references below.

Notes

1   The ruling also found that it was illegal to provide hyperlinks to content which allowed a 'new public' to get access to works that previously were unavailable to them, and to which the rights holder would object. This and other rulings have created a somewhat confused picture of the legality of hyperlinking in the EU. Ultimately there is little if any risk involved with linking to content which is either freely available to all, or to provide links to legitimate users of content that sits behind a registration or pay wall.

2   An example of a deep link is https://en.wikipedia.org/wiki/Deep_ linking#Example, compared with www.wikipedia.org, which is at the top level, or home page, of a site.

3   This depends on the institutional IPR policy. But given the nature of the intellectual property policy as a 'contract' even those that state they claim copyright in student material would be likely to have difficulty defending this in a court.

References

Amazon (2015) Conditions of Use & Sale, www.amazon.co.uk/gp/help/customer/display.html/ref=footer_ cou?ie=UTF8&nodeId=1040616 [accessed 6 April 2016].

Caddick, N., Davies, G. and Harbottle, G. (2016) *Copinger and Skone James on Copyright*, 16th edn, Sweet & Maxwell.

EBSCO (2015a) Terms of Use,
http://support.ebscohost.com/ehost/terms.html [accessed 6 April
2016].

EBSCO (2015b) EBSCO Support and Training,
http://support.ebsco.com [accessed 6 April 2016].

IPO (2014) Technological Protection Measures (TPMs) Complaints
Process, Intellectual Property Office,
https://www.gov.uk/government/publications/technological-
protection-measures-tpms-complaints-process [accessed 6 April
2016].

Jisc Collections (2009) JISC National E-Books Observatory Project: key
findings and recommendations,
http://observatory.jiscebooks.org/reports/jisc-national-e-books-
observatory-project-key-findings-and-recommendations [accessed
6 April 2016].

Jisc Collections (2010) JISC National E-books Observatory Project,
http://observatory.jiscebooks.org [accessed 6 April 2016].

Jisc Collections (n.d.) How do the Model Licences Work,
www.jisc-collections.ac.uk/model_licence [accessed 6 April 2016].

JSTOR (2015a) JSTOR Terms and Conditions of Use,
http://about.jstor.org/terms [accessed 6 April 2016].

JSTOR (2015b) JSTOR Discovery and Linking,
http://about.jstor.org/jstor-help-support/discovery-linking [accessed
6 April 2016].

Li, S. (2015) Amazon Overtakes Wal-mart as Biggest Retailer, *LA Times*,
24 July,
www.latimes.com/business/la-fi-amazon-walmart-20150724-story.
html [accessed 6 April 2016].

LSE (n.d.) Copyright Issues and Student-Made Videos, London School of
Economics,
http://lti.lse.ac.uk/copyright/Student-videos.html [accessed 6 April
2016].

National Archives (2015) The Open Government Licence for Public
Sector Information, version 3,
www.nationalarchives.gov.uk/doc/open-government-licence/
version/3 [accessed 6 April 2016].

Pedley, P. (2015) *Practical Copyright for Library and Information*

Professionals, Facet Publishing.

Project MUSE (2015) Project MUSE Institutional Subscriber Journals Licensing Agreement, http://muse.jhu.edu/about/order/license_review.html [accessed 6 April 2016].

ProQuest (n.d.) ProQuest Terms and conditions, www.proquest.com/about/terms-and-conditions.html [accessed 6 April 2016].

Reid, D. (2009) Europe Split on Google Book Plans, BBC News, 13 November, http://news.bbc.co.uk/1/hi/programmes/click_online/8357773.stm [accessed 6 April 2016].

Reuters (2015) Google Book-Scanning Project Legal, says U.S. Appeals Court, 16 October, www.reuters.com/article/2015/10/16/us-google-books-idUSKCN0SA1S020151016#W7akOiqhrLC79Y2b.97 [accessed 6 April 2016].

Thomson Reuters (2015) Subscriber Agreement for Westlaw, http://legalsolutions.thomsonreuters.com/law-products/_ui/common/webResources/subscriber-agreement.pdf [accessed 6 April 2016].

UNESCO (2015a) Copyright, www.unesco.org/new/en/terms-of-use/terms-of-use/copyright [accessed 6 April 2016].

UNESCO (2015b) Terms of Use, www.unesco.org/new/en/terms-of-use/ [accessed 6 April 2016].

Walters, W. H. (2014) E-books in Academic Libraries: challenges for sharing and use, *Journal of Librarianship and Information Science*, **46** (2), 85–95.

WIPO (n.d.) *Guidelines on Developing Intellectual Property Policy for Universities and R&D Organizations*, World Intellectual Property Organization, www.wipo.int/export/sites/www/uipc/en/guidelines/pdf/ip_policy.pdf [accessed 6 April 2016].

5 Copyright in the connected digital environment

Introduction

The internet and associated web-based technologies have developed significantly over the last decade, with a seemingly constant stream of new tools to facilitate communication and interactivity. At the same time we have also seen the devices we use to connect to internet services become significantly more sophisticated and embedded in our daily lives. There has also been a shift towards cloud computing services where data processing and storage takes place on the network rather than on the local device. This has been made possible by the increased availability and a reduction in cost of high-speed broadband networks. Recent Ofcom statistics showed that broadband access in the home in the UK grew from 13% in 2003 to 87% in 2015 (Ofcom, 2015). Increased connectivity has changed the ways in which learning can be delivered to students, so anytime, anywhere learning is becoming a real possibility in much of the UK.

This chapter focuses on current internet technologies being used in education, and the associated copyright issues. The terminology used to describe these technologies can be problematic as any attempt to categorize developments in such a fast moving environment tends to sound out of date relatively quickly. The term 'Web 2.0', which started to be used after 2004, was intended to describe the development from a read-only web of static pages to one that was inherently interactive, but was immediately criticized by many (including Sir Tim Berners Lee, the inventor of the world wide web) for being too vague or potentially misleading (Naughton, 2012). Similarly, 'mobile technology' and 'cloud computing' were buzz words in 2009 when the first edition of this book was written, but in the intervening years the technologies have become so well established that they no longer seem that remarkable. However, despite the issues with shifting terminology it is clear that digitally connected tools such as blogs, wikis, apps, social media and social networking services share certain characteristics and have transformed the way that people access information, communicate and interact with the wider world. The focus here is not on these technologies *per se*, but on any specific copyright questions that arise from their use in an educational context. Suggested further resources are included at the end of the book; for example, Cornish (2015, 176–9) examines some of the copyright issues associated with social media services.

The chapter starts by focusing on a number of tools currently used by individual teachers, students and educational institutions, including social networking and social media services. It then considers the copyright issues associated with using third-party-hosted materials, including where copyright lies in works created by multiple authors, and who owns copyright of content uploaded to social media services. The chapter provides examples of how several social media services protect their own rights when handling copyright, as many are commercial websites funded largely from advertising revenues. It also considers how these services handle a contributor's copyright, for example if you upload content to a service such as Facebook or if you want to re-use material from one of these sites. Examples are included from some of the most popular social media services such as Flickr, Facebook and Wikipedia. Finally the chapter considers emerging trends and specifically considers the copyright questions associated with MOOCs. This chapter illustrates how emerging technologies provide an opportunity to develop the digital literacies of staff and students and to embed an understanding of copyright within a wider context. The case study included in this chapter comes from Zurich International School, where primary and secondary school students (K-12) are encouraged to use class blogs and educational technologies in a responsible way that respects intellectual property.

What are social media and the cloud?

It is worth briefly explaining what social media and the cloud are. As mentioned above, the term 'Web 2.0' was popularized in 2004 by the US media company O'Reilly Media, although it has been used to describe technologies that were developed in the 1990s. The technologies that take advantage of Web 2.0 are now commonly called 'social media', as one of their features is usually the ability to share resources and communicate with other users across a network. Social media use the internet as a platform to run software and services rather than a desktop PC, so most social media are hosted remotely and can be accessed from anywhere with an internet connection. Similarly, the term 'cloud computing' is now commonly used to describe any software or digital platform that runs on the internet rather than on a device. It has become almost entirely ubiquitous in consumer technology with many people entirely comfortable with using cloud-based social networks like Facebook and Twitter but also collaborative productivity tools and storage facilities like Dropbox, Evernote, Google Docs, Apple iCloud, Amazon Cloud Drive and Microsoft OneDrive. All of these services involve the use of data storage and computing power in large server farms located many miles from their users, but instantly accessible via any internet-enabled device. Many organizations are taking advantage of cloud computing as part of their institutional or corporate IT strategy, but concerns over data protection and reliability in the education sector have limited take-up in the UK (Jisc, 2015b). Wikipedia (itself a cloud-based, social media tool) describes much of the background and definition of the terms (Wikipedia, 2015b).

While it is not necessary to debate terminology any further in this book, it is clear to many in education that the way we can interact with the internet has changed. If one examines the development of a website such as the BBC, over the last few years it is now far easier for users to contribute, share content and interact with this website. It is also clear that the concept of 'user-generated content' (content created by users of a website and uploaded to it) has become mainstream and many of the tools and services such as RSS feeds (Really Simple Syndication – a way of publishing rapidly changing web-based content), blogs and social networking sites are widely used. To summarize, these are some overall characteristics of social media:

◆ the development of social networks
◆ content created or curated by users rather than created by an organization

- information passing from 'many to many' rather than 'one to many'
- the development of user profiles
- the use of 'tagging', to attach keywords created by users, to items to aid retrieval.

UCISA recently produced helpful guidance on the use of social media (UCISA, 2015) and Jisc has also been a valuable source of advice, producing several guides on the use of connected digital technologies in education and associated copyright issues (Jisc, 2015a). In 2007 Jisc highlighted six key concepts related to Web 2.0 technologies: the creation of user-generated content, harnessing the power of the crowd, data on a large scale, participation, network effects and openness (Anderson, 2007). What was apparent from these terms is that traditional modes of content creation, 'ownership' and most importantly copyright do not sit well in the connected digital environment. When people write a document collaboratively on Wikipedia, it is not obvious who owns it. When people edit video material and upload it to YouTube, copyright matters are rarely considered. Many of these services use the term 'sharing' to describe the creation and communication of content to peers (John, 2013), which does not sit easily with copyright laws developed for a less dynamic and collaborative environment. For example, copyright laws specifically define who the author of a literary work is, but where work is created collaboratively using a social media platform such as a wiki the authorship is less clear, particularly where those contributing remain anonymous. Oppenheim (2012) addresses these and other legal considerations that apply when using social media.

In 2008 Jisc funded a series of projects to explore how institutions might respond to 'emergent technologies'. It also produced a briefing paper entitled *Web 2.0 and Intellectual Property Rights* to highlight the key concerns. Although a number of years have passed since the report was published, the findings are still relevant to the digital environment at the time of writing. These are the key issues it addressed:

- the collaborative nature of Web 2.0 – international multiple contributors who never meet results in the shifting of risks, blurring who owns copyright, who is responsible for dealing with infringements within different legal jurisdictions and/or the identity of collaborators

◆ consequential difficulties in policing and enforcing any infringements that might occur and establishing who is liable for what and when
◆ uncertainty about what may be permitted under exceptions to copyright, because of a lack of suitable case law (Jisc, 2008).

Copyright issues were mentioned again by Jisc in 2009 (CLEX, 2009), in the context of young people having a 'casual approach' to copyright and other legal constraints. Jisc also funded the Web2rights project, which provided a wealth of information and resources for further and higher education including an animation to highlight some of the key issues and an online diagnostic tool (Jisc/SLC, n.d). The project explored questions such as:

◆ Do rights exist in a virtual world; if so, who owns them?
◆ Who owns the rights in works that are a result of collective collaboration?
◆ What happens if you can't find the rights holders?
◆ What are the legal risks associated with Web 2.0 engagement?
◆ How can risks associated with content re-use be sensibly managed?

The project website has a valuable toolkit of resources for all sorts of possible scenarios. It includes a diagnostic tool to help identify IPR and copyright issues. This chapter attempts to distil some of the advice from this project and other organizations, but unsurprisingly this is an area where technology is developing rapidly and the copyright laws struggle to keep pace. The Hargreaves Review of intellectual property and growth (Hargreaves, 2011), which led the recent UK reforms, explicitly made the case for changing copyright law to support technological innovation, particularly among small to medium enterprises. However, despite the UK Government's commitment to ensuring that the UK stays at the leading edge of the global digital economy through a progressive copyright regime, considerable tension still exists between law and practice.

New technologies for learning

Over the last decade there has been an increasing number of improvements in commercial and open-source e-learning systems to include social networking functionality, or at least allow third-party tools to be embedded.

The use of social and cloud-based technologies in higher education has led to some educational establishments relaxing their policy towards hosting data on third-party sites. Until recently, university IT departments steered away from such practices, recommending that data was kept on internal systems, but many social media commercial services provide tools and software that cannot easily be run in-house. In addition, many educational institutions are keen to engage with new technologies in response to student demands. We are therefore seeing an increasing amount of 'academic' content being hosted on third-party sites, such as Flickr, YouTube or Facebook, which has implications for copyright, though this is not the case everywhere. In other institutions, typically schools and further education colleges, and in the health sector, access to many social media sites is blocked. In these institutions IT departments have taken the approach that the risks associated with using these services are too great when considered against the educational benefit.

These are some of the risks associated with using social media:

◆ the security, privacy and data protection issues that uploading content to a third-party site might create
◆ concerns about retaining control of the intellectual outputs of an organization
◆ possible confusion if official branding or logos appear on third-party sites
◆ the staff time needed to manage these sites, for example moderating comments on a blog
◆ the copyright issues if staff or students upload content that infringes copyright or use infringing material from a social media site
◆ the perception that many social media are purely social sites and not appropriate to use in the workplace – Facebook is the most common site to be blocked by employers for this reason.

The risks aside, much has been written about the potential for social media to help engage learners, particularly younger students who have grown up with access to technologies such as mobile phones, computer games and the internet. The opportunities and challenges of social media were recognized at the inaugural 2015 Social Media for Learning in Higher Education Conference, which took place at Sheffield Hallam University in December 2015 (Sheffield Hallam University, 2015). Technologies such as blogs, social networking sites, wikis and podcasts are all currently widely used, particularly in higher education. Organizations such as Jisc and the Association for Learning Technology (ALT) have been working to help ensure that educators and support staff have the appropriate skills to use these technologies effectively. This next section considers a number of technologies, specifically looking at the copyright challenges they might present to teaching staff who wish to use them and those in a teaching support role, such as librarians and learning technologists. There is considerable enthusiasm for experimentation in this field and many of the social media sites encourage collaboration and content 'sharing'. On the surface it appears that copyright issues are often disregarded by both users and creators of many of these tools. The next section includes only a brief introduction to each technology, focusing on particular copyright concerns associated with their use.

Blogs

Blogs or weblogs are essentially a website often in an online journal or diary format and usually written by a single named author who uploads entries or posts using a simple interface. The blog posts are arranged in reverse chronological order, with the most recent entry appearing at the top of the screen. Readers are provided with the ability to leave comments on the posts. A typical blog post is an opinion piece that might include links to resources and photos. Their value to the education community is considerable, particularly for teachers as a learning journal to aid reflection. There are numerous examples of blogs being used in education and some staff encourage students to write blogs to develop their communication and reflection skills. Blogging software can be installed on in-house servers or hosted externally and a number of commercial sites host blogs for free on behalf of users, such as Blogger.com (owned by Google) and WordPress.com.

Original blog entries are covered under copyright law, being original, fixed literary works; therefore, permission to re-use entries should be sought even if a teacher has asked students to write a blog as part of their studies. Some bloggers use Creative Commons licences to indicate that they are happy for their entries to be shared and re-used. The licences can be attached to a personal blog, or staff can encourage their students to use one on their blog. Blogging is less likely to present copyright issues for the author of the blog if they stick to writing their entries as original opinion-based pieces. However, if bloggers wish to reproduce an entire entry or a substantial part of an entry from another blog they are well advised to seek permission (as with any content you find on the internet) if they cannot see a Creative Commons licence or similar open re-use terms. It is usual for bloggers to include their contact details or to have a commenting facility (indeed finding an audience and engaging with them is one of the key reasons for blogging) so getting permission is usually not difficult.

Bloggers frequently write about and refer to other material on the internet and many are drawn towards blogging as a way of sharing their creativity with a wider collaborative community. A good blog is likely to include links to other material on the internet, including reports, other blog posts by the same or other authors, or recent news stories. If you wish to use photographs on your blog you are advised to use your own photos, those with no copyright restrictions or those licensed under a Creative Commons licence. It is not necessary to seek permission to link to a post on another blog, although caution should be applied if the link is to clearly infringing content (e.g. a peer to peer file sharing link). Another common practice in blogs is to embed links to third-party content such as video or images so that they appear in the body of the blog post while actually being hosted from another site. This is an effective way to make a blog post more compelling, but bloggers should be careful to find out whether this is recommended by the site hosting the content. For example, YouTube, Vimeo and Getty Images Embed (Getty Images, 2015) all provide this functionality and promote it for non-commercial use, but bloggers should avoid embedding content from sites that do not promote it, particularly where the owners of the third-party content might be unhappy about it appearing alongside advertising or other content to which they might object.

Blog services

Blogger (www.blogger.com) is a popular blog service owned by Google that allows people to set up a blog hosted remotely on external servers. Blogger uses Google's terms of use, which include a section about IPR

(Google, 2015a). This clearly states that when using this service, the blog author retains copyright in their contents:

> You retain ownership of any intellectual property rights that you hold in that content. In short, what belongs to you stays yours.
>
> When you upload, submit, store, send or receive content to or through our Services, you give Google (and those we work with) a worldwide license to use, host, store, reproduce, modify, create derivative works (such as those resulting from translations, adaptations or other changes we make so that your content works better with our Services), communicate, publish, publicly perform, publicly display and distribute such content. . . . Make sure you have the necessary rights to grant us this license for any content that you submit to our Services.
>
> Google, 2015a

This statement should reassure teachers who are concerned that by hosting their content on Blogger.com they will lose ownership of their data. In addition, as is common with many social media sites technologies, Google encourage people to license their content for re-use under a Creative Commons licence.

WordPress is an open-source blog tool that offers hosted blog services (http://wordpress.com) and allows users to download the software to run it on their own servers (http://wordpress.org). For those in educational establishments who feel uncomfortable about having content hosted on external sites, this latter option is useful. Like much open-source software, WordPress is licensed under the GNU General Public Licence (the most widely used open-source software licence; see www.gnu.org), which allows users to modify the source code freely. The terms of service set out useful 'responsibilities of contributors' including the following:

> If you operate a blog, comment on a blog, post material to WordPress.com, post links on WordPress.com, or otherwise make (or allow any third party to make) material available (any such material, 'Content'), you are entirely responsible for the content of, and any harm resulting from, that Content. That is the case regardless of what form the Content takes, which includes, but is not limited to text,

photo, video, audio, or code. By making Content available, you represent and warrant that your content does not violate these terms or the User Guidelines

WordPress, 2009

Accordingly the user guidelines include a section on IPR:

> WordPress.com is a publishing, rather than a file sharing platform, so we recognize that copyrighted materials are often used in fair use context. We strongly support this and urge copyright holders to take this into consideration before submitting complaints. If you're not sure, a good rule of thumb is to always ask the rights holder for permission before republishing their content.

WordPress, 2015

Interestingly, the WordPress terms of service document is also licensed under a Creative Commons licence, which explicitly states: 'You're more than welcome to repurpose it for your own use. Just make sure to replace references to us with ones to you, and if you don't mind we'd appreciate a link to WordPress.com somewhere on your website.'

Most VLEs, for example Moodle and Blackboard, also now have in-built blogging tools that are password protected, so only staff and students in the institution or on a particular course can view them. Password protecting blogs is seen as a way to reduce the risks associated with sharing digital content by not making it available to the wider public, though good practice in complying with copyright should never be disregarded. To avoid any potential problems, it is recommended best practice to include copyright advice as an integral part of any blog training, whether for staff or students, and regardless of whether the blog is publicly available or not. Many students might start blogging within a password-protected VLE, but then go on to set up a blog on a site such as WordPress or Blogger. Ensuring that they respect intellectual property from the outset of their studies should be part of any training and education programme.

Copyright advice for blog authors

Here is some good practice advice for blog authors:

◆ Blogs are usually opinion based, so writing an original piece that does not infringe copyright should be fairly straightforward if you stick to viewing your blog as your opinions and thoughts. Under the UK's exception for quotation, criticism and review it may be also acceptable to reproduce small amounts of a copyright work as part of your blog post.

◆ Remember that what you write is publicly available on the internet, unless you password protect the site, so common sense should tell you not to write anything libellous about other people, your employer or companies.

◆ Link to other web-based materials you are referencing, but do not copy large amounts of material from other websites.

◆ If you are going to use content from elsewhere ensure you have permissions or include only limited quotations from other works to reinforce your points.

◆ If you wish to use photos on your blog, use your own photos, or find photos that are licensed under a Creative Commons licence and credit the original photographer.

◆ If you want to embed content in your site, make sure that the copyright holder and/or the site from which you are linking to are happy for the content to be embedded.

◆ Protect your intellectual property by attaching either a copyright symbol on your materials, or, if you are happy for the content to be used by others, a Creative Commons licence symbol.

Wikis

Wikis are easy-to-edit websites that allow content to be created collaboratively by multiple authors. They are particularly useful for group work and student projects, where several writers can work collaboratively to build up knowledge in an area. One of the pedagogic rationales for using wikis is to encourage students to create new knowledge, so you would typically expect contributions to be original work (not copied and pasted) as part of any student wiki project. It might be necessary to make this clear to students at the outset of this type of project. Wikis support version control: changes can be tracked and earlier versions of a document can be retrieved even after a wiki has been published, and individual contributions from different authors can be identified. However, wikis provide an interesting example of the understanding of copyright, because work is undertaken collaboratively and even though the authors have version control functionality it is not always clear who has contributed what or even who those people are. The content in institutionally hosted wikis used by staff as part of their employment (e.g. wikis in a professional collaborative environment like Microsoft SharePoint) is owned by the employer, as with any text written in the course of employment. However, student work hosted on a wiki is jointly owned by the group of students. If a tutor wishes to re-use the content from the wiki they would be advised, as with any piece of student work, to ask permission from the authors. Even in situations where a fair dealing exception, such as illustration for instruction, applies it is best practice to be clear with the students about how their work is going to be used.

Wikipedia is the most well established and well known example of a wiki. Launched in 2000, it aimed to build an online encyclopedia as the sum of all human knowledge. The Wikipedia software is called MediaWiki and it is licensed under the GNU General Public Licence for free download. This allows individuals and organizations to install the MediaWiki software on their own servers so they can use it to set up their own wiki on any topic of interest. Again, if the wiki is used by staff as part of their employment, it is no different from any other jointly authored document.

Wikipedia and copyright

As Wikipedia becomes an increasingly accepted information resource within educational establishments, staff and students are more likely to want to or be encouraged to contribute to the site. Anyone who does so needs to consider copyright issues carefully, however. They should ensure that they do not submit any third-party copyright material without permission, and that any content they do include is their own original work. Cutting and pasting from elsewhere on the web to create a Wikipedia article infringes copyright and is not permitted in the terms of use, which specify it is only possible to add content that can be re-used under a Creative Commons Attribution Share Alike Licence. The Wikimedia Foundation (which is responsible for Wikipedia) terms of use state:

To grow the commons of free knowledge and free culture, all users contributing to the Projects are required to grant broad permissions to the general public to re-distribute and re-use their contributions freely, so long as that use is properly attributed and the same freedom to re-use and re-distribute is granted to any derivative works. In keeping with our goal of providing free information to the widest possible audience, we require that when necessary all submitted content be licensed so that it is freely reusable by anyone who cares to access it.

You agree to the following licensing requirements:

a. Text to which you hold the copyright: When you submit text to which you hold the copyright, you agree to license it under:

- Creative Commons Attribution – ShareAlike 3.0 Unported License ('CC BY-SA'), and
- GNU Free Documentation License ('GFDL') (unversioned, with no invariant sections, front-cover texts, or back-cover texts).

Wikimedia Foundation, 2015

Other wiki software

Increasingly, as with many social media services, free hosted wiki software is available to allow users to create wikis for their own use. PBworks (http://pbworks.com) and WikiSpaces (www.wikispaces.com) are two examples of hosted wikis. A hosted wiki on the PBworks site is still owned by the contributors, so PBworks makes no claims over ownership of what it terms 'user submissions' in its terms of service. PBworks also emphasizes that material posted on its site should not infringe copyright. As is typical with many social media services, copyright infringement is taken seriously and results in suspension of a user's account. The terms of WikiSpaces are very similar to those of PBworks.

Several VLEs include a wiki tool, which could be used for a student project. These tools tend to have less functionality than bespoke wiki software such as PBworks or WikiSpaces, but have the advantage of being password protected and restricted to students on a course of study. As is the case with blogs, password protection should not be viewed as a reason for permitting staff or students to copy and paste content from elsewhere onto a wiki. While using a password might potentially lower the risk of the infringing activity being noticed by a rights holder, the risk still remains. In addition, advising on this course of action creates an implied acceptance of copyright infringement. It is worth returning to the main educational value of using a wiki with students, which is the collaborative creation of new knowledge. The content should be original and so a teacher would not want students simply to reproduce content from another site unless it was in the form of short, attributed quotations.

Good practice when using wikis

Those wishing to use wikis in education should consider the following points:

◆ Consider the options carefully when deciding whether to use a hosted wiki on a third-party site, wiki software hosted on your own servers, or a wiki tool available in your VLE or e-learning platform. This may depend on the type of information or data that you are collecting on the website; any sensitive or personal data should not be hosted remotely.
◆ Establish the expectation with students that the content of the wiki is to be original, and give them plagiarism and copyright advice. If students are expected to include images the concept of Creative Commons could be included in any technical training for wiki creation.
◆ If students are expected to use a wiki for a group project, remember that the group will own the resulting project just as they would any other document.

Case Study 6   Zurich International School, Switzerland – e-learning and copyright

Mark Dilworth

Introduction
Zurich International School (ZIS) is a leading, non-profit day school offering a comprehensive education programme for students aged 2 to 18 in the greater

Zurich area. Over 1500 students from more than 55 countries attend one of the school's four campuses (Early Childhood Center in Kilchberg for students aged 2 to 5; Lower School Wädenswil Campus for students aged 5 to 11; Middle School Kilchberg Campus for students aged 11 to 14; Upper School Adliswil Campus for students aged 14 to 18).

Teaching and learning

The ZIS website (www.zis.ch) states:

> The ZIS Mission and Philosophy underpins our curriculum and its design, review, development and delivery. Learn, Care, Challenge, Lead – these give us the parameters to question what we teach and how we teach in a complex and ever-changing global environment.
>   We want our students to be:
>
> ◆ active, not passive, learners who are critical and compassionate thinkers
> ◆ inspired and challenged to develop a love of learning, and have this stay with them for the rest of their lives.   www.zis.ch

ZIS launched a one-to-one tablet programme in Grades 6–12 in 2008 and a one-to-one iPad programme in Grades 1–5 in 2012. Faculty have the same device as the one provided to their students. Classrooms are equipped with interactive whiteboards and wireless internet access is available throughout the campuses. In 2015, ZIS adopted Google Apps for Education as the primary tool for communication and collaboration.

ZIS uses a set of common learning principles as the basis for a whole school framework that guides teaching and learning and ensures that learning is connected and coherent across divisions and teaching areas. With the onset of the tablet and iPad, the Library and IT departments shifted their focus from offering IT courses or standalone lessons in IT labs to supporting integration across all subject areas.

Although ZIS does not have an explicit IT curriculum, it is an ongoing goal to integrate IT skills, information fluency and citizenship into the curriculum. To that end, we have specific roles and resources to support students and faculty. Educational technology coordinators and librarians model best practice, attend planning meetings, team-teach and offer ongoing professional development.

Moodle and class blogs provide digital platforms for communication of resources that are accessible to students outside the classroom. The introduction of policies and agreements to support responsible use are learning opportunities for students.

Roles

Educational technology coordinators are division-wide leadership roles responsible for assisting faculty with effective and meaningful integration of technology across the curriculum. Librarians offer faculty assistance in using information resources and incorporating information literacy skills in the classroom curriculum. Together, this team provides support for students and faculty, with the goal of moving them across a continuum of competence towards independent, embedded use of technology for learning. They also promote the ethical use of information technology through respect for intellectual property and adherence to copyright laws.

The web portal and the VLE

The school's web portal has been designed to provide online and/or off-site access for all members of the school community while offering a range of curriculum delivery options for faculty and students depending on their needs. The resources that can be accessed from the web portal for student learning are listed in Table 5.1.

Table 5.1 Resources available from the web portal for student learning at Zurich International School	
VLE	Moodle and Edublogs
E-mail	Gmail
Shared folders and files	Google Drive
Collaborative calendars	Google Calendars
Student portfolios	Edublogs

At our lower school we use Edublogs for class sites and student portfolios. Each grade level team publishes a grade level blog that communicates upcoming curricular and logistical information for students and parents. Each teacher publishes a classroom blog that documents and celebrates student learning. At

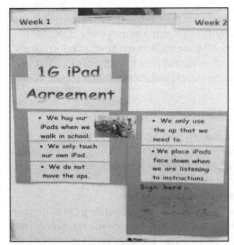

Figure 5.1 *Example classroom agreement at Zurich International School*

our middle and upper schools each teacher has a Moodle course for their class where students can access resources online.

Students and faculty have a variety of digital resources that they can draw on to support teaching and learning. They are encouraged to use these resources when appropriate and in a responsible manner. In our lower school, classroom agreements are developed at the beginning of each school year (see example in Figure 5.1). These agreements outline behavioural expectations and encompass the use of technology. This process engages students in a conversation about acceptable online behaviour and gives them ownership in the classroom agreement.

At our middle and upper schools, a responsible use policy (Figure 5.2) and a school owned device contract (Figure 5.3) guide student use of technology. These

---

Internet access is available to all students and teachers at ZIS. While the Internet offers a great deal of useful information and resources, it is also a diverse public medium. As such, it is important that pupils and faculty conduct themselves in a way which is compatible with the academic aims and the spirit of ZIS. Our goal in providing access to the Internet is to promote educational excellence by facilitating resource sharing, innovation, and communication. With access to the Internet also comes the potential availability of educationally questionable, politically controversial, and morally inappropriate material.

Although we strive to supervise Internet use, it is impossible to guarantee that users will not be exposed to, or able to obtain such materials. ZIS therefore relies heavily on mature and responsible use by students and faculty and believes that Internet usage is a chance to teach students about responsible, ethical behavior. These guidelines have been established to inform the ZIS community of the responsibilities which all users of the school's Internet facilities must carry.

Access to the Internet is provided for the express purpose of furthering studies at school, engaging in collaborative work with others, and obtaining information which is consistent with the educational objectives of ZIS. Faculty, staff, or students may not transmit or seek access to materials which violate laws, infringe on copyrights, or have threatening, obscene, or racist content unless in the context of investigative research.

Figure 5.2 *Responsible use policy at Zurich International School*

Continued on next page

Members of the ZIS community who post, discuss on the Internet, or distribute through e-mail slanderous or deliberately hurtful comments which damage the integrity of and cause personal distress to ZIS parents, faculty, staff, administrators, Board members, or students, are considered in violation of the school's mission and values, in breach of professional ethics, and/or out of sympathy with the school's Code of Conduct.

Responsible Use Policy
- I understand that my device, e-mail account, and all other ZIS IT services and resources are to be used for educational purposes;
- I understand that streaming video or music, social networking sites, instant messaging and chat, video games are not allowed during class time unless used for completion of classroom activities or permitted by a teacher;
- I understand that creating, accessing, displaying, producing, storing, circulating or transmitting pornographic or offensive material in any form or medium is against school rules and in some cases against the law. This includes sending, posting or displaying offensive images, language or any other type of offensive content including the bullying, harassment or intimidation of others. Please note this also applies to student owned devices;
- I will not intentionally disrupt school network traffic with high bandwidth use for personal entertainment such as downloading music, videos, or online gaming;
- I will not give out my password to anyone nor use someone else's password or log-in identity and I understand the dangers of giving out personal information;
- I will not deliberately introduce any harmful or nuisance program or file including executable files from untrustworthy websites, or deliberately circumvent any precautions taken by the school to prevent this from happening;
- I agree to comply with trademark, copyright laws, data protection laws and computer misuse laws, and to give credit to all sources used. I also agree not to jailbreak or otherwise hack the device in any way for any reason;
- I understand that electronic communication and computer use may be monitored at anytime, including a physical search of the device loaned to me;
- I understand that ZIS may limit, suspend or revoke access to the school's technology systems, services, or network on violation of this Responsible Use Policy.

Figure 5.2 *Continued*

policies are reviewed at the beginning of the school year with students and parents. Students and parents are expected to discuss and sign the agreements before receiving their device. These policies encourage balancing digital time with 'unplugged' time, learning from and with technology, respectful digital action and protecting self and others from negative digital situations.

School Owned Device Contract

1. The tablet remains the property of Zurich International School and as such must be returned to the school either on demand or at the end of your enrolment at ZIS.

2. The user accepts responsibility for:

   All pre-installed software on the tablet. The user agrees not to alter the core configuration of the tablet or install additional software without approval by the ZIS IT Department.

   All data contained on the tablet. This includes any pictures and information downloaded from the Internet. The user is responsible for any infringement of copyright, violation of school use policies, or any applicable statute or regulation. The downloading of material which is incompatible with the goals and values of ZIS is not tolerated.

   The physical security of the tablet. The machine is insured within Switzerland under the school's insurance policies. However, this coverage does not extend to instances where the user is deemed negligent such as:

   - Tablet left unattended (including if left unattended on school premises)
   - In view in a car or unattended in a public place
   - Left on a train or plane, etc.
   - In these cases, the user will be held personally liable for any loss or theft.

   General care and maintenance of the tablet
   Care at all times should be taken of the tablet and maintained in good condition. The user is held liable for damages caused by negligence:

   - Inappropriate usage, or abuse beyond normal wear and tear
   - Stickers, markings or decorations of any kind
   - Intentionally damaged
   - Cosmetic damage that is not covered by the Thinkpad Protection.

   Reporting the damage or loss of the school owned tablet to the IT department as soon as possible

3. The tablet has **antivirus software pre-installed.** This software requires regular updates in order to remain effective. The antivirus update system is an automatic procedure, on the tablet being connected to the school network. As such, the user agrees to connect the tablet to the network at least once a week when school is in session.

4. **The user will adhere to the ZIS Responsible Use Policies as stated in the Student Handbook.**

Figure 5.3 *School owned device contract at Zurich International School*

Conclusion

ZIS provides many opportunities for authentic learning experiences. Technology can enhance those experiences when used appropriately and responsibly. Faculty are encouraged to model and demonstrate responsible use in their own practice. Educational technology coordinators and librarians play a specific role to support faculty and student learning. Resources and policies are reviewed regularly to meet the needs that arise from new developments in technology and education. Students are engaged in these conversations to give them a voice in how they learn. An appreciation of copyright is therefore presented to students as one of a number of responsibilities they have towards the use of technology in class. We hope they will remember them in their lives outside school and stay with them as their education and careers progress.

Media-sharing sites

Media sharing (such as photos, video and audio) is a feature of many social media services such as blogs and wikis. There are also numerous services designed specifically for sharing audio, visual and audiovisual media. Some of these have been discussed in Chapter 3 and they provide interesting examples because of their differing approaches to copyright. The two examples that will be explored in greater detail here are Flickr, which is predominantly a photo-sharing website (although videos can also be uploaded), and YouTube, the video-sharing site. Both sites allow users to create a profile from which they can upload, organize and share content. The background, development and differing approaches to copyright of these two sites is explored.

Flickr

Flickr (http://flickr.com) is one of numerous media-sharing websites that allow users to upload content to share either with the wider public or to a restricted set of contacts. It was launched in 2004 by a Vancouver-based company, but has been owned by Yahoo since 2005. In February 2010 it was reported that one million images were being shared on the site every day (TechCrunch, 2015). The site is popular with many different types of users, from individuals who wish to share photos with friends to professional photographers showcasing their work. A free account provides a user with up to 1TB of storage for their photographs (up to 200MB each) and videos (of up to 1GB each), which can be tagged using keywords to facilitate searching. Users can also join groups where they can share photos related to specific topics. Those who wish to upload more photographs need to upgrade their account to a Flickr Doublr account, which has an annual subscription fee but offers 2TB of storage.

Some organizations such as libraries and museums use Flickr to showcase their photographic collections and the site allows content to be re-purposed to appear elsewhere on the web as a 'photostream'. There are a number of high profile libraries and museums in the world that now have a Flickr account, for example:

◆ the Library of Congress
 (www.flickr.com/photos/library_of_congress)
◆ the British Library (www.flickr.com/photos/britishlibrary)
◆ the Metropolitan Museum of Art in New York
 (www.flickr.com/photos/metmuseum)
◆ the National Portrait Gallery
 (https://www.flickr.com/photos/natportraitgallery)
◆ the London School of Economics Library
 (https://www.flickr.com/photos/lselibrary).

Most copyright laws in the world specify that the individual who takes a photograph owns the copyright of the resulting work. With the widespread availability of digital cameras, both dedicated cameras and those included in mobile digital devices, large numbers of people can easily create content in the form of digital photographs and videos. Photo and video-sharing has become increasingly popular as the functionality to do so is built into the devices people carry with them at all times. To respect copyright, the default option when uploading a photograph to Flickr is to protect the rights of the owner and label it as 'all rights reserved', which means that permission must be sought if someone wishes to re-use that image. However, a small but increasing number of individuals and organizations are applying open licences to their photograph collections on Flickr to indicate that they are happy to allow re-use. Flickr's use of Creative Commons licences is discussed in the next section.

Flickr's terms of use specify that users must own the copyright of any photographs that are uploaded to the site and that the company reserves the right to remove anything it considers inappropriate or infringing. While the sharing of images on the internet has become second nature to most people, many professional photographers have become deeply concerned at the way digital technology has affected their ability to make a living. Some professional photographers and photographic agencies use technical measures to control how their photographs are used. For example, techniques such as watermarking or offering only low resolution images limit the usability of photographs unless a fee is paid to download the higher resolution version, but many professional photographers do use Flickr as a showcase for their work and rely on the clear usage terms and control over whether downloads are allowed and to what resolution. Those who acquire digital photographs that they did not take themselves are strongly advised not to upload them to a photo-sharing website such as Flickr in order to avoid issues with photographers, who may be highly protective of their work. Matters can also become complicated if individuals take photographs of copyright-protected works, such as paintings or other works of art. Anyone who wishes to digitize photographs from a historical collection should be aware that photographs are artistic works and qualify for copyright protection in the UK for 70 years after the death of the author (the person who took the photo – see Chapter 1). It is also important to note that a person who commissions a photograph does not own the copyright, the photographer does so by default unless there is an agreement to the contrary.

Flickr, Creative Commons and the Flickr Commons

Flickr has done considerable work to encourage the sharing and re-use of photographs under licences such as Creative Commons Attribution Share Alike (see pages 37–9 in Chapter 1 for more detail on the Creative Commons licences). The Creative Commons Search has an embedded Flickr image search that allows you to identify photographs licensed for re-use. It is also possible to search Flickr and limit your search to specific types of Creative Commons licences. So, for example, those looking for images that can be re-used for commercial purposes will find a large collection of photographs on the site. In addition to Flickr's use of Creative Commons licences on its public service (i.e. members of the public who use Flickr can assign CC licences to their photos), it has a dedicated service for cultural heritage institutions only called the Flickr Commons (Flickr, 2015), which encourages them to upload material either in the public domain, or dedicated to it through the use of a 'no known copyright restrictions' assertion. Public awareness of Creative Commons licences and their value has grown through association and embedding within the Flickr website. Flickr is a good example of a social media service that has raised awareness of copyright issues and helped to build up good practice in the re-use of digital content.

YouTube

YouTube (http://youtube.com) is a video-sharing service that was launched in 2005. It was bought by Google in November 2006 and has now become one of the most popular services on the internet with over a billion users worldwide (YouTube, 2015a). It incorporates many features such as the user profile (called a channel), tagging to facilitate access, commenting and ratings. With the strap line 'broadcast yourself' the site capitalizes on increased ease of creating and editing video recordings without sophisticated hardware and software. An increasing number of media companies and large organizations are using YouTube to host some of their content. The functionality of digital cameras and mobile devices now allows many people to create digital video content. By using a video-sharing site such as YouTube individuals can easily share this content with others via the internet. The use of video editing software makes copying digital video from a DVD or the internet relatively straightforward and as a result a large amount of commercially produced content is uploaded to YouTube from unofficial sources.

YouTube epitomizes the problematic relationship between users of social media and copyright laws largely formulated to serve the needs of 20th-century mass media production. The service has been littered with examples of blatant copyright infringement, whereby individuals have copied copyright-protected works, such as commercial video or DVD recordings, live performances and audio content. However, like other online service providers, Google and YouTube are protected from infringement claims related to their users' actions by the DMCA safe harbor provisions (see page 35). This remains a bone of contention between rights holders and internet companies.

In order to placate major rights holders YouTube has an automated infringement detection system called 'Content ID', which identifies potentially infringing uses against a reference database of digital original files provided by film, TV and record companies (YouTube, 2015b). When the system finds a match between the reference file and the video being uploaded it alerts the rights holder, who decides whether to block access to the file, leave it as is or monetize the use. As well as the Content ID system, which is largely in place to keep commercial content publishers happy, YouTube has a system whereby anyone can request infringing use of their content to be removed. This is done through their copyright notice, which sets out how to make a complaint of copyright infringement, and is available online at YouTube Copyright Infringement Notification (https://www.youtube.com/copyright_complaint_form).

YouTube also provides a set of copyright and rights management pages (YouTube, 2015c) designed to educate users about how to avoid or report infringement. These set out what copyright is, how to identify copyright works and what the penalties might be for those who upload copyright work (their account could be closed and they could be sued). The advice offered is carefully worded in order to ensure that the interests of both rights holders and users of the service are respected, while at the same time clarifying that Google does not take responsibility for the actions of either. This reflects the lucrative arrangements YouTube has in place with broadcasters, studios and record labels, and the huge value to the company of the individuals who upload and view their content. For example:

Can YouTube determine copyright ownership?

No. YouTube isn't able to mediate rights ownership disputes. When we receive a complete takedown notice, we remove the content as the law requires. When we receive a valid counter notification we forward it to the person who requested the removal. After this, it's up to the parties involved to resolve the issue in court.

YouTube, 2015c

In order to uphold the rights of copyright holders YouTube operates a 'copyright strike' system whereby those found to be uploading infringing content have functionalities disabled from their account. After three strikes, where a rights holder has notified of infringing use, the user's account is deleted.

YouTube also tries to uphold the rights of their users by making it clear to rights holders that they must have the necessary authority to report copyright infringement: 'Do not make false claims. Misuse of this process may result in the suspension of your account or other legal consequences' (YouTube, 2015c).

In addition to these warnings YouTube provides services to users if they are accused of infringement, such as the ability to swap the audio track on a video to another one, for example one from their free-to-use audio library.

YouTube staff rely on their users to alert them to inappropriate content; the site is hosted in the USA so US copyright law is cited, where fair use could be argued. Case law has shown that the removal of content from YouTube for copyright infringement is not always straightforward despite the company's stated policy. One particularly noteworthy case was *Lenz vs. Universal Music* from 2007 onwards, also known as the 'dancing baby case' after the content of the video, uploaded by Stephanie Lenz of her 13th-month-old baby dancing to Prince's song 'Let's Go Crazy'. Universal Music, which owns the rights to the Prince recording, had the video removed, and Lenz objected on the basis that the use of the music was fair use. At the time of writing the most recent ruling on the long running case further bolstered the argument for fair use in this and similar cases (Thielman, 2015) and Google also announced it would provide legal support for those relying on a fair use defence (Google, 2015b).

YouTube and e-learning

Complaints continue that YouTube contains inappropriate content, and despite the introduction of the Content ID system and copyright takedown procedure, many still feel YouTube's approach is irresponsible. In some countries access to YouTube is blocked, as it is in many schools. Nevertheless, YouTube is being used by increasing numbers in the education community as a platform to host educational materials, and as a source for teachers to find relevant content produced by others. YouTube's education channel (YouTube EDU; www.youtube.com/edu) was launched in March 2009 and universities in the USA, UK and elsewhere are using YouTube to distribute some of their content. YouTube has several advantages as a platform for hosting video content, provided educational establishments take steps to ensure that their content does not infringe copyright. For example, it can be a useful way of getting wider publicity for training or promotional materials for an institution, and it offers storage space for high quality video content that would otherwise need to be placed on an institutional streaming server.

Using YouTube as a source of content for teaching can be more problematic than using other sources for this purpose as the content might be infringing. Unless they are using videos from official channels (e.g. TV broadcasters or TED Talks), teachers are well advised not to rely on video content from YouTube being available long after they first access it, as it can be removed with little or no warning. If an institution subscribes to a service such as Box of Broadcasts (see Chapter 4, page 100) or Planet eStream it may be best to use this service. Unlike photo-sharing sites, YouTube does not encourage (or make it easy) to download videos, so linking to resources is the safest and easiest way for a teacher to share content with students. YouTube content can be embedded into a variety of other platforms such as blogs and social networking sites relatively easily. Using the 'share' option users can obtain a link to a video and once they have a YouTube account they can bookmark resources and obtain a piece of Hypertext Markup Language (HTML) code to embed the video into a website or VLE. There is also a PowerPoint add-on, which allows teachers to embed a YouTube video into their slideshow that does not require the file to be downloaded from the YouTube site.

Here is some good advice for those using YouTube in teaching:

◆ As with all content on the web, be discerning about who produced the video, if it is good quality and if it might infringe copyright.
◆ If you are encouraging students to create content for uploading to YouTube, ensure that they do not infringe copyright by incorporating content in their videos without permission or where fair dealing would not apply. For example, give them guidance about where they can source music for their production.
◆ Explore the YouTube EDU site and TeacherTube (www.teachertube.com), which contains educational videos (check out more resources in Chapter 3).
◆ Consider advertisement-free alternatives to YouTube such as Box of Broadcasts (BoB National) if available.

Peer to peer file sharing

The most high profile area of copyright-related conflict since the rise of the internet has been the systematic sharing of music and video files using 'peer to peer' technology. The development of the MP3 audio compression format in the 1990s made the transfer of music via the internet possible when combined with software that allowed people to use their domestic computers for 'file sharing'. Although peer to peer technology and file sharing are not in themselves illegal, the unauthorized sharing of copyright-protected works (such as music or films) is. Perhaps the most notorious file sharing service was Napster, created by Shaun Fanning in 1999 and eventually shut down following legal challenges from the music industry. The story of Napster and its demise has been told many times, but is explained clearly, concisely and in the wider context of the development of the internet by John Naughton in *From Gutenberg to Zuckerberg* (2012, 70–6). Since Napster the entertainment and computer industries have done much to regulate how we access music over the internet and, more importantly, how we pay for it. There are now many legal online music services such as Apple iTunes, Spotify and Google Play Music offering nearly all the commercially available music. Although file sharing services have some applications for educational use, such as the sharing of large project files between students, it is likely that sharing third-party copyright content through this kind of platform would be a high risk activity. Those wanting to use multimedia in teaching are advised to read Chapter 3; see also Further Resources on page 245 for an additional list of reading.

Social networking services

Social networking services had been around in various guises since the launch of the world wide web, but reached relative maturity around 2002, with the appearance of sites such as Friendster (www.friendster.com) and MySpace (www.myspace.com). They have become enormously popular in recent years with growing numbers of people throughout the world. Social networking services allow individuals to create a profile to communicate with both existing friends and new contacts with similar interests. Users can upload content such as photos and videos to social networks, create and join groups and share resources with each other.

Facebook (www.facebook.com) rapidly became the social network of choice among the higher education community in the USA and the UK, after its launch in 2005. It was started by Mark Zuckerberg as a website for Harvard students in 2003, but after first extending membership to other universities, it was opened to the world in 2007. In February 2009 it was reported that 175 million people use Facebook but as of November 2015 this figure had grown to 1.55 billion monthly users (Statista, 2015). Social networking services such as LinkedIn (www.linkedin.com) are aimed at the professional sector, whereas services like ResearchGate and Academia.edu are aimed specifically at an academic audience allowing collaboration and sharing of research.

There are several copyright issues to be aware of when using social networking services. Individuals should be particularly wary of social networking services, which inevitably contain a lot of personal information. Some teachers have used social networking services such as Facebook or Twitter for teaching purposes and in December 2015 there was an entire conference devoted to the use of social media in learning in higher education (Sheffield Hallam University, 2015). It involved academics from a wide variety of disciplines exploring how students and staff use social networks in education and the opportunities, challenges and disruptive nature of social media. The Jisc report on higher education in a Web 2.0 world (CLEX, 2009) recognized the engaging nature of social networking services, which is often in contrast to more formal learning spaces such as VLEs. Nevertheless these services should be approached with caution if they are going to be used for teaching purposes. Most social networks are hosted by external companies, so personal data about students and teachers is shared with a third party. It would be unwise to compel students to use third-party services given that some students may feel uncomfortable with using them – either because they are aware of and concerned about the terms and conditions of these services, or because they already use social networking services and prefer to keep their studies and their personal lives separate. There are also several free open-source social networking tools that can be downloaded and several universities host their own social networks to retain ownership of what is often highly personal data. Probably the most widely used of these is Elgg (https://elgg.com). The disadvantage is that students may be reluctant to use a social networking service for their study, in addition to using a VLE.

In this next section we will look specifically at the copyright issues involved with using Facebook and Twitter – two extremely popular social networking sites.

Facebook

The Facebook terms and conditions have been revised a number of times since its launch in 2005, largely following changes to the company's services and in response to concerns over user privacy. The site has clearly stated copyright information that sets out how to report any copyright infringement (Facebook, 2015a). The terms and conditions also state:

- You will not post content or take any action on Facebook that infringes or violates someone else's rights or otherwise violates the law.
- We can remove any content or information you post on Facebook if we believe that it violates this Statement or our policies.
- We will provide you with tools to help you protect your intellectual property rights.

Facebook, 2015b

Facebook allow users to appeal if their content is removed on the grounds that it infringes someone else's copyright and they believe that this was a mistake, but the accounts of those who repeatedly infringe other people's IPR are disabled.

In line with many other sites that rely on user-generated content there is a risk that when an individual uploads content to Facebook, they may infringe the copyright of another. Although Facebook's approach has consistently been to put the responsibility for use of third-party copyright material on the user, it has changed its terms on the ownership of user data, including personal photographs. In early February 2009 it was widely reported in the UK media (Harvey, 2009) that Facebook intended to assert copyright in all content (for example, photographs, messages) that users uploaded to their site, even if users cancelled their account. At that time Facebook was being used by over 175 million people worldwide. Many individuals had uploaded personal content such as photos and videos to

Facebook to share with friends and relatives. The idea that a private company would now own the copyright of this content was therefore a matter of great concern. After widespread protests, this policy was withdrawn several weeks later and the old terms and conditions were reinstated. The number of Facebook users has now grown to over 1.5 billion and the terms maintain a position where users 'own' their content, but give Facebook a broad permissive licence to use it in any way while their account is live:

> you grant us a non-exclusive, transferable, sub-licensable, royalty-free, worldwide license to use any IP content that you post on or in connection with Facebook (IP License). This IP License ends when you delete your IP content or your account unless your content has been shared with others, and they have not deleted it.
>
> Facebook, 2015b

Social networking sites have many advantages over traditional VLEs when engaging students for teaching purposes. Services such as Facebook have also developed robust policies to protect themselves against allegations of copyright infringement. It is tempting to consider these policies as useful models for the e-learning community, as they provide a pragmatic way of allowing users to work creatively while managing the risk that some of them might upload infringing material.

It is worth noting that a social media company has a very different operational model, organizational culture and place in society than an educational establishment. Taking a relatively hands off approach to copyright by setting clear rules of engagement but ultimately leaving it up to rights holders to pick up on the activities of individual users might work for an internet company with millions of users with whom it has a customer–business relationship. However, educational establishments have a duty of care to their staff and students, and therefore one could argue a greater responsibility to provide more guidance and education on appropriate behaviour. This is in contrast to the reliance on safe harbor provisions by commercial internet providers (see page 35).

Twitter

Although first described as a 'micro-blogging' site, Twitter (http://twitter.com) is now regarded as one of the major social and information networking services and has several applications in an educational context. It was launched in 2006 and has attracted considerable media attention not least because of the large number of celebrities who use it. Based around the idea of sharing 'status updates', users register with the site, create a limited profile and then start posting updates. Posts are limited to 140 characters, so rather than overwhelm people with information, Twitter can be a fast and simple way of finding out what people are doing or what topics are making the news. You can choose to 'follow' people, or you can search the site for words or tags, which are indicated with the symbol #. Twitter can be a useful way of sharing links to web-based resources, including photos. The terms of service are clear that users retain the copyright of any content they post to Twitter but:

> By submitting, posting or displaying Content on or through the Services, you grant us a worldwide, non-exclusive, royalty-free license (with the right to sublicense) to use, copy, reproduce, process, adapt, modify, publish, transmit, display and distribute such Content in any and all media or distribution methods (now known or later developed).
>
> Twitter, 2015

Twitter has a copyright policy listed under the terms of service, which asks that users respect others' intellectual property when using the service. It sets out how to report any allegations of copyright infringement and warns users that if they infringe copyright they will have their content removed, and repeat offenders may have their account withdrawn. Twitter is an interesting social media example that has led some to question whether 'tweets' can be protected by copyright given the 140 character restriction, which could make it hard to create a sufficiently original creative expression (Bailey, 2008; Cuban, 2009). Bailey (2008) suggests that the likelihood of copyright infringement on Twitter is very low. It may be possible for even short passages of text (for example a haiku poem) to qualify for copyright protection. More relevantly though, many people use Twitter to share photographs, which has clear copyright implications.

Recent case law has focused on the use of photographs sourced from Twitter by news agencies, which have confirmed that Twitter's terms do not allow third-party media companies to use the images, despite them being available on the open web (Reuters, 2013). It is clear that the process of 'retweeting' content is allowed as it is stated in the terms of use and is one of the defining characteristics of the service. Nonetheless, in the absence of any case law relating specifically to use of Twitter in education, teachers and teaching support staff are well advised to treat it like any other blogging service and to ask for permission or consider educational exceptions if they find content they want to re-use outside the Twitter service.

Social bookmarking and curation tools

Social bookmarking and curation tools are particularly useful for individuals to manage their resources. Instead of using browser-based favourites or bookmarks, links to useful websites can be 'bookmarked' on a website such as Delicious. As is common with many social media services, users create a profile and then store their favourites online so they are accessible from anywhere with an internet connection. They can also be shared with others and searched. In general, most copyright laws recognize that linking to another legitimate and freely accessible website cannot by classed as copyright infringement and is a fundamental part of the web.[1] There are general good practice guidelines about how to avoid 'passing off' another's content as your own, such as avoiding frame links, but social bookmarking sites can be used in education largely without any concerns about infringing copyright. Educators who wish to keep their bookmarks private may prefer not to use a social bookmarking site.

Delicious and Diigo

Delicious (http://delicious.com) and Diigo (www.diigo.com) provide users with the ability to store weblinks. The Delicious terms of use state that users are responsible for any content they upload. While there are unlikely to be any copyright issues associated with users storing URLs to freely accessible websites, the service allows users to add other content such as commentary and tags, so the terms state: 'When you add content to the

Service you are representing that you have all the necessary rights to do so and to enable others to use the content as described in these Terms' (Delicious, 2015).

Diigo is a slightly different type of social bookmarking tool from Delicious; as well as allowing users to bookmark and organize favourites, it also allows them to annotate and archive the material they find useful on the web on a Diigo server. While UK law states that only temporary copies made in the process of communicating content via the web can be made legally, Diigo is a US-based service and operates under the fair use provision in the US Copyright Act. Users of this site in the UK might similarly be able to rely on an exception to copyright if they are using the site for private non-commercial research or study but this would have to pass the fair dealing test (see Chapter 1, pages 18–19). This is Diigo's policy towards copyright:

> You may not post, modify, distribute, or reproduce in any way any copyrighted material, trademarks, or other proprietary information belonging to others without obtaining the prior written consent of the owner of such proprietary rights. It is the policy of Diigo.com to terminate Membership privileges of any Member who repeatedly infringes the copyright rights of others on receipt of prompt notification to Diigo.com by the copyright owner or the copyright owner's legal agent.
>
> Diigo, 2015

The company has a clear policy on how to proceed if someone believes their copyright has been infringed by a Diigo user.

Mendeley and Zotero

Mendeley (https://www.mendeley.com) and Zotero (www.zotero.org) are online reference management tools that work similarly to software such as Endnote and RefWorks. Zotero is a free, open-source plug-in, which automatically senses content in a user's internet browser and allows them to store references online. The latest version of Zotero also allows users to store their PDF files. Zotero is increasingly being used by students in higher education as an alternative to proprietary reference management software. Again the software was developed in the USA where copyright law includes the concept of fair use, but fair dealing in the UK also permits copies of materials to be stored for private study or research. Fundamentally this tool is a personal reference management tool and therefore any references including the full text are stored in a personal library, rather than a public archive. Although the terms of use make it clear that users are responsible for respecting third-party intellectual property (Zotero, 2015), because sharing is restricted to links and metadata there are no real copyright implications of using this software in teaching.

Mendeley runs either in a web browser or via a mobile or desktop app and also allows references and PDFs to be stored in the cloud. It was initially developed by three German PhD students and was designed to support the open sharing of academic publications. However, the major publishing house Elsevier bought Mendeley in 2013, which led to concerns from those in the open access community that Elsevier would restrict the sharing ethos and functionality of the service. Mendeley's popularity continues to grow, not least because of the way that large collections of PDFs can be managed effectively in the cloud. As with other social media and cloud-based services the terms state that users must not:

> send, knowingly receive, upload, download, use or re-use any Academic Papers without authorization. You may perform these actions only if you are the copyright owner, have the copyright owner's permission, are permitted to do so under your publishing agreement or your institution's license agreement or under license from an Open Access database or under a Creative Commons license.
>
> Mendeley, 2015

Users should therefore be clear that from a legal perspective use of Mendeley is no different than the use any other kind of online sharing platform. Despite the ease by which PDFs can be added to the system and catalogued, the same care should be taken not to make or communicate copies of copyright content unless licences or exceptions cover the use.

Evernote

Evernote (https://evernote.com) is a popular cloud-based note-taking, organization and archive tool that works via a web browser or through dedicated mobile and desktop apps. There are a range of similar productivity tools available including Microsoft OneNote and Google Keep. Evernote allows users to create and share their own notes and scrape content from the internet. As with other similar tools, the terms of use put the responsibility for respecting copyright onto the end user (Evernote, 2015a). Evernote has an 'IP compliance program', which allows rights holders to request infringing material is removed (Evernote, 2015b). Once again users should be clear that despite the ease by which content can be 'clipped' from the internet and shared with other users, the same copyright issues remain as with any other digital service.

Dropbox

Dropbox (https://www.dropbox.com/) is a cloud-based file storage solution, which has become highly popular due to its versatility. It has a browser-based version and dedicated mobile and desktop apps, so files are available on multiple devices and backed up in the cloud. The free version offers up to 5GB of storage space and the shared folder function makes it ideal for collaborative working. Although some institutions have policies that prohibit or discourage its use because of concerns about data protection, it is widely used in higher education by academic and administrative staff. For example one US university found that 12,000 of its employees and students used Dropbox accounts (EdSurge, 2015). Shared files and folders are one of the key benefits of this service, and responsibility lies with the user to respect copyright in the material they share. If a rights holder becomes aware of anyone infringing their copyright they can provide a notice of alleged infringement (Dropbox, 2015). While there have not been many notable examples of infringing uses of copyright content using Dropbox in education to date, those providing copyright guidance should be aware of the ease with which files can be shared. This could lead to inadvertent infringement because of the way that shared folders appear to be local folders and might stop people from taking the same care as when using institutionally hosted services like a VLE.

Pinterest

Pinterest (https://uk.pinterest.com) is a visual discovery tool; since its launch in 2010 it has grown to become one of the major social media services, with 28% of online adults in the USA using it by September 2014 (Pew Internet, 2014). It was conceived as an online pinboard allowing users to curate images from the internet by 'pinning' them to 'boards' set up on their profile. The service has proved popular with some in education, partly because of the ease of sharing visually appealing information such as infographics. The service quickly raised copyright issues because of the built-in functionality to copy images from the internet regardless of their copyright status and upload them to a user's collection in a different context. This controversy has subsided somewhat with the general acceptance of 'pinning' as a way of providing links to other content. Also, recently introduced functionality, which reinstates attribution to the original source from some services (such as Flickr) if the Pinterest user has removed it, and another tool which allows other websites to 'opt out' of their content being pinned, has helped meet some concerns (Wikipedia, 2015a). However, it is clear that repinning copyright material on an open online service like Pinterest without permission is an infringement so users should be careful only to pin licensed or out-of-copyright content. As with many other social media services Pinterest's copyright policy provides a mechanism to report copyright infringements and Pinterest will terminate a user's account for repeat abuse of copyright (Pinterest, 2015). Any educators who want to promote the use of Pinterest and similar image sharing sites should ensure that all users are aware of the copyright implications and that they have a clear mechanism to alert their home institution if a question of liability occurs (Jisc, 2015c).

Massive open online courses

The purpose of this section of the book is not to provide a detailed overview or critique of MOOCs but to explore the copyright challenges that they present, which are very similar to those involved when making any openly licensed content available. MOOCs are free online courses offered to large numbers of students and made available freely and openly on the web. They are a development in distance learning and since 2008 many elite universities have entered the MOOC arena, often working in partnership with one of the large hosting platforms that now exist, such as Coursera, Udacity and EdX in the USA and FutureLearn in the UK. The name massive open online course (MOOC) was coined in 2008 following the launch of the course 'Connectivism and Connective Knowledge' by George Siemens and Stephen Downes, where 25 fee-paying campus-based students were joined by over 2000 members of the public who took the course online for free. Their model which came to be known as a cMOOC (connected MOOC) contrasted with later xMOOCs, which were often developed by universities in conjunction with commercial MOOC providers. cMOOCs tend to focus on community and the creation of knowledge by students whereas xMOOCs resemble more traditional courses, where content is delivered to students via a standard curriculum.

MOOCs arguably reached the height of their popularity in 2012 but are still a hot topic in higher education. They have been criticized for the high drop-out and low completion rate and the fact that many of the students who take these courses already have degree level education. Critics have argued MOOCs have not truly opened up education to the world for free and that finding a sustainable business model for MOOCs is one of the greatest challenges for universities (BIS, 2013). MOOCs are typically produced by a course team, similar to the production of other distance learning courses, because of the need to manage the learning process and produce engaging learning resources. This contrasts significantly with the way traditional courses are developed, which are often led by one or two members of academic staff. The nature of the way the courses are developed means that ownership of the resulting intellectual property can be far more complex. They 'present complex copyright questions that can challenge the relationship between the institution and its faculty and students' (EDUCAUSE, 2013) largely because of their open nature. Some of the challenges EDUCAUSE (2013) identified were the need to:

◆ educate academic staff about copyright and open content to populate their course, particularly if it is based on a course they may teach in a traditional 'closed' fashion and where material might have been used under a licence or copyright exception
◆ determine ownership of a MOOC if it includes content and probably significant contributions from several members of staff in its design and associated learning resources

◆ protect the intellectual property of the institution that is making content available in an open way
◆ determine ownership of student generated content when students are not registered at the university in a traditional way, or paying fees
◆ determine the terms of use entered into with a commercial MOOC-hosting platform and ownership of the course content.

Educational establishments considering launching a MOOC or similar open course typically investigate copyright and IPR to avoid potential issues. Guidance and advice is offered by the MOOC platform hosts and bodies such as Jisc (Kernohan, 2014). Case study 4 in Chapter 3 discusses the approach taken at UCL to develop open courses and the steps taken to avoid copyright issues. One method advocated by Kernohan (2014) is to rely on open content, such as material licensed under Creative Commons for use in a MOOC. This avoids the need to obtain copyright clearance. Typically permission costs by publishers are based on student numbers and therefore the open nature of MOOCs may incur high permission charges. Many MOOCs include content such as video that has been created in-house and relies on open access readings. Copyright exceptions may be used to include small amounts of content in MOOCs, provided it falls under fair use or fair dealing, but this involves an element of risk, because of the open nature of the course. Fowler and Smith (2013) outlined the way a copyright and permissions service for MOOC instructors was created at Duke University in the USA. They highlight how MOOC platforms such as Coursera strongly discourage academics from relying on third-party content to include in MOOCs. Fowler and Smith found that the time required to negotiate copyright and permission was one of the greatest challenges – almost 300 hours were spent negotiating this (Fowler and Smith, 2013). However, in many cases permission was obtained for free, and in some instances with the payment of a fee. Any institution considering and exploring developing MOOCs should seek advice from the institutional copyright officer or librarians with an understanding of licences and exceptions to copyright at an early stage. In many ways MOOCs are no different from other forms of online learning, but because of their open nature – where anyone around the world can register on the course and gain access to the content – they are more visible. There is a far greater risk of a copyright infringement being noted by a rights holder, so institutions have tended to become more aware of copyright and IPR issues. Consequently they are more likely to look for openly licensed content, rather than rely on educational exceptions or licences.

Emerging trends

The pace of technological change shows no sign of slowing and there are huge numbers of tools with educational applications being developed all the time. While trends such as wearable technology, 3D printing and immersive virtual reality are becoming mainstream, it is impossible to know exactly how these will manifest themselves and what the impact might be on education and its relationship with copyright. As we have seen from the current breed of cloud-based services summarized in this chapter, a tension remains between the ease by which copyright laws can be infringed through the use of sophisticated technology and the terms of use of these tools. These products and services put the responsibility on the shoulders of the end user, many of whom do not understand the legal implications. If computing power and data transfer speeds continue to increase exponentially it is possible that digital technology will disrupt copyright even further, although we do not yet know how. Most of the technologies described in this chapter did not exist ten years ago and many of those who created the technology did not understand exactly how it would be used and what its wider implications would be. For example the founders of Twitter could not have predicted that they would be creating the global interlinked information system that exists today.

Jisc (2016) has recently identified some areas that they recommend institutions should consider when thinking about the use of digital technologies for education, many of which have major implications for copyright. First, Jisc argues that cloud computing will inevitably become more powerful and cost-effective, so institutions could start to use these technologies to the same extent as private consumers. Therefore educational establishments will have to face the IPR challenges that cloud computing presents, as discussed earlier in this chapter.

Second, Jisc suggests that the ability for people in organizations to make decisions based on the data created in and around them provides a major opportunity. Digital services and devices generate huge amounts of data about people's behaviour, which many commercial organizations already use to understand and predict what their customers want. Educational institutions could do something similar with students, which in turn could help inform more inclusive and personalized learning experiences. Learning analytics technologies can track how a student is responding to their studies, not just in the classroom but whenever they interact with an online educational resource like a VLE. Although there are a number of ethical considerations with tracking people's activity in this way (Kay, Korn and Oppenheim, 2012), this could lead to the creation of more personalized teaching materials. However, once again copyright presents yet another challenge to those wanting to take this more flexible approach. Providing many different types of copyright learning resources to students, potentially remixed and recontextualized according to their specific needs, is difficult when the terms under which they are provided are restrictive and do not allow adaptation or inclusion in new works (Kalshoven, Teunissen and van Ginkel, 2015). This in turn presents another argument for investment in open educational resources that allow teachers to work more flexibly, but does not resolve the issue of using third-party material, which is not available under permissive re-use terms. Therefore pressure from educational users to adopt harmonized, global copyright exceptions is likely to continue as the potential for technologically enhanced learning gets even greater.

Many believe that adoption of so called 'open practice' will increase and initiatives such as the Open Textbook Network (https://research.cehd.umn.edu/otn) in the USA may gain more traction throughout the world. If the consistent growth of Wikipedia over the last 15 years from zero to over five million articles (Wikipedia, 2016) or the number of Creative Commons licensed works to over one billion is any indication, there is widespread support for this way of perceiving human creativity. Any further adoption of open practice in education is likely to inform and drive more development of devices and services that specifically take advantage of it.

The use of unmonitored and illicit digital spaces shows no sign of declining. Technologies such as the 'dark web' allow people to transact with each other without control from government or industry (Bartlett, 2015). This facilitates illegal trading, but also appeals to those who want to maintain privacy for other reasons. The widespread use of Sci-Hub, an illegal repository of academic papers set up by Kazakhstani student

Alexandra Elbakyan in 2011, was receiving significant media coverage in early 2016 (Bohannon, 2016). The legal action taken against the site by Elsevier is likely to have a major impact on the way copyright is perceived in education.

One current development that is likely to have an impact on copyright and education is the Copyright Hub (www.copyrighthub.co.uk), which was set up as a non-profit organization following a recommendation in the Hargreaves Review (see Chapter 1, pages 17–18). This in turn led to a review by Richard Hooper (IPO, 2012) to explore the idea of a 'digital copyright exchange'. The idea was to make medium to low value licensing transactions more efficient. This would therefore address the widespread use of copyright content without permission, or situations where people decide not to use or license copyright content because clearing it was too difficult or expensive. Although the Copyright Hub has a website, it is not primarily a web location that a user is expected to navigate to, rather it is an organization that is developing tools to automate the licensing process. The technology it has developed acts as an enabling service, identifying copyright works and connecting the owner with potential users, wherever they or the work happens to be located. Although the Copyright Hub has not yet reached its full potential the basic technology has been developed which proves it is possible to link potential users of copyright works with the owners, allowing copyright owners to use their preferred licensing mechanism regardless of where the user finds the work. All of this is done in the background without the need for in-depth investigation on behalf of the user. The obvious application of this in an educational context is to check whether those accessing material from an educational institution are covered by a blanket licence. However, if the Hub is adopted by individuals and organizations it could become a key component in the discussion of how licences and exceptions operate in the world of education. In addition to the Copyright Hub potentially giving rights holder representatives an argument that use of exceptions do not apply to an online learning context, it could also disrupt the business models of the collecting societies (such as CLA), which have to run relatively large organizations to acquire and process data relating to copyright ownership and usage. If the Hub were to create a truly level playing field for licensing of content, this could support innovative ways of providing licensed teaching materials such as finding and compiling them at the point of need.

It could also give educational institutions, and those who work in them, greater opportunities to exploit and maximize the impact of the copyright material that they create, without relying on traditional content aggregators.

Despite the potential of the Copyright Hub to bring efficient licensing to the wider internet, collecting societies like CLA will continue to build their own digital platforms in an attempt to reinforce their relationships with educational customers and sell them additional products such as consultancy and additional content storage. The Copyright Hub intends to make all rights based digital platforms interoperable so this could make these platforms smoother and easier to use, particularly when using different types of copyright work. It is not yet clear what the future picture will be, but it is likely that within the next five to ten years the environment will once again have shifted dramatically.

Conclusion

There are a number of common issues regarding emerging technologies and how they protect both an individual's copyright and the copyright of others. One of the greatest considerations when using many of the services described here in an educational context is who takes responsibility for any resulting copyright infringement. Many of the most popular social media services are now owned by one of the large internet companies (such as Google or Yahoo) and have well established copyright and privacy policies in addition to detailed terms and conditions of use, all of which are designed to protect their private interests. At the same time as these services are evolving, e-learning practitioners are struggling to understand to what extent they can or should influence the online behaviour of teachers or students who are less familiar with copyright law. Staff often feel uncomfortable acting as a 'policing' body over what can and cannot be uploaded into the VLE, but an understanding of copyright and other ethical issues needs to feature in any digital literacies programmes whether they are for staff or students. This chapter emphasizes that by placing the responsibility on the individual, through clearly stated terms of use, social media services have found an effective way of managing risk in the use of their services.

Currently, many in education perceive that responsibility lies with an institution to inform teachers about copyright law, and that if something goes wrong the institution should simply cover this under its insurance arrangements. However, in today's internet-enabled world everyone is individually responsible for taking an ethical approach to the use of copyright material. Drawing direct comparisons between the ways in which educational establishments and internet companies manage copyright risk can be problematic. The answer to the question 'if Google can do it, why can't my school, college or university?' involves many factors. These include the fact that Google's service is based on US jurisdiction, which involves fair use, and the company's enormous economic power and access to legal expertise. Google also has a unique relationship with its customers and third-party rights holders, some of whom it partners, others of whom it is being sued by. Educational establishments therefore need to develop holistic approaches to the use of copyright content in the connected environment, which balance their need to manage institutional risk while providing support and creative freedom to their staff and students. Ideally this should be done by creating clear policies including takedown procedures for services such as the VLE, and guidance communicated clearly and in a way that is practical, relevant and available to its audience at the point of need. It makes sense to provide a consistent set of messages about copyright that apply to use of the VLE and the institutional website, social media and other internet services. For more on communicating messages about copyright through education and training initiatives see Chapter 6.

Note

1 Recent EU case law has proved rather confused on this point, although for the purposes of this book one can assume that as long as the content is not clearly infringing and the link does not deliberately circumvent some kind of registration or pay wall there is no problem.

References

Anderson, P. (2007) *What is Web 2.0? Ideas, technologies and implications for education*, JISC Technology and Standards Watch, www.jisc.ac.uk/media/documents/techwatch/tsw0701b.pdf [accessed 6 April 2016].

Bailey, J. (2008) Copyright and Twitter, *Blog Herald*, 5 May, www.blogherald.com/2008/05/05/copyright-and-twitter [accessed 6 April 2016].

Bartlett, J. (2015) Jamie Bartlett: how the mysterious dark net is going mainstream, video file, June, https://www.ted.com/talks/jamie_bartlett_how_the_mysterious_ dark_net_is_going_mainstream?language=en [accessed 6 April 2016].

BIS (2013) *The Maturing of the MOOC: literature review of massive open online courses and other forms of online distance education*, BIS Research Paper 130, Department for Business, Innovation & Skills, www.gov.uk/government/uploads/system/uploads/attachment_ data/file/240193/13-1173-maturing-of-the-mooc.pdf [accessed 6 April 2016].

Bohannon, J. (2016) Who's Downloading Pirated Papers? Everyone, *Science*, **352** (6285), 29 April, 508–12, www.sciencemag.org/news/2016/04/whos-downloading-pirated-papers-everyone [accessed 6 April 2016].

CLEX (2009) *Higher Education in a Web 2.0 World*, Committee of Inquiry into the Changing Learner Experience, Jisc, www.jisc.ac.uk/media/documents/publications/heweb20rptv1.pdf [accessed 6 April 2016].

Cornish, G. (2015) *Copyright: interpreting the law for libraries, archives and information services*, 6th edn, Facet Publishing.

Cuban, M. (2009) Are Tweets Copyrighted?, Blog Maverick, http://blogmaverick.com/2009/03/29/are-tweets-copyrighted [accessed 6 April 2016].

Delicious (2015) Delicious Terms of Service, https://delicious.com/terms [accessed 6 April 2016].

Diigo (2015) Diigo.com Terms of Use Agreement, https://www.diigo.com/terms [accessed 6 April 2016].

Dropbox (2015) Dropbox DMCA Policy, https://www.dropbox.com/dmca [accessed 6 April 2016].

EdSurge (2015) Dropbox Hops to School With New Education Team, https://www.edsurge.com/news/2015-06-29-dropbox-hops-to-school-with-new-education-team [accessed 6 April 2016].

EDUCAUSE (2013) Copyright Challenges in a MOOC Environment, *Educause Brief*, 29 July, www.educause.edu/library/resources/copyright-challenges-mooc-environment [accessed 6 April 2016].

Evernote (2015a) Evernote Terms of Service, https://evernote.com/legal/tos.php [accessed 6 April 2016].

Evernote (2015b) Evernote, IP Compliance Program, https://evernote.com/legal/ip_compliance.php [accessed 6 April 2016].

Facebook (2015a) Facebook Desktop Help: about copyright, https://www.facebook.com/help/249141925204375 [accessed 6 April 2016].

Facebook (2015b) *Terms of Use*, https://www.facebook.com/legal/terms [accessed 6 April 2016].

Flickr (2015) Flickr Commons, https://www.flickr.com/commons [accessed 6 April 2016].

Fowler, L. and Smith, K. (2013) Drawing the Blueprint as We Build: setting up a library-based copyright and permissions service for MOOCs, *D-Lib Magazine*, **19** (7/8), www.dlib.org/dlib/july13/fowler/07fowler.html [accessed 6 April 2016].

Getty Images (2015) Embed, www.gettyimages.co.uk/resources/embed [accessed 6 April 2016].

Google (2015a) Google Privacy & Terms, https://www.google.com/intl/en/policies/terms [accessed 6 April 2016].

Google (2015b) Google Public Policy Blog: a step toward protecting fair use on YouTube, http://googlepublicpolicy.blogspot.co.uk/2015/11/a-step-toward-protecting-fair-use-on.html [accessed 6 April 2016].

Hargreaves, I. (2011) *Digital Opportunity: a review of intellectual property and growth*, Intellectual Property Office, https://www.gov.uk/government/uploads/system/uploads/attachment_data/file/32563/ipreview-finalreport.pdf [accessed 6 April 2016].

Harvey, M. (2009) Users Force Facebook to Withdraw Controversial 'Copyright' Plan, *Social Network Times*, https://socialnetworktimes.wordpress.com/2009/02/21/users-force-facebook-to-withdraw-controversial-copyright-plan [accessed 6 April 2016].

IPO (2012) Rights and Wrongs: is copyright licensing fit for purpose for the digital age? The first report of the Digital Copyright Exchange Feasibility Study, http://webarchive.nationalarchives.gov.uk/20140603093549/ www.ipo.gov.uk/dce-report-phase1.pdf [accessed 6 April 2016].

Jisc (2015a) Guides, https://www.jisc.ac.uk/guides [accessed 6 April 2016].

Jisc (2015b) The Future of Cloud Computing, https://www.jisc.ac.uk/reports/the-future-of-cloud-computing [accessed 6 April 2016].

Jisc (2015c) Pinterest, Image Sharing Websites and the Law, https://www.jisc.ac.uk/guides/pinterest-image-sharing-websites-and-the-law [accessed 6 April 2016].

Jisc (2016) Horizon Scanning: what's next in digital technologies and how can we help?, https://www.jisc.ac.uk/rd/projects/horizon-scanning [accessed 6 April 2016].

Jisc (2008) Web 2.0 and Intellectual Property Rights, www.webarchive.org.uk/wayback/archive/20130607094401 http://www.jisc.ac.uk/publications/briefingpapers/2008/bpweb20iprv 1.aspx [accessed 6 April 2016].

Jisc/SLC (n.d.) Strategic Content Alliance Blog: Intellectual Property Rights (IPR) and Licensing, https://sca.jiscinvolve.org/wp/allpublications/ipr-publications/ [accessed 6 April 2016].

John, N. (2013) The Social Logics of Sharing, *The Communication Review*, **16** (3), 113–31.

Kalshoven, L., Teunissen, B. and van Ginkel, C. (2015) Copyright & Education: innovation made difficult, Communia, https://medium.com/copyright-untangled/copyright-education-innovation-made-difficult-98dea4437664#.f2kwg35ap [accessed 6 April 2016].

Kay, D., Korn, N. and Oppenheim, C. (2012) *Legal, Risk and Ethical Aspects of Analytics in Higher Education*, http://publications.cetis.org.uk/wp-content/uploads/2012/11/ Legal-Risk-and-Ethical-Aspects-of-Analytics-in-Higher-Education-

Vol1-No6.pdf [accessed 6 April 2016].

Kernohan, D. (2014) Risky Business: make sure your MOOCs are not exposing you to legal challenge. Jisc Blog, 6 March, www.jisc.ac.uk/blog/risky-business-make-sure-your-moocs-arent-exposing-you-to-legal-challenge-06-mar-2014 [accessed 6 April 2016].

Mendeley (2015) Terms of Use, https://www.mendeley.com/terms/ [accessed 6 April 2016].

Naughton, J. (2012) *From Gutenberg to Zuckerberg: what you really need to know about the Internet*, Quercus.

Ofcom (2015) *The Communications Market Report*, http://stakeholders.ofcom.org.uk/binaries/research/cmr/cmr15/CMR_UK_2015.pdf [accessed 6 April 2016].

Oppenheim, C. (2012) *No Nonsense Guide to Legal Issues in Web 2.0 and Cloud Computing*, Facet Publishing.

Pew Internet (2014) Social Media Update 2014, www.pewinternet.org/2015/01/09/social-media-update-2014/ [accessed 6 April 2016].

Pinterest (2015) Copyright, https://about.pinterest.com/en/copyright.

Reuters (2013) News Outlets Improperly Used Photos Posted to Twitter: judge, www.reuters.com/article/us-socialmedia-copyright-ruling-idUSBRE90E11P20130115.

Sheffield Hallam University (2015) 2015 Social Media for Learning in Higher EducationConference, https://blogs.shu.ac.uk/socmedhe [accessed 6 April 2016].

Statista (2015) Leading Social Networks Worldwide as of November 2015, Ranked by Number of Active Users (in Millions), www.statista.com/statistics/272014/global-social-networks-ranked-by-number-of-users [accessed 6 April 2016].

TechCrunch (2015) Flickr at 10: 1m photos shared per day, 170% increase since making 1TB free, http://techcrunch.com/2014/02/10/flickr-at-10-1m-photos-shared-per-day-170-increase-since-making-1tb-free [accessed 6 April 2016].

Thielman, S. (2015) YouTube 'dancing Baby' Case Prompts Fair Use Ruling on Copyrighted Videos, *Guardian*, 15 September, www.theguardian.com/technology/2015/sep/15/youtube-dancing-baby-copyright-videos [accessed 6 April 2016].

Twitter (2015) Terms of Service,
http://twitter.com/tos [accessed 6 April 2016].

UCISA (2015) Social Media Toolkit: copyright and IPR, Universities and
Colleges Information Systems Association,
www.ucisa.ac.uk/groups/exec/socialmedia/chap9/chapt9_2.aspx
[accessed 6 April 2016].

Wikimedia Foundation (2015) Terms of Use,
http://wikimediafoundation.org/wiki/Terms_of_Use [accessed
6 April 2016].

Wikipedia (2015a) Timeline of Pinterest,
https://en.wikipedia.org/wiki/Timeline_of_Pinterest [accessed
6 April 2016].

Wikipedia (2015b) Web 2.0,
https://en.wikipedia.org/wiki/Web_2.0 [accessed 6 April 2016].

Wikipedia (2016) Modelling Wikipedia's Growth,
https://en.wikipedia.org/wiki/Wikipedia:Modelling_Wikipedia%27s_
growth [accessed 6 April 2016].

WordPress (2009) Terms of Service,
http://en.wordpress.com/tos [accessed 6 April 2016].

WordPress (2015) WordPress Support: user guideline,
https://en.support.wordpress.com/user-guidelines [accessed 6 April
2016].

YouTube (2015a) Statistics,
https://www.youtube.com/yt/press/en-GB/statistics.html [accessed
6 April 2016].

YouTube (2015b) How Content ID works,
https://support.google.com/youtube/answer/2797370?hl=en-GB
[accessed 6 April 2016].

YouTube (2015c) Copyright on You Tube,
https://www.youtube.com/yt/copyright/en-GB/ [accessed 6 April
2016].

Zotero (2015) Zotero Terms of Service,
https://www.zotero.org/support/terms/terms_of_service [accessed
6 April 2016].

6 Copyright education and training

Introduction

As the digital learning environment develops it is becoming increasingly important to offer copyright education and training for teachers, lecturers, librarians, learning technologists, administrative staff, students and researchers. Acquiring and demonstrating the appropriate knowledge, skills and behaviours to enable the ethical creation and use of copyright material has been referred to as 'copyright literacy' (Morrison and Secker, 2015). An IPO and NUS study (NUS, 2012) found that students in all disciplines, not just creative subjects, wanted to know more about copyright, and a discussion paper by the UK Government's intellectual property adviser (Weatherley, 2014) recommended that copyright education should be embedded in the school curriculum within a range of subject areas. In some universities an understanding of copyright is being taught to students as part of digital literacy or entrepreneurship programmes, so students understand how to respect others' intellectual property and protect their own. It can be far easier to infringe copyright in the online environment than in the classroom because digital technology facilitates the copying and sharing of learning materials, and learning activities that previously took place face to face are far more visible and open to scrutiny in a digital space. For example, in the UK higher education sector, the CLA periodically audits institutions by checking their VLE. In Chapter 4 this book discussed the relative ease with which lecturers and students can distribute many born digital files without realizing the legal implications that follow. This chapter describes how copyright literacy can be embedded into existing teaching and training programmes and regarded as part of improving teaching quality and developing open practices for the sharing of teaching materials.

A range of external bodies provide copyright education services for staff in educational establishments. Professional bodies for librarians such as the Chartered Institute of Library and Information Professionals (CILIP) and Aslib offer copyright training courses and have done so for many years, and several independent consultants also work in this area. Other organizations offer copyright training that focuses on particular types of resources; for example, Jisc Digital Media, the BUFVC and the Open University offer copyright courses for those producing multimedia content. There are also a range of training opportunities available for those in the cultural heritage sector, for example from bodies such as the Archives and Records Association and the Collections Trust. The Association of Learned and Professional Society Publishers offers courses for those working in the publishing industry. For a full list of copyright training providers, including some recently produced copyright MOOCs, see the section 'Further resources'.

Some courses offered by external bodies may only be suitable for particular groups of staff, such as library or archives staff, and not appropriate for teaching or administrative staff. Therefore, often the most cost-effective and efficient means of delivering training to groups of staff or students is through in-house education and training programmes. This chapter outlines the set up and organization of copyright education programmes and identifies suitable resources to support staff who deliver them in higher education organizations. The case study describes how an innovative games-based approach to learning, developed by the authors of the book, can help engage staff and students in copyright education and provide a more informal approach to learning about copyright. Where there is an institutional copyright officer it is likely that they are the best person to deliver the teaching; in other institutions it may be appropriate for a number of staff to take on this role in order to deliver a comprehensive and embedded copyright education programme. The chapter goes on to examine the intended audience of the training programme and the method of training – whether face-to-face or online. Finally it looks at how to develop support materials, such as paper or online guides, and strategies for dealing with the host of queries that copyright discussions inevitably lead to.

Throughout this book we have considered a wide variety of copyright issues that arise when teaching and learning in an online environment. It is essential that those working in this field get a good overview of copyright so they understand what they can and cannot do and to mitigate risk. For this reason, being able to offer in-house copyright training should form an important component in any organization's staff development provision. However, although addressing institutional risk is important, the consideration of copyright and IPR issues needs to be reframed within organizations as part of a wider discussion about ethics and respect for others because it is central to how the institution uses the information and data that it owns, and that which belongs to others. With an increasing move towards more open models of publishing, open education and open educational practices (see Chapter 1), knowing what rights exist within works and how they can be used is essential to enhancing teaching quality.

The copyright educator, trainer or teacher

Deciding who should deliver copyright education or training may be a straightforward matter in institutions where there is a designated copyright officer who has responsibility for advice and support in relation to such matters. Needless to say, apart from in very small institutions copyright education cannot remain the preserve of one person if it is to become part of the institutional culture. Therefore an important part of the copyright officer's role is to cascade their learning to others. In many smaller organizations, such as further education colleges and schools, or in public sector and charitable organizations, copyright officer roles are relatively rare. In a UK survey of the library and cultural heritage sector (Morrison and Secker, 2015), 64% of institutions were found to have a copyright officer or designated person with responsibility for copyright issues in particular. This figure was much lower outside the higher education sector and elsewhere in Europe. Consequently, many people reading this book may well be doing so because there is no copyright officer in their institution. The decision to create such a post requires some consideration, not least because of the knowledge and experience such a person requires. Nonetheless, institutions are urged to consider establishing such a post, or to ensure that one or more dedicated members of staff have responsibility for copyright issues written into their job descriptions. Case Study 1 in Chapter 1 provides an example of how one institution, Brunel University, deals with copyright matters through a dedicated post.

Many smaller educational establishments may not have the resources to create a dedicated copyright officer role. If this is the case, it is recommended that managers support one or (ideally) more individuals to develop their understanding of copyright so they can provide training and advice, within the institution, and highlight areas of concern. This responsibility may fall on a member (or members) of staff within the library, learning resources centre, educational development unit or learning technology department. It may be someone responsible for signing and managing collective licences (such as the CLA Licence), or licences for software and electronic resources. Some institutions might consider it more appropriate that a senior member of administrative staff should take on this responsibility and others may have a legal or information compliance team that deal with matters such as data protection and freedom of information requests. Copyright and IPR issues are sometimes seen as sitting naturally with these responsibilities. Whoever has responsibility for copyright does not need a legal qualification but should have:

◆ a good overview of the copyright laws of their respective country as described in this book – there are also training courses and guidance from professional bodies, other books and a variety of online resources that provide an excellent grounding (see the list at the end of this book)
◆ familiarity with licences in the digital environment for subscription and freely available online resources
◆ an understanding of broader intellectual property issues around scholarly communication, such as knowledge of open-source software, open access, open education and the Creative Commons licensing model
◆ an understanding and an ability to communicate that they are not providing formal legal advice and are not personally responsible for the actions of others; decisions relating to copyright risk are best made in collaboration with the person or team carrying out the activity
◆ a network of support for referring questions that go beyond their

knowledge or understanding, which may involve some means of gaining access to legal counsel if the need arises or advice from academics in a law school. In higher education in the UK Jisc employs a legal specialist who can offer advice on copyright and IPR issues. Membership of the JISCmail list LIS-Copyseek, to which queries can be routed, enables those dealing with copyright to seek advice from colleagues in similar roles at other institutions.

Finally it is highly recommended that more than one person has a good working knowledge of copyright in order to cover staff absences, ensure a reasonable workload and provide different perspectives on an issue. There is also considerable value in building a network of people within an organization who have a broad understanding of copyright, rather than relying on one person to deal with this alone. Building up a network of contacts in other institutions can also be invaluable to provide support and guidance when new topics of concern arise, or when seeking a second opinion on a complex or contentious question.

Developing a copyright literacy programme

As we have seen in earlier chapters, the widespread use of VLEs and other online learning systems in education makes it far easier than in the past for staff to inadvertently infringe copyright by sharing files with students. Many academic staff are unaware that e-mailing files to students or uploading copyright materials to the VLE is a 'restricted act'. Most institutions have invested significantly in education and training programmes that provide staff with the pedagogical and technical skills they need to design and create effective online learning. While there is no legal requirement also to offer copyright education, it is good practice to do so. For those in UK higher education, the CLA Licence requires institutions to undergo periodic audits of their scanning process. The CLA audit (CLA, 2014) looks for evidence that staff and students in licensed institutions receive guidance and training about the terms of the licence and copyright issues more generally. The audit also looks for evidence about how an institution tells its student population about restrictions on scanning, and how the institution 'pursues infringement of copyright-protected material by staff'(CLA, 2014).

Aside from any legal obligations, providing copyright education forms an important part of a well rounded staff development programme and helps ensure quality is maintained in teaching materials. Institutions that do not offer any copyright education are well advised to undertake a risk assessment to explore the possible implications of a copyright infringement claim. In the worst case scenario a rights holder, for example a large publisher, might decide to pursue a case of copyright infringement. A comprehensive education programme, alongside robust terms of use for the VLE and a notice and takedown policy (see section 'Further resources' for examples), all indicate that the institution takes copyright infringement seriously. Institutions that can demonstrate that all staff received copyright training might be better placed to defend themselves in a copyright infringement case. Those without an education programme might be seen as negligent or even complicit in fostering a culture where copyright infringement is tolerated. It is standard practice in many organizations for staff contracts or terms of employment to state explicitly that during the course of their employment staff must respect copyright and other laws, therefore ignorance is rarely a defence. At many universities respect for copyright and IPR is also part of the conditions of use of IT facilities. Ultimately copyright infringement cases can result in the organization paying a fine, but they are perhaps a greater risk to an institution's reputation. While individual members of staff are unlikely to face personal prosecution, their reputation may also suffer if they are shown to be acting without due care and attention. To avoid blame on either side, a robust copyright education programme and a clear policy on the responsibilities of all staff and students is advised. This is particularly important when preparing materials for use on the VLE, as teaching staff may also implicate other staff members such as learning support staff or administrative staff by asking them to upload infringing materials.

Embedding copyright literacy in the institution

Once the decision has been taken to provide a copyright education programme, some thought should be given to the method of delivery. Standalone copyright courses inevitably suffer from poor attendance, with many teaching staff citing lack of time and viewing copyright as a low priority for their professional development. Very few educational institutions make copyright education mandatory and therefore some staff can easily avoid attending copyright courses or view it as a session that might tell them about all the things they cannot do. Therefore it is essential to develop a positive message about copyright literacy and to offer a range of tailored (and well publicized) courses and online support materials. Any online materials should avoid legal jargon and be written in an accessible 'what you need to know' style, for example including frequently asked questions about copyright issues. By providing a suite of copyright support options, organizations go some way towards protecting themselves from possible litigation. Offering training to new staff (particularly new teachers) is also important, but an embedded approach to copyright literacy is often the most successful approach, providing copyright advice in context, for example as part of the technical hands-on training sessions attended by teachers using the VLE, or giving advice and guidance about how to find copyright-free or openly licensed images in a workshop about finding and using images in teaching. This type of workshop raises the issue of copyright in the context of a positive activity that members of staff will find helpful for their teaching. In this case staff may want to illustrate their lecture slides using images, so the focus can be on providing good sources of images that can be re-used (such as those in free image banks, or images licensed using Creative Commons). See Chapter 3 for more details about sources of openly licensed image collections that can be recommended in this type of workshop.

In developing a copyright education programme it is useful to carry out a review or audit of the training courses currently on offer at your institution and whether it might be appropriate to embed some copyright advice into any existing workshops; for example, a course about creating a website, or uploading resources to the VLE, could remind staff that they should only use material where they own the copyright or else they will need to obtain permission. The review or audit is likely to involve speaking to as many different people and teams as possible about the training and advice that they currently provide to staff. The in-house staff development unit is a good place to start for supplying a list of courses currently on offer to staff. If your institution does not have a dedicated staff development team, you may find that training is offered by various departments such as the IT department or the Library, by the e-learning team or incorporated in teaching and learning support, such as teacher training programmes.

The review should attempt to identify not just formal workshops, but also informal training and advice that is given to staff, to build up a complete picture of the copyright support available. This will enable you to plan to fill any gaps in support, or to spot opportunities to embed aspects of copyright into existing courses.

Your audience

When devising your programme it will be helpful to divide your potential audience into different categories in order to tailor the training to their specific needs. What a person needs to know about copyright and the level of detail of that knowledge varies significantly depending on their role. For example, the requirements of departmental administrators, researchers and teaching staff vary and differ from those of people who work in the finance department. In many cases rolling out copyright training to all staff is difficult and trainers should concentrate on specific groups where the needs are greatest. Similarly providing copyright education to all students is not feasible for those in learning support and needs to be cascaded by teaching staff or other students as appropriate. This chapter will examine training for the following groups:

◆ library staff
◆ learning support staff, educational developers and learning technologists
◆ reprographic unit staff or staff responsible for scanners
◆ departmental administrators and personal assistants
◆ teaching staff
◆ students
◆ researchers.

Library staff

Copyright concerns often arise among those working in a library and a basic knowledge of copyright features in most library professional qualifications. Therefore library staff are often more enthusiastic than other categories of staff when it comes to attending copyright training and developing best practice. Queries are often related to users wanting to copy materials in the library collection by photocopying or scanning. Copyright issues can also arise in the course of general queries sent to librarians or library staff either via e-mail or face to face at service points so it is important to ensure that all staff are kept up to date with the latest developments in copyright. For example, following the 2014 amendments to the CDPA in the UK (see Chapter 1), several new exceptions to copyright were introduced and some exceptions were amended. As the law and licences change it is good practice to offer copyright refresher training. In addition some of the provisions in UK law specifically allow libraries and librarians to undertake certain unique types of copying, for example for interlibrary loan purposes, for preservation or for disabled users, and some of the exceptions relevant to librarians were updated in the UK in 2014.

Library staff working in certain areas of the library might require more focused copyright training, for example anyone preparing scanned or photocopied materials under the CLA Licence should have a good understanding of the terms of the licence. They need to consult the CLA website regularly and use the CLA Check Permissions tool (http://he.cla. co.uk/check-permissions) because CLA Licences do not cover all publications. This tool helps to determine whether a work is included in the CLA Licence and if it can be photocopied, scanned and/or copied digitally. Staff dealing with journals should be familiar with the different types of journal licences and what standard clauses say about making multiple copies of articles available. Interlibrary loan staff need a good working knowledge of copyright. Librarians working with special collections or archival materials might deal with material where the copyright status is unclear, such as orphan works, and need guidance on taking the best approach. Staff involved in digitization programmes for preservation or to improve access to a collection need a practical knowledge of copyright so they can establish whether the material is in copyright or not and if permission is required and can be obtained. Finally, those involved in supporting open access initiatives such as publishing via the institutional repository or an open access publishing platform require a good working knowledge of copyright as they are making copyright materials available on open access. They need to know when copyright permission might be required and must be able to identify and understand specific publisher policies on open access, such as embargoes and restrictions on full-text submission.

It might be helpful to offer specific copyright sessions for library staff, so that the training can focus on the information key to their role. Amongst library staff there are many different roles and this will affect the level of understanding they need about copyright; as previously mentioned, those staff dealing with organizations such as the Copyright Licensing Agency (CLA) may need separate, more detailed training on this licence. However, there is also some merit in library staff attending copyright training alongside other staff, for example teachers or researchers, as they can learn from each other and share experiences. Sometimes library staff might attend specialist externally run copyright training, but for staff in generalist library roles who need a working knowledge of copyright, one approach might be for a copyright specialist to attend external training and then to pass on their learning to other members of staff.

Learning support staff

The term 'learning support staff' covers a growing number of professionals now employed in educational establishments to work alongside teachers and lecturers. Many organizations employ staff with specific responsibility for technology-enhanced learning, online learning and the VLE who might be called learning technologists, educational technologists, instructional designers or e-learning specialists. Educational developers are another important group who advise staff about pedagogy and good teaching practice. Learning developers provide study skills advice to students and might support specific groups of students such as those with disabilities. Most universities and increasing numbers of colleges employ staff in this area, although in schools this is less common. All of these groups of staff should ideally receive an overview of copyright issues as part of their induction process, so they are aware of the key subjects of concern that can arise, particularly around uploading material to the VLE. However, probably of greater importance is for these staff to know where to refer copyright queries if anyone raises a query, or if they have any uncertainty themselves.

Learning technologists and other staff who support the use of educational technologies frequently help staff prepare online learning materials and are ideally placed to advise on copyright matters and provide technical and pedagogical advice. As with many groups of staff the need for copyright training might be met with some reluctance as these staff may perceive copyright laws as being overly restrictive, leading them to have to tell teachers they cannot do certain things. Many learning support staff like to be seen as 'enablers' who find ways to make things happen. There is a danger that copyright may be seen as preventing teaching staff from undertaking their primary role. One way to counter this belief is to link copyright education with the promotion of open practices (see Chapter 1, page 41) and the improvement of teaching quality. It is also important that learning support staff are aware of copyright, to avoid being personally implicated in any infringing activity a teacher might undertake. If learning technologists are familiar with the basics of copyright law they can advise staff on the best technical and legal ways to put materials online. They may also be able quickly to resolve common problems that arise through teaching staff being unfamiliar with copyright issues. For example they can remove journal article files from a course and show lecturers how to link to these resources.

Increasingly HEI managers are expecting academic staff to undertake formal postgraduate teaching qualifications. While mandatory for a long time in the schools sector, teacher training is a relatively new area in higher education. Currently the curriculum of many teaching qualifications in the UK, for example those that are accredited by the Higher Education Academy, only looks very briefly at issues such as legal compliance and copyright, and there is a potential opportunity to embed copyright education in these types of programmes.

Administrators and professional services staff

In the education sector it is extremely important to give copyright training to administrators, department or faculty managers and other professional services staff. While it is now less common in universities for lecturing staff to have their own personal assistants, much of the administration of teaching is still undertaken by administrative support staff who might work for a group of lecturers or a department. In the past, administrative staff prepared photocopies and paper course packs for students; nowadays they are increasingly uploading content to the VLE on behalf of lecturers. If these staff have an understanding and awareness of copyright issues they can help prevent copyright infringement within a department. They can also spread good practice across their department and influence the behaviour of teachers. Conversely, if these staff do not understand or recognize the importance of copyright, infringement might occur and teaching staff might continue to infringe copyright, unaware that they are doing something wrong. It is important that these staff understand the basics of copyright law, and the main terms and conditions of licensing schemes such as the CLA Licence. A good practice guide for administrators was recently published by the Association of University Administrators (Morrison and Secker, 2016).

Teaching staff

Teaching staff are likely to be a challenging audience, as traditionally they may perceive copyright as a restriction that gets in the way of the education process. The restriction is not just perceived from an ideological perspective – the process of getting copyright permission is often seen as time consuming and overly complicated. Ideally copyright training should be offered to these staff as part of their induction when first joining the institution, framed in a positive way by associating an awareness of copyright with quality teaching and innovative, open practice. Many new teaching staff are now required to complete a teaching qualification, for example, a postgraduate certificate in teaching, so if copyright training is delivered in induction briefings, alongside health and safety instruction, for example, it can reach a wide audience. However, there is a danger that when staff are obliged to attend certain training sessions they view a subject fairly negatively. Induction sessions also tend to be pitched at basic level for a general audience. Copyright training for teaching staff should ideally be delivered at an appropriate and relevant time, for example when they are preparing or updating course materials. Teaching staff may also need to be kept up to date with any new developments in copyright law, so while copyright could be briefly mentioned in the induction process, it should feature in a range of workshops and programmes offered to these staff. Copyright education for learning support staff and administrative staff within departments helps reinforce good practice among teachers. Ideally if teachers feel supported by those with copyright expertise they will approach them if they have questions or require assistance.

Students

Students are a challenging audience largely because of their sheer numbers, and therefore embedding copyright literacy into relevant discipline teaching may be the best approach. For example, in subjects such as art and design students need to understand how to use other people's ideas without infringing copyright. In subjects such as engineering, patents are likely to be a more important topic to cover and students involved in an entrepreneurial scheme or creating start-ups need an understanding of all types of intellectual property to help them protect their ideas.

It is now increasingly common to offer doctoral level students copyright training, often because many institutions now publish theses in an open access repository. PhD students are therefore required to address the use of third-party content in their theses before submission and will benefit from a practical understanding of the issues involved.

Researchers

Researchers are another important audience that benefit from copyright education, and are becoming an increasingly receptive group as they increasingly recognize that they need to understand a host of IPR matters relating to scholarly communication and the dissemination of their research findings and data. The increased focus on open access in higher education, with many funding bodies now mandating that publicly funded research is available openly under permissive licence terms, has raised awareness of copyright issues and the policies of specific journals and publishers. For example in the UK, following the Finch Report (Finch, 2012), which recommended that authors rather than readers should pay for publication, Research Councils UK issued an open access policy for any research funded from April 2013 (Research Councils UK, 2014). Researchers are becoming increasingly aware of the implications of the copyright transfer agreements they are asked to sign by publishers, and many university libraries now have specialist research support teams to advise staff on open access and scholarly communications. Some universities' copyright training and advice therefore fits neatly into the training and services that are offered in this area. It is also increasingly common to include PhD students in research support activities as they need to consider where to publish, the copyright policies of specific publishers, and how to comply with institutional and research councils' requirements on open access. This training can involve the use of third-party content as described above.

Case Study 7   Copyright the card game: a games-based approach to copyright education

Chris Morrison and Jane Secker

Background

This case study describes a games-based approach to copyright education, how the game and associated resources were developed, and the evaluation data collected, which demonstrates that this new approach engages learners more effectively than traditional methods.

In June and October 2014 there were several significant changes to UK copyright law, including some new exceptions relevant to educational establishments. SCONUL (the Society of College, National and University Librarians) recognized the need for the sector to understand how these changes might apply in practice and asked the copyright consultant Naomi Korn to devise some training. Naomi approached Chris Morrison and Jane Secker to work with her to create a new half-day training course and they agreed to collaborate to deliver these sessions.

Development work

Planning began by establishing the broad aims and learning outcomes of the session and discussing previous approaches the three trainers had used before. Despite feeling that their training was effective, the group was looking for an opportunity to try something different, in particular the use of visual cues to anchor delegates' understanding of what often seem abstract legal concepts. All agreed that the use of representative icons was an important aspect of the popularity of the Creative Commons licences. The group felt that practical scenarios needed to be integral to a training session, but in these half-day sessions timing would be critical to explain the relationship between licences and updated fair dealing exceptions. Another important consideration was the delegates' varying knowledge and experience, which the training ideally needed to take account of.

There was some consideration of the value of quizzes, practical exercises and a copyright snakes and ladders game, which had been developed by Annette Moore from the University of Sussex. Meanwhile Chris suggested creating a card game to explain how copyright works. It was agreed that this approach was worth exploring and the idea developed of creating four 'suits', one each for types of copyright works, usages, licences and exceptions. At this stage it was envisaged that the cards would be developed and used as part of a discrete exercise at the end of the session.

The card game evolves

As time went by Chris felt that to get the most out of the card concept it should be used as an integral part of the session. He was inspired by how his son had learned his numbers and letters using a puzzle peg board and foam bath toys. By holding something in his hand his son had mentally grasped the concepts, a phenomenon known as embodied cognition where intellectual thought is influenced by the relationship between body and mind (Wilson, 1999). The group members were also mindful of the inevitable glazing over or drooping eyelids of some delegates who attend copyright training so interaction was important. If people were kept on their toes by interacting with each other and carrying out exercises throughout the session it was hoped that they would stay engaged.

Embracing the card game concept and using it throughout the session would allow the trainers to intersperse the introduction of factual information seamlessly with the application of new learning. Chris developed a running order of the session, explaining the concepts of the game, identifying what should be on the cards and what should happen in each round. Going with this new format was a risk. Never having done it before no one could say whether this would work or whether it would be too costly to develop and too complicated to deliver in a half-day session. Despite these concerns, the group agreed to carry on with the idea working on various aspects of the training course. It was important to link the cards to the information in the slides and decide if delegates would need additional information provided on handouts or elsewhere. On referring back to the original concept behind the card game it was decided that the cards had to be the ultimate containers for the relevant knowledge otherwise the whole idea would probably not work.

Preparing for the training

As the day of the training got closer Chris worked on the visual cues that would link the cards with the information and instructions on the accompanying PowerPoint slides. The website openclipart.org contains openly licensed images that can be incorporated into publications and presentations without additional permissions, and this provided many of the images used on the cards and slides. Eventually a final version of the cards (printed double-sided on thick, A6 size paper) was ready, with the key copyright information that delegates would need, integrated with a set of slides outlining the framework of the session. The key to the success of the game was the extent to which delegates would intuitively understand what they were being asked to do. It was important that the way in which the session was structured helped people to reflect and learn, and the use of the icons was fundamental to this. The selection of these fell into three categories:

◆ generic icons taken from openclipart.org, which represented an aspect of copyright (e.g. a microphone denoting a sound recording)
◆ existing copyright-related icons (e.g. Creative Commons icons or the associated public domain mark)
◆ newly created or amended icons usually denoting the more abstract or niche elements of copyright (e.g. orphan works or collective rights management bodies' names).

The rules of the game

The rules of the game are relatively simple. Players are put in teams and the game consists of four rounds, which should be played in a specific order: works, usages, licences and exceptions. In each round the teams are given scenarios to consider and they must lay their cards as appropriate. The final round of the game uses all four sets of cards, plus some additional risk cards. Full instructions are included in the downloadable resource available on Jorum (http://find.jorum.ac.uk/resources/19369) and the UK Copyright Literacy website (https://ukcopyrightliteracy.wordpress.com/about-2/copyright-the-card-game).

The training sessions

From the first session run in late January 2015, it has been clear that the card game instinctively makes sense. The continual back and forward between the trainer and the delegates encourages people to consider the different aspects of copyright, building up the complexity as the game progresses and constantly testing people's critical faculties. This creates a buzz in the room in a way not typically experienced in copyright training. This approach gives delegates time and space to test their knowledge and assumptions, and to voice their concerns about whether they are getting things right.

Rather than focusing on 'right' or 'wrong' answers, the card game format allows an appreciation of the subjective nature of how to apply the law. This builds up gradually throughout the session so that the relatively clear cut aspects of copyright are introduced first, with a subjective 'risk' judgement introduced only at the end once the delegates are confident with the basics.

The teamwork aspect makes good use of the differing levels of knowledge within each group. It was initially proposed that people would be split into groups based on their perception of copyright knowledge but this idea has proved unnecessary. Therefore typically in sessions the group allocation is random, based on where people sit when they come into the room.

Feedback to date

The feedback received from each of the four SCONUL sessions (run in Cardiff, Manchester, London and Leicester) was unanimously positive with people rating the training either 'excellent' or 'good'. The only criticism received was that delegates would have liked more time to go through more scenarios. This was a limitation of the SCONUL sessions, which incorporated an update from the CLA in the afternoon, but meant that the card game needed to fit into a short morning session. Chris and Jane now use the card game at their respective institutions, the University of Kent and LSE, in workshops ranging from 1.5 to 3.5 hours. The sessions with a longer duration provide more time to consider multiple scenarios and allow deeper discussion within the group, whereas the shorter sessions have been created in order to reach a wider number of people with limited time. However, at 1.5 hours the game is rather rushed with little time to consider the scenarios properly, so ideally 2 hours is needed as a minimum. The game has also been run as part of a workshop on information literacy and games-based learning, attracting over 40 librarians, and various other events. Because it is available under a Creative Commons licence it is also being used throughout the UK higher education sector by other copyright support practitioners. Feedback collected through online forms has remained consistently positive and natural feedback in the room suggests that delegates enjoy the session and the depth of discussions about copyright that it provokes. In recent training sessions an element of competition has been introduced with points awarded to each team for the rounds, and an overall winning team announced at the end.

Find out more

The resources are available for free download from the UK Copyright Literacy website (https://ukcopyrightliteracy.wordpress.com) and have been downloaded from Jorum over 2300 times between March 2015 and January 2016. Jane and Chris have been working to adapt the game, writing new scenarios. They are currently making modifications so it can be played with research students, and also to explore the copyright challenges of social media. The card game is proof that copyright training can be fun and suggests that a games-based approach to learning about copyright, where people play as part of a team, has benefits both for learners and teachers.

References

Wilson, F. R. (1999) *The Hand: how its use shapes the brain, language, and human culture*, Vintage.

Face-to-face training sessions

Offering face-to-face training sessions may seem the obvious approach to providing copyright education and it is possible to deliver training to people in large groups via a lecture-style presentation. However, in general, more effective learning should include an opportunity for discussion and interaction between the teacher and the learners. People attending face-to-face copyright sessions often bring along specific queries and therefore teaching smaller groups (of around ten to 15) is advisable to allow time for questions. Copyright education should be approached like any teaching: first consider the learning outcomes of the session, then design appropriate activities and any assessment, which all need to be aligned. Practical issues are important, such as finding the right time and duration for the session and an appropriate learning space to suit the type of activities. The intended learning outcomes should guide the approach to the session. For example, very few teaching staff need an in-depth knowledge of copyright legislation but they might need to understand what copyright exceptions allow them to do for their own private study or research. They probably also need to know what they can photocopy or scan under their institutional CLA Licence, and when they might need to seek copyright permission to copy material on the internet or upload files to the VLE. Ideally trainers should focus on several key points, rather than overwhelm trainees with details, which can be provided in a printed guide or on a website. It may be enough for participants to leave the session knowing that there is someone who can advise them in the future and they should think twice before they copy or scan material.

Topics to include

This varies from one organization to another. These are some of the topics that are often included in copyright education:

◆ factual contextual information about copyright laws including which works qualify for copyright protection and for how long, why the laws are in place, what protection they offer to rights holders and how these work in practice
◆ information about licences the institution holds that allow copying by way of legal contract: the CLA, the ERA, the NLA, etc.
◆ copyright exceptions and important principles such as fair dealing and fair use
◆ copyright and the internet: terms and conditions of online services
◆ the practicalities of getting copyright permission.

Depending on the audience, it might also be worth including subjects such as open access, digitization and how to handle 'orphan works'. Practical scenarios are often useful to help people understand how copyright works and to test their understanding. For example, you could ask your group to consider the following situations:

◆   A teacher wants to make 50 copies of a specific book and to put it on a website; what are the issues?
◆   A lecturer is showing and recording a video in class; what licences or copyright exceptions might apply?

Games are another helpful way to run copyright training, as illustrated in Case Study 7 in this chapter. The element of interactivity is particularly important to help engage learners, but people are more inclined to attend training if they think it is going to be fun and informative.

Practical considerations

As with any teaching, scheduling sessions requires careful consideration of the time of year they are offered and the time of day they are delivered. It might be worth experimenting with advertising a course at different times of year to see if this affects attendance. For example, in an academic institution, offering training right at the start of the academic year is rarely a good idea as people are often busy dealing with new students and have heavy teaching commitments. Conversely, offering courses to academic staff in the summer is unlikely to be successful in a university, as lecturers and researchers are usually away from their institution. Trial and error is often the only way to find the right time at your organization. For example, lunchtime sessions (where lunch is provided) can be effective. In UK universities late spring (March–May) seems to be a popular time of year for staff development activities after much of the teaching has finished but before the exam period. Other times of year might be more appropriate in other institutions, but in general it is best to avoid peak times. In schools it might be appropriate to include an element of copyright training as part of a staff training day.

Marketing and publicity is vital in order to ensure good attendance at courses. It is also important to try to devise an appealing title for the session – while it may seem disingenuous, avoiding calling it 'copyright training' helps to get a good turn out! It is worth spending some time brainstorming names for courses and running them past a few volunteers to get feedback about the titles that sound appealing. In addition, spelling out some clear objectives of what people will learn in a session and why they need to attend are key to success. Publicity, whether in electronic (via e-mail or on the web) or paper form (leaflets or posters), needs to be simple, clear and eye-catching. It often pays to employ design professionals in this area.

Other more practical issues to consider include the location for the training session and available facilities. You need to find a room in your institution that is conveniently located but also has a projector (if you need one) and is a flexible learning space so you can move the furniture around should group discussions or activities require this.

It is important to develop a set of resources for use during the session, for example handouts, resources or example materials. The copyright card game described in Case Study 7 requires a number of materials to be prepared in advance: the sets of cards, the PowerPoint slides and objects used in the first round where participants have to identify the type of copyright works (see Case Study 7 for details of where to download the resources for free). See the section 'Booklets, guides and leaflets' below for some information on producing booklets and leaflets to supplement a face-to-face training session; it is useful to distribute these at the end of a workshop to provide more detail or reminders of the key areas covered.

Using the web

The web is an important source of material about making copyright information available to staff. Not only can staff access the information as and when they require it, having copyright information on your website demonstrates to both your internal audience and to external bodies or organizations that your institution takes copyright seriously. The website can be a useful point of reference for copyright queries you receive via e-mail and over time you may develop frequently asked questions to which you can point staff or students when they ask similar queries. Many universities now provide copyright advice for staff and students on their websites, usually with a disclaimer stating that it is not legal advice. Those planning to devise copyright web pages should consult the list of guidance from universities produced by the University of Loughborough (2015), which includes links to the copyright advice pages produced by many UK universities. The intended audience for university copyright pages is usually the university's own staff members, although increasingly universities provide advice for students as well. Many of the pages are created by librarians or dedicated copyright officers, and some of the copyright guides are licensed under Creative Commons so can be re-used with attribution. The advice given by different HEIs is often very similar: many provide a brief overview of UK copyright law, a guide to what can and cannot be copied or scanned, information about using material from the internet, specific guidance on the use of the VLE and links to further resources. A number of the sites now include information for specific groups of staff or students. It may be that all that is required of organizations that currently provide no copyright advice is a simple copyright web page, which can be added to over time as queries arise. Consider keeping usage statistics of your website to monitor the numbers of people who view this information.

If you already have copyright web pages or do not feel happy with this content being available on the internet to those outside your organization you might want to consider using the VLE to develop an online course about copyright. The tools available in the VLE allow you to monitor who has completed the course. You can also use assessment or communication tools to make the course more interactive. Figure 6.1 shows a screenshot from the online course 'Copyright, the internet and teaching online', which is available to all staff at the LSE. This course complements the face-to-face training session offered to staff throughout the year. In addition to

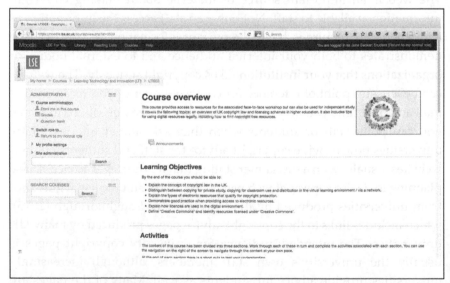

Figure 6.1 *LSE learning technology and innovation: copyright, the internet and teaching online: an online course for staff*

including resources from the class, such as the presentation and handouts, content is available to work through online, split into bite-sized chunks. The materials have been divided into three sections, each of which is followed by a short quiz to check the participants' understanding.

The course includes links to useful external resources, such as the CLA's website and the UK IPO website. It is available on demand; the number of staff who enrol on the course is relatively low, and attendance at face-to-face training is more popular at LSE. When preparing any online information, be aware that many staff and students like to talk to someone in person when faced with a copyright concern, because they perceive the subject to be complex. This anxiety about copyright was highlighted in the recent UK Copyright Literacy Survey (Morrison and Secker, 2015, 91). Therefore, in practice online copyright guidance is not a substitute for timely advice and guidance from a named individual, although MOOCs on copyright may involve discussion forums and mentors, which go some way to providing some support from others involved in the course.

Booklets, guides and leaflets

In the digital age it might be assumed that traditional help in the form of booklets and leaflets is redundant. However, the authors' experience suggests that teaching and administrative staff respond favourably to a hard copy guide they can hold in their hand and they seem to be more likely to refer to this, rather than to remember to read a web page. The provision of booklets and leaflets gives a useful outward signal to your internal audience and external bodies that you are taking copyright issues seriously. You do not necessarily need to have a large budget to produce such materials. They can be given to staff during training sessions and included in induction packs for new staff. A well written and concise guide has the advantage of tangible immediacy over online materials, despite being less easy to keep up to date. There are two staff copyright guides produced at LSE, both in the form of responding to frequently asked questions. The short guide to copyright for LSE staff (Figure 6.2 on the next page) is complemented by a guide to copyright and e-learning. The guides can be consulted online (LSE, 2015a; LSE, 2015b); those wishing to see the printed booklets can contact the authors for more details. A printed copyright guide for PhD students is also currently under production.

Figure 6.2 *A short guide to copyright for LSE staff (http://lti.lse.ac.uk/copyright/ LSEGuideToCopyright2015.pdf)*

One final issue with producing written guides (whether in printed form or on the web) is to ensure that they are easy to read and any direct advice they contain is accurate. You may wish to include a disclaimer so staff are aware that the guide does not give legal advice, and give the name of the person whom readers should contact if they require further guidance. Some institutions employ an external consultant or a lawyer to oversee or proofread their guides. Printed guides should be kept up to date and synchronized with any web-based publications that may exist to make certain there are no discrepancies in the content.

Dealing with queries

Copyright officers inevitably receive a number of queries from staff and students in their organization, often from those who have recently attended a workshop or training session, or from people who have read a guide or booklet but require further advice. It is important to consider how your organization might manage these queries and to decide:

◆ who is the best person to answer the query
◆ what to do if a query goes beyond their understanding
◆ whether queries should be managed in any way in order to keep track of their type and frequency, for example tracking or logging them in a customer support system.

It is worthwhile first to decide who is responsible for answering specific copyright queries. Clearly if your organization is fortunate enough to have a dedicated copyright officer, this might be one person. However, in many organizations several people might share the responsibility for copyright, and even dedicated copyright advisers may want to get a second opinion when faced with a new or complex query.

The key point when offering copyright advice is to be clear about the limits of your knowledge. If you are unsure of the answer, it is better to take further advice from a colleague, or to undertake further research into the issue using resources such as those listed at the end of this book. Reference books such as *Copyright for Archivists and Records Managers* (Padfield, 2015) and *Copyright* (Cornish, 2015) are helpful for those in the UK; Cornish's book is set out in the form of frequently asked questions. Many aspects of copyright include grey areas and are open to interpretation. For example in the UK some terms in the CDPA, such as 'fair dealing' and 'substantial', are not precisely defined and subject to interpretation and case law. In some instances answering a copyright query may involve making a judgement based on a risk assessment. There may be instances where providing someone with a concrete answer is difficult; while copyright officers may want to be helpful, they may also need to be cautious in their advice. Anyone who provides copyright advice, but who is not legally qualified, should frame his or her advice with suitable disclaimers. It is important to stress to staff looking for advice that ultimately it is down to their judgement whether they go ahead with the activity in question. In practice, the organization rather than individuals are likely to be pursued in court in the case of an allegation of copyright infringement. Therefore some copyright decisions may need to be referred upwards and should ideally involve a discussion at senior management level about the organization's appetite for risk.

Sources of further advice and support

There is a growing way of building up your knowledge about copyright issues, with several excellent websites now available. For example in the UK, Copyright User (http://copyrightuser.org), which launched in 2014, is an independent online resource which aims to make copyright law accessible to creators, media professionals, entrepreneurs, students and members of the public. The IPO website offers guidance and there are several copyright-related MOOCs available in the USA and Europe.

Professional bodies offering copyright training courses and sources of further advice are listed in the section 'Further resources'.

Arguably one of the most important things that copyright officers can do is to develop a support network by contacting others in similar roles in other organizations. This network can provide invaluable advice and support if a copyright officer is unsure how to answer queries from members of staff at their organization. For staff new to this role, networking can also be a useful way of developing their knowledge of copyright issues. In the UK e-mail lists maintained by JISCmail can be good sources of advice and many copyright officers in universities are members of LIS-Copyseek (www.jiscmail.ac.uk/lists/lis-copyseek.html). This is a closed mailing list for those interested in copyright matters in the higher education community. It does not deal specifically with e-learning, but covers all types of copyright concerns; increasingly queries about online learning and technology feature in the postings. For those who work in the museums or cultural heritage sector there is a JISCmail list for the Museums Copyright Group (https://www.jiscmail.ac.uk/cgi-bin/webadmin?A0=mcg). SCONUL has a copyright sub-group that provides periodic guidance to the higher education sector and runs training for academic libraries on copyright matters. Advice is also available from Jisc Customer Service team, which has copyright guidance online and maintains a helpdesk for queries.

In the USA there is a mailing list for librarians involved in the scanning of copyright materials for teaching purposes (known as electronic reserves). This is managed by Princeton University and is a useful source of advice for those running electronic reserves services. You will find it listed in the section 'Further resources' along with some other country specific sources of advice.

Personal contacts are invaluable for those providing copyright advice and these are often obtained through attending copyright-related events, training courses or workshops where you are likely to meet individuals in other organizations with responsibility for copyright. It can be hugely beneficial to share the copyright queries that you receive with others and to compare your own advice with that others give.

Conclusion

This chapter examined the design and delivery of copyright training within an organization. It considered the copyright educator and their needs, the audience for training sessions and the format, and publicity materials. The chapter included a case study describing a games-based approach to copyright education and sources of further help and advice. While no approach is fail safe, establishing a professional and timely copyright training programme that is well supported with online resources, leaflets and other documentation should go a long way to ensuring that staff within an organization are informed about copyright and follow good practice. It is also important to be realistic about your role, whether you are formally a copyright officer, or if it is just one of your responsibilities. Some staff might remain resistant to attending training sessions, or following your advice. Ultimately the decision to abide by copyright laws is the responsibility of each individual and an organization with a mature attitude towards copyright literacy will accept that 100% compliance is not possible. Provided you take reasonable steps to offer copyright education and advice at the point of need, and make it clear to those to whom you give advice that it is for them to take appropriate action, this should offer protection for your organization. Ideally your role should be to help embed a culture of copyright literacy where staff and students understand the importance of behaving ethically, are given accurate information in order to make the best decisions they can, and feel that they are being given adequate support in doing so.

References

CLA (2016) Audit Materials, Copyright Licensing Agency, http://he.cla.co.uk/complying-with-your-licence/audit-materials [accessed 6 April 2016].

Cornish, G. (2015) *Copyright: interpreting the law for libraries, archives and information services*, 6th edn, Facet Publishing.

Finch, J. (2012) *Accessibility, Sustainability, Excellence: how to expand access to research publications*, report of the Working Group on Expanding Access to Published Research Findings, www.researchinfonet.org/wp-content/uploads/2012/06/Finch-Group-report-FINAL-VERSION.pdf [accessed 6 April 2016].

LSE (2015a) Learning Technology and Innovation: copyright frequently asked questions, London School of Economics, http://lti.lse.ac.uk/copyright/copyright-faqs.php [accessed 6 April 2016].

LSE (2015b) A Short Guide to Copyright for LSE staff, London School of Economics, http://lti.lse.ac.uk/copyright/LSEGuideToCopyright2015.pdf [accessed 6 April 2016].

Morrison, C. and Secker, J. (2015) Copyright Literacy in the UK: a survey of librarians and other cultural heritage sector professionals, *Library and Information Research*, **39** (121), 75–97.

Morrison, C. and Secker, J. (2016) Nine things You Need to Know about Copyright: a good practice guide for administrators, librarians and academics, LSE Impact Blog, http://blogs.lse.ac.uk/impactofsocialsciences/2016/04/05/nine-things-university-administrators-and-academics-need-to-know-about-copyright [accessed 6 April 2016].

NUS (2012) *Student Attitudes Towards Intellectual Property*, National Union of Students, www.nus.org.uk/PageFiles/12238/IP%20report.pdf [accessed 6 April 2016].

Padfield, T. (2015) *Copyright for Archivists and Records Managers*, 5th edn, Facet Publishing.

Research Councils UK (2014) RCUK Policy on Open Access, www.rcuk.ac.uk/research/openaccess [accessed 6 April 2016].

University of Loughborough (2015) Guidance from other Universities, http://copyright.lboro.ac.uk/copyright/training/guidance-other-universities [accessed 6 April 2016].

Weatherley, M. (2014) *Copyright Education and Awareness, a discussion paper*, www.cubismlaw.com/wp-content/uploads/2015/06/mweatherly-copyright-education-awareness.pdf [accessed 6 April 2016].

7 Conclusion

This book has considered a wide range of copyright issues associated with online learning. It has sought to provide practical advice for those working in education and to give readers a working knowledge of copyright law as it applies in this field. Copyright and e-learning is a compelling and complex subject. Copyright exceptions provide special privileges for research and education, yet despite the best efforts of governments around the world, people still struggle to interpret how the law applies to new technologies. The problems arise from the inherent nature of digital technology and the ease with which it allows information and knowledge to be shared. The very reasons why educators want to teach online – to open up education, to break down geographical and physical barriers to learning – are some of the reasons why those in the cultural industries fear technology. Sharing information in a digital format allows it to be freely distributed and not easily controlled, and therefore attempts are made by commercial publishers and other media organizations to lock information through digital rights management technologies.

There have been many developments in the six years since this book was first published. The law has been updated around the world, most notably in the UK, and there has been a major shift in scholarly communications with a continuing growth in the uptake of open access publishing models. We have also seen the embedding of cloud-based and 'always connected' technologies, along with the widespread use of social media, changing the way people communicate and share information. We have seen a proliferation of digital devices, the introduction of wearable technologies and the generation of data on a massive scale. In the education field we have seen increased globalization, increasing commoditization of education as a product and 'experience', the rise of MOOCs, and in many countries a decline in public sector funding of higher education.

Clearly copyright and e-learning is still an area of considerable interest and concern, and many people are uncertain about what they or their institutions should be doing. Arguably many of the fears and anxieties about copyright stem from people approaching it as a rigid and unhelpful framework that they try to apply as an afterthought. There is much that could be gained if copyright were reframed in the wider context of the practical and philosophical considerations that come into play in any educational establishment. People are now able to use social media to create their own norms to navigate the ethics of what the latest technology enables them to do, as well as what the companies that provide the technology suggest is acceptable. This sort of online behaviour can compound the problem as people mistakenly believe that all online content is free and can be shared. In education, in particular, one of the tensions seems to be related to the view that copyright is a set of clearly defined rules that need to be adhered to. In reality most copyright disputes inevitably become hugely complex when courts attempt to determine what rights exist and explore the web of agreements and legal provisions that may or may not relate to the contentious activities. The pragmatic approach to copyright in education involves understanding risk in a shifting environment. It empowers people to make their own decisions according to the specific circumstances they find themselves in, having been first equipped with an understanding of what the law says. Educational establishments have a responsibility to understand these issues and invest in embedding a culture of copyright literacy. This is not simply to manage compliance, it is about providing quality teaching and supporting innovation in a way that encourages a discussion of the wider ethical issues of knowledge creation.

You may have read this book thinking it will give you all the answers – and in many ways we hope that the information helps you to make decisions within your organization. Some of the most challenging questions faced by practitioners include determining whether specific types of content can be uploaded to the VLE; whether linking to resources is always legitimate; how images, video and audio can be used in online education; and whether it is possible to post third-party copyright content legally on social media. In practice a whole range of factors go into working out the best response to any given copyright situation, including the nature of the technology (which is constantly evolving), the types of work being used and how much of it is being used. Your institution's attitude towards risk and senior management's understanding of the implications of what is actually happening are also key. Educational establishments have varying approaches to copyright policies including some which do not have a policy at all. Where policies exist they range from those that are flexible (which some might read as 'vague and unhelpful') to those which provide much more clarity, but are seen as overly restrictive. Some institutions are keen to cover their backs and adopt risk-averse approaches, whereas others might be happier with a greater level of risk. Regardless of the conditions you are working in, understanding (and indeed influencing) the culture of your institution is important when you are involved in responding to copyright questions.

In this book we have provided a framework to gain a better understanding of copyright issues. Through the case studies we have illustrated how copyright works in practice and the types of procedures and organizational structures that institutions have developed to provide support to staff and students. Ultimately the application of high quality copyright support and policy development is as much of an art as it is a science. It often involves working with high levels of ambiguity and no small amount of contradiction, while at the same time requiring communication techniques that simultaneously engage, comfort and challenge colleagues and students at all stages of their careers. This cannot be done in isolation and the communities of practice that exist around copyright support (such as LIS-Copyseek in the UK) are some of the most valuable resources to any copyright support professional.

The work that we, the authors, have done to develop creative and interactive ways of allowing people to understand copyright issues and relate them to practical examples is the first step towards rethinking copyright within a wider set of digital literacies. There is much that can be learned from other approaches to embedding digital literacies within an institution. Often a process of review or audit across the entire institution can be a catalyst for organizational change. Policies, frameworks and models help to engage senior managers, but the reality is that creating a culture of copyright literacy involves working from the ground up as well.

Practical examples are needed to illustrate the key benefits to all the stakeholders involved. For students, it might be learning how to protect their ideas if they are interested in creating a start-up company. Research staff need to understand copyright to know how to make their research compliant with open access policies; teachers looking for inspiration will appreciate the time saved when developing learning resources if they search for existing content under open licences such as those issued by Creative Commons. For those tasked with educating others about copyright it involves devising realistic scenarios and using empathy to understand people's motivations and behaviours. This can give greater insight into why common misconceptions occur and in turn help to create a shared understanding about copyright that will underpin effective communication and collaboration within an organization.

We will end this book by listing six ideas, which we hope are helpful for any educator when they are approaching a copyright issue related to teaching online:

1   Realize that everything is about risk and there are ways of mitigating the risk. For example, devise helpful and timely education and training programmes, but also have institutional policies such as notice and takedown policies publicized on the VLE or any online platform where content can be shared.
2   Break down any copyright query into its constituent parts – what type of copyright works does it concern, how will they be used, are there any licences that might apply and finally could a copyright exception come into play? This inevitably requires developing your technical knowledge to tackle these queries and we have provided practical advice and numerous examples in this book, as well as links to further resources.
3   Use empathy – in any given situation understanding what someone is actually trying to do when they approach you with a copyright query is helpful. Empathy is important from both sides so try to get the person to think about what the creators and rights holders of a work had in mind too. Ideally this will help you put your copyright support work in context and frame it as a collaborative enterprise.
4   Understand that there is lots of great material available for free or under liberal licence terms. Many people are happy to share their

work with you provided they are credited, particularly when it is for educational use, but recognize that there are often good reasons why some content costs money or is not available to you.

5   Recognize that good manners go a long way – asking nicely, giving credit and building creative networks are a fundamental component of education and research. Over time you can build up your network of contacts, and often knowing the right person to ask will give you access to a wider network of resources, which can be used at little or no cost.

6   Remember, you are not alone. It is easy, particularly if you are faced with a tricky copyright situation, to feel you are expected to know all the answers, but no one is an island. So build up your support network within your organization and externally, and come join our network!

No book on this topic can hope to answer every question that the reader might have. Educational technology is developing rapidly, giving rise to new scenarios and new copyright challenges. Around the world, countries continue to respond to technological developments and to adapt and modify their copyright laws. The book therefore ends with some useful resources for keeping up to date in this area. The resources are organized by topic broadly related to each of the chapters of this book, and include some specific country-related resources. The listing includes books, websites, online courses, blogs and mailing lists that should provide useful sources of further advice, training and support.

If you found this book useful and would like to find out more, please visit our website (http://ukcopyrightliteracy.wordpress.com). Here we maintain an online list of resources to complement the book. You can also join us as part of a growing supportive community that can help educators work through the complexities of copyright and e-learning together. We end by urging everyone, particularly those in senior management and leadership roles, to recognize that copyright is an important issue that educational establishments need to take seriously and invest in as people teach and learn in the increasingly digitally connected digital environment.

Further resources

An online version of this resource list is maintained at: https://ukcopyrightliteracy.wordpress.com/publications/copyright-and-e-learning/.

General resources on copyright
Mailing lists

JISC-DRM (2015) JISC Digital Rights Management Discussion List, https://www.jiscmail.ac.uk/lists/JISC-DRM.html, JISC-DRM@JISCMAIL.AC.UK.

Library E-reserves discussion list, LIB-ERESERVES@PRINCETON.EDU, https://lists.princeton.edu/cgi-bin/wa?A0=LIB-ERESERVES.

LIS-Copyseek (2015) JISCMail Closed Discussion List for Copyright Queries, https://www.jiscmail.ac.uk/lists/LIS-COPYSEEK.html, LIS-Copyseek@jiscmail.ac.uk.

Museums Copyright Group (2015) JISCMail Closed Discussion List for Staff in Museums and Galleries, https://www.jiscmail.ac.uk/lists/MUSEUMS-COPYRIGHT-GROUP. html, MUSEUMS-COPYRIGHT-GROUP@JISCMAIL.AC.UK.

Copyright courses and MOOCs

Copyright – DIY, http://platform.europeanmoocs.eu/course_copyright_diy.

Copyright Clarity,
    https://www.canvas.net/courses/copyright-clarity.
Copyright for Educators & Librarians,
    www.coursera.org/learn/copyright-for-education.
Copyright for Librarians from EIFL and Berkman Center for Internet and
    Society,
    http://cyber.law.harvard.edu/copyrightforlibrarians/Main_Page.
Copyright for Multimedia,
    www.coursera.org/learn/copyright-for-multimedia.
UK Intellectual Property Office, IP Tutor,
    www.ipo.gov.uk/blogs/iptutor.
Unlocking Film Rights: understanding UK copyright, FutureLearn,
    https://www.futurelearn.com/courses/film-copyright.

Copyright law resources by country
The UK

1709 Blog,
    http://the1709blog.blogspot.co.uk.
British and Irish Legal Information Institute website,
    www.bailii.org.
    Open access case law and legislation resource.
Centre for Copyright and New Business Models in the Creative
    Economy (CREATe) website,
    www.create.ac.uk.
Copyright, Designs and Patents Act (1988) (amendments from 2014 still
    pending at the time of writing),
    www.legislation.gov.uk/ukpga/1988/48/contents.
Copyright, Designs and Patents Act (1988) (unofficial consolidated
    version as amended in October 2014),
    www.gov.uk/government/uploads/system/uploads/attachment_
    data/file/308729/cdpa1988-unofficial.pdf.
Copyright User website,
    http://copyrightuser.org.
Cornish, G. (2015) *Copyright: interpreting the law for libraries, archives and
    information services*, 6th edn, Facet Publishing.
Library and Archives Copyright Alliance (LACA) website,

www.cilip.org.uk/cilip/advocacy-awards-and-projects/advocacy-and-campaigns/copyright/laca-libraries-and-archives.

Padfield, T. (2015) *Copyright for Archivists and Records Managers*, 5th edn, Facet Publishing.

Pedley, P. (2012) *The E-Copyright Handbook*, Facet Publishing.

Pedley, P. (2015) *Practical Copyright for Library and Information Professionals*, Facet Publishing.

UK Copyright Literacy website, https://ukcopyrightliteracy.wordpress.com.

UK Intellectual Property Office website, www.gov.uk/government/organisations/intellectual-property-office.

Weatherley, M. (2014) *Copyright Education and Awareness: a discussion paper*, www.cubismlaw.com/wp-content/uploads/2015/06/mweatherly-copyright-education-awareness.pdf.

International

Electronic Frontier Foundation website, www.eff.org.
US-based global organization defending civil liberties, including those that restrict the use of information and data in the digital world.

Electronic Information for Libraries (EIFL) Copyright and Libraries Programme, www.eifl.net/programmes/copyright-and-libraries-programme.

WIPO Lex website, www.wipo.int/wipolex/en.
One-stop search facility for national laws and treaties on intellectual property of WIPO, WTO and UN members. This database provides access to intellectual property legislation from a wide range of countries and regions, and to treaties on intellectual property.

World Intellectual Property Organization website, www.wipo.int/portal/en/index.html.

Europe

EDRi website,
> https://edri.org.
> EDRI is an association of civil and human rights organizations set up to defend civil rights in the information society and foster co-operation in Europe on the internet, copyright and privacy issues.

European Bureau of Library, Information and Documentation Associations (EBLIDA) website,
> www.eblida.org/activities/information-law.
> EBLIDA is an independent umbrella association of library, information, documentation and archive associations and institutions in Europe that lobby on various aspects of information law. This includes a strong focus on copyright and intellectual property rights..

The Irish Copyright Licensing Association (ICLA) website,
> www.icla.ie.

LIBER (Association of European Research Libraries) website,
> http://libereurope.eu/copyright-reform.
> Copyright reform is an important aspect of the advocacy work that this organization undertakes. LIBER established a working group on copyright reform in 2014 and lobbies on related issues such as text and data-mining and open access.

Canada

Access Canada website,
> www.accesscopyright.ca.

Canadian Library Association (2016) Copyright Issues,
> www.cla.ca/cla-at-work/advocacy/copyright-issues.

Geist, M. (2015) Michael Geist's blog,
> www.michaelgeist.ca.

Universities Canada website,
> www.univcan.ca.

New Zealand and Australia

Australian Copyright Council website,
> www.copyright.org.au.

The Copyright Council of New Zealand website,
www.copyright.org.nz.
Copyright Licensing New Zealand website,
www.copyright.co.nz.
IP Australia – Australian Government website,
www.ipaustralia.gov.au.
LIANZA (n.d.) Copyright: guidelines for librarians, Library and
Information Association of New Zealand Aotearoa,
www.lianza.org.nz/copyright-guidelines-librarians.
An online course for New Zealand librarians covering all aspects of
the relation between New Zealand's copyright law and its libraries.
LIANZA (n.d.) Copyright Resources, Library and Information
Association of New Zealand Aotearoa,
www.lianza.org.nz/our-work/voice-profession/copyright/copyright-
resources.

The USA

ALA (n.d.) Copyright, American Library Association,
www.ala.org/advocacy/copyright.
The ALA website contains a large number of resources and
information for US librarians and teachers, covering many aspects of
copyright including specific guidance on fair use and distance
education and the TEACH Act.
Association of Research Libraries (2015) Know your Copy Rights: using
copyright works in academic settings,
www.knowyourcopyrights.org.
Baruch College, CUNY (2009) Interactive Guide to using Copyrighted
Media in your Courses, City University of New York,
www.baruch.cuny.edu/tutorials/copyright.
Brewer, M. (2008) Fair Use Evaluator, ALA Office for Information
Technology Policy,
http://librarycopyright.net/resources/fairuse.
Columbia University Libraries/Information Services (2016) Copyright
Advisory Office,
https://copyright.columbia.edu.
Copyright Advisory Network (ALA Office for Information Technology

Policy) website,
http://librarycopyright.net.
Copyright Clearance Center website,
www.copyright.com.
US reprographic rights organization offering licensing and permissions to copying beyond statutory limits. Also provides advice and training.
Copyright Crash Course,
https://copyright.lib.utexas.edu/index.html.
A resource produced by Georgia W. Harper, the scholarly communications adviser at the University of Texas until 2015. The resource has a Creative Commons licence and is particularly useful for those working in higher education in the USA.
Copyright Librarian Blog, run by Nancy Sims Copyright Program Librarian at University of Minnesota,
http://simsjd.com/copyrightlibn.
Crews, K. (2012) *Copyright Law for Librarians and Educators: creative strategies and practical solutions*, 3rd edn, ALA Editions.
Library Copyright Alliance website,
www.librarycopyrightalliance.org.
Scholarly Communications @ Duke, blog,
http://blogs.library.duke.edu/scholcomm.
Strong, W. S. (2014) *The Copyright Book: a practical guide*, 6th edn, MIT Press.
US Copyright Office website,
www.copyright.gov.

Further reading on e-learning

There are numerous resources focusing on e-learning, learning technologies and classroom technologies, including monographs and journals. Those wishing to get a general overview of this topic are advised to consult the websites listed below.

The Association of Learning Technology

The Association of Learning Technology (ALT; www.alt.ac.uk) is the UK's professional and scholarly body for those with an interest in the use of learning technology. It publishes an open access journal, *Research in Learning Technology* (www.researchinlearningtechnology.net), and a newsletter, and organizes an annual conference and other events.

The European Distance and E-learning Network

The European Distance and E-learning Network (EDEN; www.educause. edu) exists to share knowledge and improve understanding among professionals in distance and e-learning and to promote policy and practice across the whole of Europe and beyond. It has over 200 institutional members and over 1200 members.

EDUCAUSE

EDUCAUSE (www.educause.edu) is a US not-for-profit membership organization that aims 'to advance higher education through the intelligent use of information technology'. It provides advice, resources and publications in a variety of areas including copyright, and advises on using digital media and lecture capture. The resources can be browsed or searched.

E-learning Network of Australasia

The E-Learning Network of Australasia (https://www.linkedin.com/ groups/ 2116103/profile) is an Australian membership organization for e-learning professionals in business and education. It organizes events, provides a news service, has a range of resources related to e-learning on its website and publishes an online journal.

Jisc

Funded by UK higher education and further education funding bodies to provide world-class leadership in the innovative use of ICT to support education and research, Jisc (www.jisc.ac.uk) manages and funds a range of projects and services for the higher education and further education community, including e-learning. It organizes events and training, and provides news, resources and publications from its extensive website.

SURF

SURF (https://www.surf.nl/en) is the Dutch equivalent of Jisc and has a website providing advice and support on a variety of topics including e-learning, open access and open education.

Copyright, e-learning and open education

Eduserv (2007) Copyright Toolkit,
    http://copyrighttoolkit.com/index.html.
Electronic Frontier Foundation (n.d.) Teaching Copyright,
    https://www.teachingcopyright.org.
HEFCE (2006) Intellectual Property Rights in e-Learning Programmes:
    guidance for senior managers,
    http://webarchive.nationalarchives.gov.uk/20100202100434
    www.hefce.ac.uk/pubs/hefce/2006/06_20.
Hobbs, R. (2010) *Copyright Clarity: how fair use supports digital learning*,
    Corwin.
Jisc (2014) Intellectual Property Law,
    https://www.jisc.ac.uk/guides/intellectual-property-law.
Jisc (2014) Open Educational Resources,
    https://jisc.ac.uk/guides/open-educational-resources.
Jisc (2015) Intellectual Property Rights in a Digital World,
    https://www.jisc.ac.uk/guides/intellectual-property-rights-in-a-
    digital-world.
OER Commons website,
    https://www.oercommons.org.
    A global digital library and network of open education resources.
Secker, J. (2004) *Electronic Resources in the Virtual Learning Environment:
    a guide for librarians*, Chandos Publishing.
Strategic Content Alliance/JISC (2009) IPR Toolkit,
    http://sca.jiscinvolve.org/files/2009/10/sca_ipr_toolkit-v2-01_intro.pdf.
UNESCO (2016) Open Educational Resources,
    www.unesco.org/new/en/communication-and-information/
    access-to-knowledge/open-educational-resources.

Social media and copyright

Australian Copyright Council (2009) *Websites: social networks, blogs & user-generated media*,
www.copyright.org.au/acc_prod/ACC/Information_Sheets/
Websites__Social_Networks__Blogs___User-generated_
Media.aspx?WebsiteKey=8a471e74-3f78-4994-9023-316f0ecef4ef.

Cornish, G. (2015) *Copyright: interpreting the law for libraries, archives and information services*, 6th edn, Facet Publishing, 176–9.

Jisc (2014) Crowdsourcing – the wiki way of working,
https://www.jisc.ac.uk/guides/crowdsourcing.

UCISA (2015) Social Media Toolkit: a practical guide to achieving benefits and managing risks,
www.ucisa.ac.uk/socialmedia.

Copyright and digital media

Aside from the relevant collective rights management organizations there are several specialist organizations offering advice for those interested in using digital media content in e-learning. The following is just a selection of these resources and does not constitute a comprehensive list.

ALA (2014) Video and Copyright, factsheet, American Library Association,
www.ala.org/tools/libfactsheets/alalibraryfactsheet07.
A useful online guide to copyright and digital media (largely video resources) in the USA. It includes links to various sources of additional advice and support for using video in libraries and classrooms.

BUFVC website,
http://bufvc.ac.uk.
A useful source of advice, training and support largely aimed at those in the education sector in the UK. The British Universities Film and Video Council is a membership organization and members include higher and further education institutions, schools, specialist institutes, commercial companies and broadcasters.

Frankel, J. T. (2009) *Teacher's Guide to Music: media and copyright law*, Music Pro Guides.

254254COPYRIGHT AND E-LEARNING

Jisc Digital Media website,
www.jiscdigitalmedia.ac.uk.
Jisc Digital Media is a source of advice, training and support for those working in higher and further education in the UK. Covering all types of digital media including images, moving images and sound recordings.

Movie Licensing USA website,
www.movlic.com.
Movie Licensing USA offers licences to K-12 schools and public libraries to allow them to show movies legally for entertainment (as opposed to teaching) purposes. An annual site licence or a one-off licence can be purchased. Site includes information about the education exemption under US copyright law and when this applies.

Smartcopying website,
www.smartcopying.edu.au.
Smartcopying provides advice for staff in schools in Australia on all aspects of copyright, including details about format shifting and multimedia copying of film, video and DVDs and musical works. The website is produced by the National Copyright Unit on behalf of the Copyright Advisory Group (schools and technical and further education institutions).

Sample of university intellectual property rights, terms of use and takedown policies

British Library (2016) Notice and Takedown,
www.bl.uk/aboutus/legaldeposit/complaints/noticetakedown [accessed 6 April 2016].
Brunel University (2007) Intellectual Property Rights Policy,
www.brunel.ac.uk/__data/assets/word_doc/0018/7155/INTELLECTUALPROPERTYRIGHTSPOLICYfinal.doc [accessed 6 April 2016].
Columbia University (2000) Columbia University Copyright Policy,
www.columbia.edu/cu/provost/docs/copyright.html [accessed 6 April 2016].
Jisc and Strategic Content Alliance (2011) Sample Notice and Take down Policy and Procedures,

http://sca.jiscinvolve.org/wp/portfolio-items/template-notice-and-take-down-policy-and-procedure [accessed 6 April 2016].

MIT (n.d.) MIT Policies & Procedures, http://web.mit.edu/policies/13/13.1.html [accessed 6 April 2016].

UCL (2015) UCL Staff IPR Policy, https://www.ucl.ac.uk/library/copyright/ipr [accessed 6 April 2016].

University of Cambridge (2016) *Intellectual Property Rights*, www.admin.cam.ac.uk/univ/so/pdfs/ordinance13.pdf [accessed 6 April 2016].

University of Glasgow (2014) Policy for Intellectual Property and Commercialisation, www.gla.ac.uk/media/media_185772_en.pdf [accessed 6 April 2016].

University of Kent (2016) Moodle Notice and Takedown Request, https://www.kent.ac.uk/itservices/forms/moodle/notice.html [accessed 6 April 2016].

University of Otago (2012) Intellectual Property Rights Policy, https://www.otago.ac.nz/administration/policies/otago003229.html [accessed 6 April 2016].

Queensland University of Technology (2015) Intellectual Property, www.mopp.qut.edu.au/D/D_03_01.jsp [accessed 6 April 2016].

Sources of further copyright training

A number of organizations offer copyright training. A list of training providers, largely from the UK, that offer courses and events related to copyright is given below.

Archives and Records Association (UK and Ireland), www.archives.org.uk/training.html

Aslib Training, www.aslib.co.uk.

Association of Learned and Professional Society Publishers, www.alpsp.org/Home.

Association of Learning Technology, www.alt.ac.uk/events.

Australian Copyright Council Learning and Events, www.copyright.org.au.

British Universities Film and Video Council,
    http://bufvc.ac.uk/courses.
CILIP (Chartered Institute of Library and Information Professionals),
    www.cilip.org.uk/products-services/onsite-training.
Collections Trust,
    www.collectionstrust.org.uk/events.
Copyright Circle,
    www.copyrightcircle.co.uk.
Copyrightlaws.com (2016) Lesley Ellen Harris's website,
    www.copyrightlaws.com.
e-LAWnora Copyright Consultancy,
    http://e-lawnora.com.
Jisc Digital Media,
    www.jiscdigitalmedia.ac.uk.
Naomi Korn Copyright Consultancy,
    www.naomikorn.com.
TFPL,
    https://www.tfpl.com/training.

Index